#1350

The
TAROT

The
TAROT

History, Mystery and Lore

CYNTHIA GILES

Paragon House
New York

First edition, 1992

Published in the United States by

Paragon House
90 Fifth Avenue
New York, NY 10011

Library of Congress Cataloging-in-Publication Data

Giles, Cynthia Elizabeth
    The tarot : history, mystery, and lore / Cynthia Giles.—1st ed.
      p. cm.
    Includes bibliographical references and index.
    ISBN 1-55778-312-8
    1. Tarot.   I. Title.
  BF 1879.T2G55 1992
  133.3'2424—dc20   91-46040
                                    CIP

Manufactured in the United States

CONTENTS

Acknowledgments

I would like to thank those people who have contributed to the birth and growth of this book by their personal generosity. Dr. Mary Lou Hoyle, as always, provided a ready source of moral support and practical assistance. Charlotte Gordon, also as always, has been patient, kind, effortful, and wise. Robert Alexander deserves much credit for sharing with me—freely and frequently—his library, his insights into a variety of matters, and his critical acumen.

To my family, my colleagues, and my friends in general, thanks for your enthusiasm about the book. I am especially grateful to George Holman for the important part he plays in my life.

Finally, my most sincere appreciation to all the people who have been willing, over the years, to share their lives with me in Tarot readings. It is through their candor, their confidence, and their spirit of discovery that I have come to know the rich possibilities of the Tarot.

AN INTRODUCTION TO THE TAROT

Tarot. The "great philosophical machine." The "key to the secrets of the ages." The "infallible instrument which foretells the future." Is it any of these? Is it all of them? What *is* the Tarot, anyway?

If a random sample were taken—say, stopping people on the streets or in the malls, and asking them, "What do you think the Tarot is?"—most people would probably say the Tarot is a set of pasteboard cards used for fortunetelling. And that is true. But the truth must obviously go much deeper, for over the centuries, there have been many popular approaches to divination, and none has inspired so much interest among scholars, artists, poets, and other students of consciousness.

To understand its nature, one must begin where the Tarot begins—in the realm of the imagination. Imagination is the faculty that allows us to *experience the immaterial*. Ordinary perception operates through the senses, and so is confined entirely to experience of the *material* world, but imagination is not bound by the rules of space and time which govern materiality. Through the mode of imagination, it is possible to travel instantaneously into the past or future, to other lands, beyond the earth, and even to realms that don't exist in the material dimension. Imaginatively, people encounter things they've never seen—flying dinosaurs, the dark side of the moon—and things that never *can* be seen—the colors of feelings, for example, or a landscape of pure crystalline forms.

Precisely because the imagination is so vast and powerful, its domain so different from the solid, sensible world of the material, it is both very seductive and very frightening. Human beings have a great yearning to adventure in imaginary realms—but at the same time, they recognize the fact that explorers occasionally get lost there and can't find their way back to "reality." So people look for ways to journey imaginatively without getting too far away from familiar landmarks. They surrender themselves to horror movies, for example, but they keep one hand in the bag of popcorn, to serve as a comforting reminder of reality; they play at the Ouija board, but if it begins to seem too real, someone quickly turns on the lights.

When people journey into the imagination, they commonly keep themselves on a tether held by the conscious mind. For some people, this tether is so short that they never really venture far from the literal world of facts and matter. But there are also those who travel on a tether that is daringly long, and they are the ones we depend on for what might be called "imaginary reconnaissance." An important way of keeping safe in imaginative terrain, after all, is to civilize this wild place, and some brave souls must go first. These explorers—poets, shamans, mystics, artists, and such—venture into the imagination, make notes and sketches, put up signs, lay out paths, and create maps that will guide the rest of us safely on our journeys. Tarot is just such a map, made by unknown explorers. It is given to us in a form similar to that of medieval maps, whereon far-off lands are marked with pictures of the various marvels to be found there.

Tarot images are pictures of the things, people, events, ideas, and emotions that shape and populate the imagination. These same things, people, events, ideas, and emotions are recorded in many other works of the creative mind— in fairy tales and dreams, in soap operas and sitcoms, in Greek tragedy, in the Bible, in history books, movies, and music videos—for they make up the stock characters and plots, the predictable crises, the continuing conflicts of human life. From the "other woman" to the idea of God, from the rite of passage to the travelling flimflam man, all the constant figures and themes of experience are essentially just continuing variations on a group of basic forms—forms which come as standard equipment with every human imagination.

These devices of the imagination have been christened *archetypes* (from the Greek, meaning "first forms"), and they are found in all times and places and modes of expression, though their outward manifestations differ. One useful way to look at Tarot is as an illustrated map of this archetypal realm. But this is only one way. Another approach to understanding the nature of Tarot is to think of it as a language—a language composed of symbolic representations, like Egyptian hieroglyphics or Chinese pictographs. Yet a third way is to conceive of the Tarot images as notes in a musical scale, each one having a different effect on the nervous system. And we may also envision the Tarot as chapters in an enormous book, where the parts can be read in any order, and each story will be complete and true.

There are many ways of approaching Tarot, and each person must decide which way (or combination of ways) makes the most sense, feels most comfortable, works most effectively. But for the purpose of common communication, Tarot can be reduced to this essential description: It is a set of seventy-eight images which, taken together, depict all the forces that affect human life, along with all the characters, events, emotions, and ideas that provide the material of which human life is composed.

To understand the nature of Tarot, it is necessary at the beginning to separate the Tarot *images* from the Tarot *cards*. Tarot is first and foremost an imaginative system, totally apart from any tangible medium. The Tarot images exist in a nonspatial, nontemporal relationship to each other, and it is possible to memorize them and use them entirely mentally. But Tarot images may also be put into material form, such as drawings or paintings—and, in this way, Tarot cards can be created. Once the images are placed on cards, it is possible either to isolate one image from all the others, or to arrange the images in different sequences, purposefully or "randomly" (by shuffling). Also, once actualized on cards, the images become capable of achieving spatial and temporal relationships, so that they can be part of material life; in this way, they can provide an interface between the realm of imagination and the material level of existence.

When the Tarot images are actualized on cards and organized in a group, we have a Tarot *deck* or *pack*. The conventional Tarot deck consists of two parts. First, there are twenty-two cards with full-sized pictures, each usually bearing both a name (The Chariot, The Hanged Man, and so forth) and a number, from zero to twenty-one. This is the *major arcana* (which means "greater secrets"), and its cards are called "trumps," "keys," or sometimes "atouts." The major arcana images are individual archetypal units, all of them well-known in art, in literature, in mythology. Each image is complete in itself, and each has its own richness and reasonance.

The Empress, for example, is the archetypal mother—fertile, nurturing, enveloping, and (on the darker side) perhaps smothering. Look for her in Demeter, the mothering Greek goddess who wouldn't let go of her daughter Persephone; in the Biblical Esther, who took Ruth to her bosom; in Snow White, with her irrepressible nurturing of the Seven Dwarfs. The High Priestess, on the other hand, is the mysterious, the cool, the hidden side of femininity (the Mona Lisa); she is the eternal virgin, who seduces and yet remains untouchable (Marilyn Monroe); she is the woman of intuitive knowledge and power (the Sybilline Oracle).

The major arcana cards are generally considered to be more powerful and more universal than the other cards in the Tarot deck, but they are not necessarily more important. The second part of the Tarot is called the *minor arcana* (or "lesser secrets"), and its purpose is to represent the day-to-day events and concerns of human life. The minor arcana has fifty-six cards, which are divided into four *suits*: Cups, Wands (or Batons), Swords, and Pentacles (or Discs). Each suit in the minor arcana contains fourteen cards: four *court* cards (King, Queen, Knight, and Page) and ten *pips*, or number cards, which run Ace through Ten.

Here's an illustration of the relationship between major and minor arcanas. The major arcana card called The Star represents the principle of hope. It symbolizes the power of hopefulness, and also that part of a person's nature which looks beyond the present and seeks greater things. The minor arcana card Nine of Cups also deals with hopefulness—but in another way, representing the fulfillment of actual, specific wishes a person may have. A second minor arcana card, the Seven of Cups, is concerned with hopefulness too—but, this time, in the form of imagined possibilities, desires, ideas.

THE MINOR ARCANA

Although the minor arcana cards—the aces, the court cards, and the pips—are often thought of as the "mundane" portion of the Tarot, they actually have more clear esoteric associations than the trumps. The minor arcana of the Tarot is best understood through several structures of correspondences; these not only reveal the symbolic significance of the minor arcana, but also shape the use of the cards in divination.

The Suits

The four suits express the same qualities as the four elements traditionally believed to be the building blocks of the material world. Through the correspondence with the elements, the suits are also linked to the four humors (bodily fluids) and their associated temperaments, and to the four divisions of the zodiac.

Suit	Element	Humor/Temperament	Zodiacal Signs
Pentacles	Earth	Bile/Melancholic	Capricorn, Taurus, Virgo
Swords	Air	Pneuma/Sanguine	Libra, Aquarius, Gemini
Wands	Fire	Choler/Choleric	Aries, Leo, Sagittarius
Cups	Water	Phlegm/Phelgmatic	Cancer, Scorpio, Pisces

Jungian interpreters also find correspondences with the four personality types defined by Jung: Pentacles/Earth/Sensation, Swords/Air/Thinking, Wands/Fire/Intuition, Cups/Water/Feeling.

The Aces

The aces, having the indivisible value of one, represent the purest form of each suit. All the numbers of the pip cards are contained in the ace and unfold from it, when the ace is viewed as the first card in the sequence. Thus the ace represents beginning and possibility. On the other hand, all the numbers of the pip cards are resolved in the ace when it is viewed as the final card in the sequence, and in this way the ace represents fullness and achievement.

All three of these cards deal with the same quality, but the major arcana card does so on the level of *character* and *destiny*, while the minor arcana cards operate on the level of *circumstance* and *behavior*. Since our lives are shaped by the interaction of these two levels—the level of cosmic forces and the level of personal choices—one of the greatest strengths of the Tarot deck is the fact that it can represent both levels and illustrate their interaction.

Of course, this two-part scheme still doesn't provide a complete operational picture of human life. There remains a third shaping element: the influence of other people as they act out their own combinations of character and circumstance. Tarot uses the *court* cards to portray these other people. The various figures in the court cards have distinct qualities that allow them to designate sex, general age, temperament, and position in life, so there is a card which will effectively represent almost any type of person.

The Court Cards

The court cards represent human diversity. They can depict almost any person, through a combination of several variables. The suit of the court card suggests the general temperament/orientation of the person, according to the correspondences described above. The gender of the card suggests the person's sex. (Pages can be either male or female.) The rank of the card suggests the person's age and/or station in life, ascending from the Page (childhood) to the King (maturity). The court cards also form the archetypal family—father, son, mother, and daughter.

The Pips

Certain qualities are assigned to each of the numbers from two through ten, and those qualities are reflected in the pips. The aspects of the suit, in combination with the number quality of the pip, define the nature of each of the pip cards. Each number also has an astrological ruler, which enriches the whole complex of minor arcana associations.

Number	Quality	Ruler
2	Antithesis	Mercury/Moon
3	Synthesis	Venus
4	Completion	Earth/Sun
5	Conflict	Mars
6	Reconciliation	Jupiter
7	Limitation	Saturn
8	Expansion	Uranus
9	Integration	Neptune
10	Culmination	Pluto

One final structure of the Tarot rounds out its symbolic capabilities. The four suits, like the traditional four elements, are related to the great categories of human experience: Pentacles refer to the material aspect of life (earth), Wands to the creative and energetic (fire), Cups to the emotional and relational (water), and Swords to the mental, abstract aspect of life (air). The special nature of each suit is captured in the *ace*, which represents in a reading the influence of that suit's particular aspect in the life of the querent.

To summarize all this briefly: The Tarot provides a storehouse of images from which can be assembled a symbolic representation of almost any human drama, from *Hamlet* to one's own life. These images are organized by two primary structures—the *major and minor arcanas*; one of these structures, the minor arcana, has four "superstructures" (the *suits*) and three "substructures"—the *court*, the *pips*, and the *aces*. The *major arcana* cards

THE TRUMPS			
CUPS	**WANDS**	**SWORDS**	**PENTACLES**
ACE	ACE	ACE	ACE
COURT	COURT	COURT	COURT
KING	*KING*	*KING*	*KING*
QUEEN	*QUEEN*	*QUEEN*	*QUEEN*
KNIGHT	*KNIGHT*	*KNIGHT*	*KNIGHT*
PAGE	*PAGE*	*PAGE*	*PAGE*
PIPS	PIPS	PIPS	PIPS
2 . . . 10	*2 . . . 10*	*2 . . . 10*	*2 . . . 10*

The Tarot deck is divided into two main structures—the major arcana, composed of twenty-two trumps, and the minor arcana. The minor arcana is subdivided into four categories or suits. Each suit has three parts, the aces, the court cards, and the pips, or number cards.

express aspects of fate and character, while the *minor arcana* cards depict matters of circumstance and behavior. People are symbolized by the court cards, mundane events by the pip cards, and spheres of influence by the aces.

If you actually wanted to use the Tarot to symbolize *Hamlet*, the structures outlined above would help you find what you need quickly, much as would the table of contents in a reference book. First you would analyze the major forces at work in the story—violence, love, loyalty, indecision—and select cards from the major arcana to represent them; then you would look among the court cards for representations of the characters, and among the pip cards for the events (Ophelia's death, the stabbing of Polonius, the visit to the grave-yard, and so on). And soon, presto! *Hamlet* in pictures.[1]

Which is all very well and good when you already know the story. But of course, the purpose of Tarot isn't to create shorthand versions of famous plays. What, then, *is* the "purpose"—the *nature*—of Tarot? The answer to that question is as complex as the Tarot itself, for the Tarot takes many forms, and lends itself to many uses. The cards may very well record secret knowledge; they may provide a process for attaining higher consciousness; they may hold magical powers. They may do all these things . . . and more.

No two people who approach the Tarot will see it in quite the same light or use it in quite the same way. In the pages of this book are opinions, facts, insights, and ideas that will help each reader move beyond limited definitions to shape his or her own unfolding relationship with the Tarot.

THE TAROT TRUMPS

The major arcana cards are multi-leveled in their meanings, and much has been written about the varied implications and the archetypal powers of each card. I've chosen five key words or phrases which represent the most frequently encountered associations for each image. (Though these varied meanings may sometimes seem disconnected or even contradictory, there is usually an underlying theme which, when grasped, will illuminate the nature of the card). Also given here is the traditional "core image" for each card.

The Fool: a walking man.
　The spirit. A quest or journey. Innocence. Chaos. Heedlessness.
The Magician: a man and a table with objects on it.
　The will. The Hermetic arts. The Trickster. Manipulation. Changefulness.
The High Priestess or Papess: a seated woman in religious attire.
　The intuition. Isis Veiled. The unconscious. Hidden knowledge. Mystery.
The Empress: a seated woman in regal attire.
　Creativity. Isis Unveiled. Nature, or the material world. The mother. Sensuality.
The Emperor: a man in regal attire.
　Reason. Society. The father. Virility. Authority.
The Heirophant or Pope: a man in religious attire.
　Wisdom. Religion. Orthodoxy. Morality. The teacher.
The Lovers: a man and a woman.
　The soul. Attraction. Choice. Sexuality. A relationship.
The Chariot: a man in a chariot.
　Mastery. War. Triumph. The persona. Progress.
Justice: a woman holding a pair of scales.
　Balance. Law. Equilibrium. Fairness. The conscience.
The Hermit: a man with a lantern or staff.
　Inwardness. Philosophy. Withdrawal. The seeker. Meditation.
The Wheel of Fortune: a wheel ridden by human or animal figures.
　Chance. Fate. Irony. Instability. Evolution.
Strength: a woman with a lion.
　Courage. Force. The serpent power. Endurance. Goodness.
The Hanged Man: a man hanging upside down by one foot.
　Ambivalence. Transition. Suspension. Sacrifice. Initiation.
Death: a skeleton.
　Transformation. Profound change. Destruction and renewal. Mortality. Ending.
Temperance: a woman pouring from one pitcher into another.
　Moderation. Caution. Prudence. Combination. Reflection.
The Devil: a horned demon.
　Materiality. Lust. Obsession. Bondage. Temptation.
The Tower: a building struck by lightning.
　Catastrophe. The unexpected. Divine intervention. Punishment. Reversal.
The Star: a woman kneeling by water.
　Hope. Aspiration. Healing. Beauty. Promise.
The Moon: animals baying at the moon.
　Instinct. Secrecy. Psychic powers. The irrational. Dreams.
The Sun: a stylized sun.
　Growth. Success. Reason. Splendor. Abundance.
Judgment: figures arising from coffins.
　Rebirth. Completion. Evaluation. Revelation. Reward.
The World: an androgynous dancing figure.
　Synthesis. Wholeness. Perfection. Eternity. Cosmic consciousness.

Notes

1. Personally, I would choose The Tower, Death, The Hanged Man, The Empress, The Emperor, Judgment, and The Moon for *major arcana* cards; the King of Pentacles for Claudius, the Queen of Swords for Gertrude, the Knight of Wands for Hamlet, the Knight of Cups for Horatio, the Page of Cups for Ophelia; and the Ace of Swords to mark the governing aspect of conflict.

Part 1
HISTORY

PROLOGUE

At the beginning is the word itself. "Tarot." Where does it come from? And . . . how is it pronounced?

Because we don't know the answer to the first question, there is no sure answer to the second! I have heard "Tarot" pronounced several different ways: tare-oh´, tare´-oh, tare´-ut, tah-row´. Since we have no idea what the derivation of the word is, there is no way of assigning a "correct" pronunciation, so everyone can make a personal choice.

The only thing we can say for certain about the word "Tarot" is where it last stopped before arriving in the English language. "*Tarot*" is the French term for a deck of seventy-eight cards which are employed both in games (though rarely today) and in divination. The cards as we now know them seem to have reached France by way of Italy, where the Italian word for the deck is "*Tarocco*." In other European countries the name for the cards is given as "*Taro*," "*Taroc*," or "*Tarok*."

The Italian "*Tarocco*" appears to have been the first of these words to come into use, but the striking fact is that the name "*Tarocco*" was not used until well *after* the deck itself appeared. During the fifteenth century, when the cards seem to have appeared in Italy, the Tarot deck was called simply "*cartes da trionfi*," meaning "cards with trumps." It was not until 1516 that the name "*Tarocco*" was first recorded in an account book.

There are, of course, many theories about the origin of the word "Tarot" and its "tar-" siblings. Some of these theories are esoteric, having to do mainly with the history of cards and their manufacturing process.[1] More interesting—and numerous—however, are the esoteric hypotheses, which

3

suppose that the Tarot is associated with an ancient (and later hidden, or "occult") tradition. One school of thought, for example, suggests that the name "Tarot" may have been taken from the name "*Tara*," which is found in several mythic traditions. A Hindu myth tells of the liaison between Soma (the god of ecstasy) and Tara, the wife of another god; out of this union, Buddha[2] ("Wisdom") was born. Another Tara, consort of the enlightened Avalokitesvara, is revered in Tibetan Tantrism as one of its great *Matrika-devis*, or mother-goddesses.[3] The same sound is found in the Roman word "*terra*," meaning earth, and the appellation "*Terra Mater*" (Earth Mother) was applied to the Roman goddess Tellus.

This entry in the Tarot name-game is, like most of the other derivations that have been suggested, related to a particular theory of the "true" meaning and the "real" history of the Tarot—in this case, to the assertion that Tarot preserves remnants of an ancient matriarchal belief system centered around goddess-worship. But those who think the origin of the Tarot is instead to be found in Egyptian hieroglyphics and temple paintings would have "Tarot" come from an ancient Egyptian phrase "*Ta-Rosh*," meaning "the royal way"; and those who stress the association of the Tarot cards with the Kabbalah,[4] a Jewish mystical system, point out that the word "Tarot" is similar to "*Torah*," the Hebrew name for the first five books of the Old Testament.

Yet another theory is that "Tarot" is an anagram of the word "*rota*," Latin for "wheel"; the Egyptian goddess-name "Ator," a form of "Hathor" (often used interchangeably with "Isis") might also be the basis for an anagram. From the sound-alike category come such possibilities as the Chinese word "*Tao*" and the Arabic "*Tariqa*," both of which mean "the Way." A different approach employs geography. One such theory suggests a connection between "Tarot" and the River Taro in northern Italy (a locale thought by some to have been the site of the introduction of the Tarot cards into Europe), while another relates "Tarot" to the Hill of Tara, seat of Irish kings from ancient times until the sixth century.

All of this speculation[5] finally "proves" only that a particular combination of sounds ("t/vowel-r/vowel") is frequently found in association with divine figures and occult practices. It's possible that the sound goes back to a once-universal and now-unknown "original language." Or it may be that there is something in the vibrations of the sound itself that connects with the basic neurological programming of human beings, linking the sound sequence imaginatively to a certain type of phenomenon. But so far there has not been enough study of these tantalizing possibilities to provide reliable illumination in our search for the etymology of "Tarot."

The origin of the word "Tarot" remains unknown—and so does the origin of the deck itself. Our factual knowledge of the existence of Tarot goes back only to 1442, when the earliest extant documentary reference to "trump" cards was made in an account book from the court at Ferrara, in Italy. The earliest surviving examples of trump cards date from the same general time and place.

But could the Tarot just have appeared out of nowhere in Renaissance Italy? Did someone invent it, find it, dream it? If not, how did it come into being?

How did the trumps become linked (and then unlinked) to the suit cards? Are the esoteric properties of the Tarot merely a creation of imaginative occultists . . . or have we rediscovered important meanings of the Tarot which were for hundreds of years obscured by the belief that it was merely a game?

There are certainly no clear answers to these questions. And there may never be. Many contemporary writers on the Tarot simply dismiss the question of origins, and treat the cards as if they were ahistorical symbols. But as Manly P. Hall, a capable modern explicator of the esoteric, comments in his book *The Tarot: An Essay*, "Anyone attempting an analysis of the cards should first acquaint himself with their historical descent in order to protect his conclusions from popular errors and concepts." And besides, what we do know about the history of Tarot is fascinating, provocative, and well worth exploring. So let's begin with some indisputable information, and see where it leads.

Notes

1. For example: The familiar pattern found on the backs of playing cards was called "*tarotee*" and a small border of dots on some old cards was called "*tares*," but it's impossible to know if "Tarot" was derived from these terms or vice versa. It seems unlikely that there is a useful connection here, since only decks with trumps were called "Tarot," and the trumps probably developed separately from the fifty-two-card deck.
2. This mythical child was not Gautama Buddha, a historical person whose teachings form the basis of Buddhism.
3. "Tantrism" will be mentioned from time to time throughout the book. It is an ancient Indian cult, thought by some to have been influenced by Chinese philosophy and practice. The aspects of Tantrism best known in the West are its techniques of esoteric sexuality and of intense meditation, but even these are not very well understood. The sexual side of Tantrism is more emphasized in Hindu Tantra, while the meditative portion is stronger in Buddhist Tantra. Tantric Buddhism was developed especially in Tibet.
4. The more common spelling of this word, "Cabala," is a Latinized version generally used by scholars; alternative spellings, "Q'balah" and "Quabala" are more often used by occultists. Rather than choosing between the two, I have chosen the spelling "Kabbalah," which tends to be preferred in the Hebrew context.
5. The theory of a goddess-worship background for the Tarot is discussed in great detail by Barbara G. Walker in *Secrets of the Tarot*. The "*Ta-rosh*" etymology was introduced by Court de Gébelin, "father" of the esoteric Tarot. Elizabeth Haich explains the "*Torah*" connection in *Wisdom of the Tarot*. See Papus's *The Tarot of the Bohemians* for an explanation of the "*Rota*" derivation. The suggestion of "*Tariq*" comes from Idries Shah, *The Sufis*. Sylvia Mann, in *Collecting Playing Cards*, proposes the River Taro connection. Stuart Kaplan mentions a number of other ideas about the etymology and origins of Tarot in chapter 2 of *The Encyclopedia of Tarot*, Vol. 1.

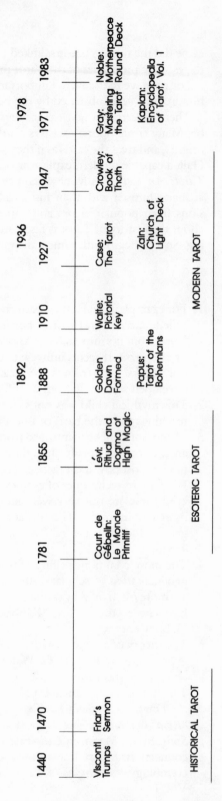

A TAROT TIMELINE

| 1440 | 1470 | 1781 | 1855 | 1892 | 1888 | 1910 | 1936 | 1927 | 1947 | 1978 | 1971 | 1983 |

Visconti Trumps

Friar's Sermon

Court de Gébelin: Le Monde Primitif

Lévi: Ritual and Dogma of High Magic

Golden Dawn Formed

Papus: Tarot of the Bohemians

Waite: Pictorial Key

Case: The Tarot

Zain: Church of Light Deck

Crowley: Book of Thoth

Gray: Mastering the Tarot

Kaplan: Encyclopedia of Tarot, Vol. 1

Noble: Motherpeace Round Deck

HISTORICAL TAROT

ESOTERIC TAROT

MODERN TAROT

TRANSFORMATION OF THE TAROT

6

1.

THE HISTORICAL TAROT

Facts and Interpretations

SOMETIME between 1450 and 1470, in Umbria, deep in the mountainous heart of Italy, a Franciscan friar preached a sermon on the subject *utilis de ludo*—the use of games.[1] He posed the question "Who invented gaming?" then gave his own somewhat oblique reply: "I answer that there are three kinds of games of chance, namely the dice, the cards, and the trumps."

This sermon, which was collected with a number of others in a manuscript thought to date from around 1500, is the first detailed reference we have to the Tarot trumps. It's clear from the sermon that the trumps were then considered separate from ordinary "playing cards"; and as the sermon continues, it also becomes clear that the trumps were thought of in quite a different light:

> Concerning the third class of games, that is trumps. There is nothing so hateful to God as the game of trumps. For everything that is base in the eyes of the Christian faith is seen in trumps, as will be evident when I run through them. For trumps are said, so it is believed, to have been given their names by the Devil, their inventor, because in no other game does he triumph (with the loss of souls to boot) as much as in this one. In it not only are God, the angels, the planets and the cardinal virtues represented and named, but also the world's luminaries, I mean the Pope and the Emperor, are forced, a thing which is degrading and ridiculous to Christians, to enter into the game. For there are 21 trumps which are the 21 steps of a ladder which takes a man to the depths of Hell.

7

One curious thing about the friar's diatribe is that he mentions God as being "represented" and "named"; yet in the list he gives of the trumps, there is certainly no card called "God," any more than there is in the packs that have come down to us today. It's interesting to speculate on which of the cards he might have been referring to. (While Justice seems the most likely candidate, another intriguing possibility is *La sagitta*—The Arrow—which was later called The House of God and today is known as the Tower.)

By the time of the friar's sermon, card-playing had been going on for about a hundred years, and was the rage in Italy and in some other parts of Europe. Written references to cards and gaming had begun to appear sometime in the latter half of the fourteenth century, but there is nothing definite to link these references to the Tarot. For example, a Swiss monk described a four-suited card deck in 1377, but made no mention of the trumps, so we cannot know if the cards he referred to were of the Tarot type.

Given the fact that there are no traces of the trumps from this period, it seems unlikely that they yet existed. The most probable scenario is that early card games were not unlike our own modern ones, such as gin or canasta, and were played with the four-suited deck. Then, some time in the first half of the fifteenth century, a game appeared which required the use of twenty-two picture cards, and these were referred to as "triumphs" ("*trionfi*" in Italian, and eventually "trumps" in English) because they could win over any of the suit cards. In later times, when the twenty-two fixed trumps were no longer used with the four-suited deck, the notion of trumping was preserved in games such as bridge by designating one suit as trumps during the course of play.

From the time of its first documented appearance, the game of Tarot seems to have gained popularity swiftly; by the end of the fifteenth century, cards were being produced in considerable quantities, and the game was played at all levels of society throughout Italy. It had many variants, but there was a common pattern, as described by Tarot historian Michael Dummett in *The Visconti-Sforza Tarot Cards*:

> The game is a trick-taking one in which the *trionfi*, exclusive of the *matto* [The Fool], serve as permanent trumps. A player must follow suit, or, if he cannot, must play a trump if he has one. The *matto* has no power to win a trick, but may be played regardless of the obligation to follow suit or trump; it does not in normal circumstances go to the winner of the trick to which it was played, but is placed among the cards won by the one who played it. A player scores one point for each trick, but, in addition, extra points for other cards captured or brought home in tricks.

In the earliest Tarot decks, the trump cards displayed neither names nor numbers, and players were expected to memorize the order in which trumps were valued. It's only thanks to the sermon described above that we have a record of how the trumps were identified in early times; the righteous friar named off the cards, and the order in which he gave them is close to the order which appears in the first numbered decks, printed several decades later. The friar's list appears in the left hand column of the table below.

Although this order was frequently found in popular decks when they began to be numbered, some of the early numbered decks had rather different orders, and other decks contained more or fewer than twenty-two trumps, so there is no certainty at all about what the sequence of the trump cards was "supposed" to be—if, indeed, there ever was an original order.[2] We do know that a different trump order was used in each of the various places where the early game of Tarot was played.

The matter of sequence is only one of many unanswered questions about the Tarot trumps and their history. Our knowledge of the early Tarot is extremely limited because it comes almost entirely from such sources as book-keeping records and legislative references. We know, for example, that three packs of hand-painted cards were purchased for the King of France in 1392—but we don't know if these decks included trumps. (Again, probably not, for the first documentary references to trumps are not found until more than fifty years later.) Similarly, we know that in 1441, the Magistracy of Venice banned the importation of cards in order to protect its own card-making industry, and that by 1464, the Parliament of England had followed the Venetian example;

	NOW KNOWN AS:
1. *El bagatella* (The Mountebank)	The Magician or The Juggler
2. *Imperatrix* (Empress)	
3. *Imperator* (Emperor)	
4. *La papessa* (The Papess)	The High Priestess
5. *El papa* (The Pope)	The Heirophant
6. *La temperentia* (Temperance)	
7. *L'amore* (Love)	The Lovers
8. *Lo caro triumphale* (The Triumphal Car)	The Chariot
9. *La forteza* (Strength)	
10. *La rotta* (The Wheel of Fortune)	
11. *El gobbo* (The Hunchback)	The Hermit
12. *Lo impichato* (The Hanged Man)	
13. *La morte* (Death)	
14. *El diavolo* (The Devil)	
15. *La sagitta* (The Arrow)	The Tower
16. *La stella* (The Star)	
17. *La luna* (The Moon)	
18. *El sole* (The Sun)	
19. *Lo angelo* (The Angel)	Judgment
20. *La iusticia* (Justice)	
21. *El mondo* (The World)	
0. *El matto sine nulla* (The Fool)	

A list of the twenty-two trump cards, as given by a Franciscan friar around 1500. Many of the titles were the same as those we know today. A few titles have changed over time, and their modern versions are given at right.

The composite figure of Ardhanari (depicting a fusion of the Hindu god Shiva's male and female aspects) holds in its four hands tokens which seem very similar to the suit markers of the Tarot minor arcana. Such parallels, along with the fact that playing cards appeared centuries earlier in the East than in the West, have suggested to many that our Western cards may have been derived from Eastern sources, but there is no direct evidence of such a link.

but still, we don't know what proportion of the many decks being manufactured at this time included trumps, and therefore were true Tarot decks rather than just playing-card decks.

A good deal of our historical knowledge concerning the Tarot comes from research into the history of playing cards, not from the study of symbolism or the history of ideas, and so may be somewhat biased. But as a matter of fact, the origin of playing-card decks is just as mysterious as the origin of the Tarot trumps. Though playing cards were known in the East—Korea, China, Persia, Arabia—well before they made their way into Europe, there is no clear information about who invented these cards or how they evolved; and while it is frequently supposed that Eastern cards (most likely brought home by the Crusaders) were the basis for Western cards, there is no evidence at all to support this idea.

In fact, the original Western suit markers of Swords, Batons, Cups, and Coins[3] don't seem to correlate with any of the Eastern suits (such as Korean Crows and Antelopes, or Hindu Shells and Water Jars), so if Eastern cards were brought to the West, it appears likely that they provided the inspiration, rather than the model, for European-style cards. One link as far as symbolism goes is with the Hindu image of the androgynous deity Ardhanari, one of Shiva's incarnations, which holds in its four hands a cup, a scepter (or wand), a sword, and a ring (or circular shield). These tokens could well have been translated into the Western suits, but even if this is true, the motives and mechanisms behind such a process remain a complete mystery. If these objects in particular were chosen from among the many different objects found in other representations of Indian deities—why?

The whole matter of the origin of playing cards was apparently not given

10

much thought until early in the nineteenth century. The first serious study of the topic was published in 1816 by Samuel Weller Singer, and in 1848, another classic work on the subject appeared, this one by W. A. Chatto. Both men suggested a Hindu origin for the cards, and related the history of cards to the early development of chess. These basic speculations about the history of playing cards have since been refined and elaborated, but never proven. The general approach of playing-card history has been applied to the Tarot, however, and has produced a modern school of Tarot inquiry which can generally be called "exoteric," since it doesn't suppose any occult background for the cards.

Exoteric approaches draw not only on the history of games, but on the history of art as well, in an attempt to date and trace the origins of Tarot by establishing—through comparisons of style, subject matter, and so on—the painter(s) responsible for existing hand-painted cards, among which are the earliest known examples of trumps. There has been a good deal of confusion about the attribution of particular cards to particular painters, however. The best-known example of this confusion concerns the cards frequently referred to as the "Gringonneur" or "Charles VI" deck.

This line drawing of The Moon, from the so-called "Gringonneur" or "Charles VI" deck, reveals clearly the details of the composition, but doesn't show the rich colors and the accents of silver and gold leaf with which the cards are embellished. Although the deck—from which seventeen cards remain in the Bibliotheque Nationale—was once thought to date from 1392, it is now generally believed to be of late fifteenth-century Venetian origin.

The confusion arose in the early eighteenth century, when someone proposed that seventeen illuminated cards (some of them Tarot trumps) in the archives of the Bibliothèque Nationale were in fact surviving examples of the cards mentioned in an account book of the treasurer to Charles VI, King of France from 1380–1422.[4] There a payment was recorded to a painter named Jacquemin Gringonneur "for three packs of cards, gilt and colored, and variously ornamented." The date of the entry was in the year 1392, and if the Bibliothèque Nationale cards, which include trumps, were really those painted by Gringonneur, the introduction of Tarot cards would have to be placed at the end of the fourteenth century.

Such dating has, indeed, been widely accepted until quite recently, in spite of the fact that as early as 1910 at least one author wrote pointedly that the ascription of the cards to Gringonneur had been disputed for more than fifty years and had fallen out of favor.[5] Even in 1910, it was already being suggested that the cards were actually Venetian and dated from the late fifteenth century, and today this idea is generally accepted by scholars as fact. In spite of the historical evidence, however, many well-known modern Tarot books still begin the known history of Tarot in 1392, citing the "Gringonneur" or "Charles VI" deck.

Misdating the appearance of the trumps in this way can make a considerable difference in interpreting the origin and nature of the Tarot.[6] For example, the 1392 date would effectively dispose of a once-popular theory that the Tarot was brought into Europe by Gypsies, since the Gypsies didn't arrive in Europe until 1411. But if the Tarot trumps appeared in the fifteenth century, it is possible that they were, after all, part of the Gypsy lore.

Possible, yes. But there is nothing to substantiate this idea—or any other, for that matter—about the earliest days of Tarot. Our best starting point for an historical analysis of the cards is probably with the group of hand-painted trumps that we *do* know (with reasonable certainty) were created sometime between 1420 and 1450. These cards are truly beautiful—radiant miniature scenes on elegant gold-leaf backgrounds, so imaginatively and delicately rendered that some of them compare with the best work of the early Italian Renaissance. There are more than 250 of them extant, apparently from as many as fifteen different packs, but all are generally referred to as "Visconti-type" since they seem to be connected with the so-named Duke of Milan and his family. Michael Dummett gives this account in *The Visconti-Sforza Tarot Cards*:

> Documentary sources and surviving cards indicate that by the end of the fifteenth century the game of tarot was known in most cities within the quadrilateral formed by Venice, Milan, Florence, and Urbino. The principal centers of the game were Bologna, Ferrara, and Milan, and from these comes the earliest evidence of the existence of tarot cards. The first certain documentary reference from Bologna is dated 1459. There are several references from Ferrara from 1442 onwards, while from Milan come the earliest surviving tarot cards themselves. These are two hand-painted decks closely related to the Visconti-Sforza deck [the best-known and most complete deck, with seventy-four extant cards]. One, which is known as the Brambilla pack after a former owner, and is now in the Pinacoteca de Brera in Milan, was certainly painted for Filippo Maria Visconti, Duke of

Milan from 1412 until his death in 1447. The other, the Visconti di Modrone pack, also named after an owner, is in the Cary Collection in the Beinecke Library at Yale University. [These three decks are also known as the Pierpont Morgan-Bergamo deck, the Brambilla-Brera deck, and the Cary-Yale deck, respectively.]

These three decks are so similar in style that it is widely believed they were painted by the same artist, but there are various problems with trying to determine exactly who that artist was. Stuart Kaplan wrote in volume 2 of his *Encyclopedia of Tarot*:

> Art historians and researchers of fifteenth-century tarocchi cards face a baffling problem in trying to determine which artist and workshop active in Northern Italy might properly be credited with the illuminated cards. There are no artists' signatures or initials on any of the cards, and documents, such as letters, court transcripts or manuscripts identifying the artists, are also lacking. . . . For many years it was thought that the artist of the early tarocchi cards was Marziano of Tortona, a scholar who lived at the court of Duke Filippo Maria Visconti and acted as his secretary. Another artist frequently mentioned was Antonio Cicognara, a painter and miniaturist. A strong case in behalf of the Zavattari brothers was advanced by Giuliana Alger (1981) . . . Roberto Longhi (1928) was the first researcher to suggest that Bonifacio Bembo was the tarocchi artist.

Today, Bembo is most frequently named, but Francesco Zavattari also remains a strong candidate. Attribution to Bembo would place the cards after 1440, while an attribution to Zavattari would allow for a date as early as 1420.[7]

It is particularly noteworthy that there are both strong similarities and significant differences among these three decks. The Visconti di Modrone pack, for example, includes among its eleven remaining trumps the theological virtues of Faith, Hope, and Charity—cards which are not found in the other two decks and which did not become part of the standardized deck. It also appears to have had six court cards for each suit, giving male and female counterparts for each rank. Since none of the decks is complete, it's impossible to know if the other decks followed the same pattern, but the fact that none of the virtues or the additional court cards remains in the other packs suggests that they did not share the Modrone pattern.

The Visconti di Modrone pack and the Visconti-Sforza pack do share one odd feature: They both have straight swords on the number cards of the Swords suit, while the Brambilla pack has the usual type of curved Italian sword. But then, the Brambilla and the Modrone packs have something in common too: Both have arrows rather than batons on *some* cards. In the Brambilla pack the arrows are on the court cards, while in the Modrone, they are on the number cards, which makes the connection seem even more curious.

As these facts suggest, the composition of the decks must have varied at first. All of the twenty-two trump images we are familiar with today (with the possible exceptions of The High Priestess, The Devil, and The Tower) seem to have been present in all decks from the beginning, but some decks added additional trumps, and/or had more or fewer court cards. The original depiction of some of the trumps also departed from the standard symbolism with

The most famous of the early hand-painted Tarot decks are the three Visconti groups, the Sforza, the Brambilla, and the Modrone. The remaining originals of these Italian cards, thought to have been created in the mid-fifteenth century, are in museums and collections around the world. However, the Visconti-Sforza deck has been reproduced and is now widely available. Shown here is The Fool, whose ragged bewilderment seems emphasized by the gold leaf background of the cards.

which we are familiar today. The Fool, for example, was typically a tattered beggar, or sometimes a wild man; The Hermit was usually on crutches, sometimes with wings, and sometimes carrying an hourglass to represent the passage of time. Both of these symbolic figures were well-known "characters" in early Renaissance art and story.

Even though the details of the Tarot trumps differed from deck to deck, and from then until now, most of the essential iconography was in place from the very beginning and has been passed along intact for several hundred years. By about 1500, the Tarot deck was apparently more or less standardized in its content, for the same images—basically, those listed by the friar—are seen in most sets of trumps from that time on. Many later decks differed from this "standard" content, but these differences seem to be the effect of political exigencies (the Emperor and Empress became the Grandmother and Grandfather during the French Revolution, for example) or of artistic creativity.

The standardization of the Tarot deck involved more than just the specific images on the cards: There were also such matters as the numbering of the cards, the suits (one type of mid-sixteenth century deck, for example, had peacocks, parrots, lions and monkeys for suit symbols), and the names attributed to the images. Though there was never one set of "rules" followed by all decks, a general pattern—now known as the Tarot of Marseilles—did evolve,

The most influential form of the Tarot images was created by the cardmakers of Marseilles, France. The basic Marseilles style, exemplified here by the Magician, appeared in many versions during the seventeenth and eighteenth centuries. The shape of the Magician's hat was no doubt originally dictated by French fashion, but its figure-eight sweep was later interpreted by occultists as a "lemniscate," the classic symbol of infinity.

beginning in the late fifteenth century; by the eighteenth century, most decks were of the Marseilles type. The styles of the cards and minor details might differ, but the basic iconography was that established by the cardmakers of Marseilles.

The Marseilles deck introduced many of the images we are familiar with today. The Fool became a handsome, carefree young man with a pack and a dog or cat, while The Hermit traded his crutches and hourglass for a staff and lantern. The Star, typically represented in early cards by a stylized star (sometimes being viewed by a group of astronomers) was changed to the figure of a nude woman pouring water from two pitchers into a stream or pond. Similarly, The Moon began as a simple astronomical object, but its image changed as other elements were added during the development of the Marseilles-type deck: The crayfish and towers appeared in the mid-sixteenth century, the dogs were added in the seventeenth century.

Clearly, some of the images which are today seen as puzzling and mysterious may once have been simple references to science, history, or politics. A classic example is The Hanged Man, the card that has provoked perhaps the most speculation of any Tarot image. Is he a pagan symbol, perhaps a sacrifice to Odin? Is he Peter, the disciple who, according to legend, wished to be crucified upside down? His face is calm, sometimes smiling. Is he a Tantrist, his position—with one leg crossed to create a triangle—symbolic of suspension? Michael Dummett offers one historical explanation of The Hanged Man's position:

> The hanged man was sometimes called *l'impiccato* and sometimes *il traditore*. He is shown hanging upside down by one foot, a posture in which traitors were

15

depicted. The walls of the Bargello in Florence were often adorned by such paintings, and the pope ordered the *condottiere* Muzio Attendolo, Francesco Sforza's father, to be so represented on all the gates and bridges of Rome; Ludovico Sforza gave a similar order concerning the treacherous governor of Milan, Bernardino da Corte, who surrendered the Castello to the French.[8]

This connection was first pointed out by Gertrude Moakley, another Tarot scholar, in her groundbreaking book *The Tarot Cards Painted by Bonifacio Bembo*. She explains a second mystery—the unlikely presence of the "Papess," or "Female Pope"—by this means:

> The Popess in the Visconti-Sforza tarocchi is not one of these legendary women [such as Pope Joan]. Her religious habit shows that she is of the Umiliata order, probably Sister Manfreda, a relative of the Visconti family who was actually elected Pope by the small Lombard sect of the Guglielmites. . . . The most enthusiastic of her followers believed that she was the incarnation of the Holy Spirit, sent to inaugurate the new age of the Spirit prophesied by Joachim of Flora. . . . Naturally, the Inquisition exterminated this new sect, and the "Popess" was burned at the stake in the autumn of 1300.

These historical references are persuasive, and suggest to scholars of the exoteric Tarot (Michael Dummett most notable among them) that the trumps, with their distinctive images, were "invented" in one of the courts of northern Italy, from which they quickly spread among the nobility. A plausible scenario is that some imaginative prince—perhaps one of the d'Estes, who patronized such romantic and fantastical writers as Ariosto and Tasso—decided to add more complexity to the popular games played with four-suited cards. Once the notion of "trumps" was born, the prince may have commissioned the court painter to create suitably intriguing pictures for the new cards. And since the pastimes of the rich are often eagerly adopted by the not-so-rich, it would at first glance seem reasonable to suppose that the trumps were quickly incorporated into inexpensive printed decks, and so was born the Tarot tradition.

But if this is the true tale, then the painter—or prince or courtier—who thought up the trump images was as remarkable in his own way as Shakespeare, for he created a symbolic masterpiece that has inspired attention and emulation for centuries. Is it not surprising that we never heard anything else of this person—that he or she was not credited anywhere with the creation of the trumps, and that no similar ideas or artworks by this person seem to exist?

Gertrude Moakley has advanced a somewhat different version of the historical origins of Tarot. She suggests that the trump images were derived from the floats which made up popular Renaissance parades called "triumphs." These floats represented virtues, and they were accompanied by walking attendants who represented the faults or vices over which a particular virtue "triumphed." Moakley's reasoning is that this festival event—particularly as it was allegorically depicted in Petrarch's poem "I Trionfi"—was translated into a card game, wherein certain cards could "triumph" by taking tricks.

One problem with Moakley's thesis is that the trump cards don't seem to fit very exactly the pattern of virtue-over-vice. Moreover, while there are some very definite parallels between Petrarch's triumphs and the early Tarot trump images (for example, Petrarch's Cupid, Time, Fortune, Death, and Eternity can be seen as very similar to the cards Love, Father Time, The Wheel of Fortune, Death, and The World), other cards—such as The Fool and The Hanged Man—don't seem to correspond at all to the triumphs. And even where there are obvious correspondences, they are not exact, as Robert V. O'Neill shows in a well-reasoned critique of Moakley's explanation.[9] (Moakley accounts for this lack of fit by suggesting that the card game was in the nature of a parody or lampoon of the triumph, but it is really very difficult to see the humorous connections that would make the joke a successful one.)

Both Dummett's and Moakley's ideas about the origin of the Tarot depend largely on the belief that the hand-painted cards were the earliest Tarots. In fact, the whole social-historical approach to the Tarot has generally been based on the assumption that the Visconti-type painted cards were the prototypes of the deck, since the surviving examples of painted cards are older than any known printed trumps by at least twenty or thirty years.[10] But O'Neill disagrees with this assumption. He points out that valuable hand-painted decks were likely to have been carefully preserved, whereas printed ones would have been discarded when they became worn—so it should not be surprising that painted cards have survived longer.

The "which-came-first" question is important because, as O'Neill observes, the early printed trumps were more interesting in their symbolism than the hand-painted decks. In the Visconti cards, for example, the figures riding on the Wheel of Fortune are human; the asses' ears that symbolize their foolishness are not actually growing out of their heads, but are part of the gold background. By contrast, the early printed cards have animal figures, or figures that are part animal and part human; in one late fifteenth-century printed deck, the Wheel is surmounted by an animal figure resembling the jackal-headed Egyptian god, Anubis.[11]

Because the painted decks have little of the overt psychological and/or magical symbolism that is found in the popular printed decks, the question of which came first is very important in deciding whether the original Tarot was in some way "meaningful," or was merely a form of popular entertainment. O'Neill argues that in the fifteenth century, court painters were expected to produce art which flattered their patrons, and since relations between the Italian nobility and the common people were not warm, it seems unlikely that the populace would be eager to imitate the imagery of court decks. Also, he contends that painters in those days were not usually creators, but rather craftsmen, which suggests that the artists who created the hand-painted Tarot decks were probably elaborating on existing images. But most intriguing of all is O'Neill's last argument on this subject, presented in his thoughtful book, *Tarot Symbolism*:

> There are seven partial decks now existing which appear to be derived from the original deck designed by Bembo. Among all of these survivors there is not a single example of the Devil or Tower cards. The probability of losing these cards

17

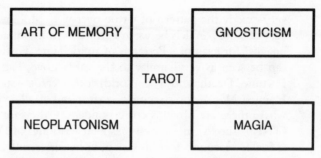

A confluence of four philosophical influences shaped the Italian Renaissance, and very likely contributed to the development of the Tarot.

by chance from among the surviving decks is twelve in 10,000! So I would argue that they were not lost by chance. They never formed a part of the hand-painted decks [because] when the ducal patron commissioned a deck to be played at court, he requested that these dismal cards be omitted from the deck since they were unsuitable for the royal ladies.

Whatever the reason may have been for the omission of The Devil and The Tower from the hand-painted decks, the fact of their absence does argue strongly in favor of the primacy of the printed decks. It seems very unlikely that these two "dark" cards would have been added by cardmakers to a set of images already established by the painter or patron of the trumps, but it's quite believable that the nobles would choose to leave out of their own decks images they thought to be common or unsuitable.

Moakley and Dummett have made very interesting contributions to Tarot scholarship, but as O'Neill points out, they and others who would explain the Tarot solely in terms of social history or art history have limited themselves severely by neglecting the symbolic dimension of the cards. Just because the cards originated in Renaissance Italy—rather than in Egypt, Atlantis, or India—it doesn't necessarily follow that they have no symbolic significance. In fact, O'Neill shows very effectively that the imaginative atmosphere of the early Italian Renaissance was more than sufficient to produce all the symbolic power captured in the Tarot.

In part 2 of this book, we will explore the occult tradition in much more detail. For now, we can look briefly at the main lines of occult influence that came together in the Renaissance, and consider whether they may have incubated the Tarot. These forces included the early stirrings of Neoplatonist scholarship, the revival of interest in magic, the continued survival of Gnostic beliefs and the revitalized tradition of the *ars memoria*. Perhaps the strongest of such influences was Neoplatonism, a philosophical construction based on the works of Plato, as elaborated by third- and fourth-century syncretist philosophers such as Plotinus and Iamblicus. The Neoplatonists held that mystical experience is the true goal of life, and this notion proved fascinating to the adventurous scholars of Renaissance Italy. By 1440, a Platonic Academy, dedicated to the study of Neoplatonist doctrines, was begun in Florence.[12]

The Florentine academy was to become a focal point of the Renaissance interest in *magia*, a Christianized magical doctrine based on the idea that a network of sympathetic relationships linked every facet of creation, and that these relationships could be used by the "magus," or magical practitioner, to manipulate the material world. Both *magia* and Neoplatonism inherited a good deal of their conceptual background from Gnosticism, a religious and philosophical movement of the Hellenistic and early Christian eras. Gnostic doctrine held that the whole universe expresses a conflict between the spiritual and the material, between good and evil, and that the power to overcome this duality is available only through special knowledge—*gnosis*. This idea also gave rise to the basic concept of the mystery religions, which hold that *gnosis* is transmitted through some type of initiation.

A fourth stream flowing into the Renaissance imagination was the *ars memoria*, or art of memory. The technique of creating mental structures (such as a journey or a building) for storing and recalling information had originated in ancient Greece as a simple device for expanding the capacity of the memory in a time when written materials were scarce. But the practice was developed much further in the thirteenth century, with the addition of Jewish letter and number mysticism, to become a tool for achieving mystical experience.

All of these ideas (and many more which flourished in the Renaissance) have been linked with the Tarot. Several authors have suggested that the Tarot images may have been used by hidden groups of Gnostic heretics—such as the Waldensians or the Albigensians—to preserve and disseminate their theology. Others have proposed that the Tarot images were used for the practice of *ars memoria*, or for magical meditation. But while it is certain that similarities can be seen among Gnostic doctrines, Neoplatonic philosophy, and the Tarot images, there is no clear evidence to be found of any direct links among these systems. It seems apparent, however, that an abundance of esoteric themes was abroad at the very time the Tarot trumps appeared, quite possibly accounting for the creation of those images.[13]

Whatever the origins of Tarot symbolism may have been, in the early days of the cards, there seems to have been only a little recognition of their symbolic power. There is scant evidence that the cards were perceived as anything more than gaming devices, and what little evidence there is can be seen mainly in the sensitive renderings of some of the early Tarot artists and in the occasional use of the trumps as allegories in poetry. One Italian poet, around 1550, compared the ladies of the court of Isabella D'Este of Ferrara to the trumps, saying that one of the ladies was like The Chariot because she "triumphs as a woman by her greatness," while another was like The Fool, because her beauty included her craziness!

There may also have been some early awareness of the *psychological* richness of the Tarot trumps. Girolamo Gargagli wrote in 1572 of seeing the game of *tarocchi* played, and "each participant was given the name from a card, and then the reasons were stated aloud why each participant had been attributed to such a tarocchi card." This provocative note suggests that even in those days, the Tarot could have been used to probe the depths of personality.

Still earlier, in 1527, the trumps had appeared in a play by Merlini Cocai, used in a way that could be described as "fortunetelling." In the play, the protagonist Limerno is asked to compose sonnets based on four "readings" with the Tarot trumps. These readings were apparently accomplished by dealing out the cards (five each for the men, six each for the women) and interpreting the "fates" they described.[14] Limerno's version of these fates, however, seems more along the lines of character-reading and general philosophizing than true divination. No reference to divination with cards is recorded until 1540, and in that instance, there is no clear mention of the trumps. In fact, there are in these early records no references to the Tarot trumps in any sort of esoteric connection whatsoever.

Consider this: During the Renaissance, the study of esoteric systems was a thriving enterprise. Alchemy, astrology, and natural magic were the preoccupations of many great men, such as Giordano Bruno, John Dee, and Isaac Newton; quantities of books were written on metaphysical subjects of all kinds—but *not a word* about the Tarot. And that is a very curious fact, because the Tarot deck seems so naturally suited to esoteric interpretation. Certainly, as soon as people began to look for esoteric structures and correspondences in the Tarot, they found an embarrassment of riches. That wellspring of speculation was opened up at the end of the eighteenth century, and there begins the next chapter in our investigation of the Tarot.

Notes

1. The sermon was recorded in a document (dated about 1500) which is now known as the "Steele manuscript." A reproduction of the manuscript page may be seen in Stuart Kaplan's *Encyclopedia of Tarot*, Vol. 1, on p. xvi.
2. Gareth Knight, building on the work of Michael Dummett, gives a first-rate presentation of trump order variations in *The Treasure House of Images*, chapter 3.
3. The suits which eventually became standard—Spades, Clubs, Hearts, and Diamonds—seem to have been invented later, in the 1470s, by French cardmakers.
4. Richard Cavendish, historian of magic and the occult, suggests that this connection was made by a priest named Menestrier, in 1704.
5. A. E. Waite, *The Pictorial Key to the Tarot*, p. 39.
6. The acceptance of this attribution has significantly affected the understanding of Tarot in what might be called "nonspecialist" scholarship. For example, the noted writer on mythology, Joseph Campbell, wrote an interesting essay on the Tarot, but since he begins with the assumption of the 1392 date, the validity of his whole discussion—which relates the Tarot to the works of Dante—is questionable.
7. Stuart Kaplan's treatment of the Visconti cards in his three-volume *Encyclopedia of Tarot* is absolutely exhaustive, and provides much interesting information about the possible early history of the cards. See especially Vol. 2, chapters 2 and 3.

8. Dummett's article, "Tracing the Tarot," appears in a beautiful issue of *FMR* magazine, January/February 1985, which contains a lengthy special section on the Tarot.
9. Robert V. O'Neill, *Tarot Symbolism*, pp. 78–84.
10. The earliest surviving woodblock-print playing cards were manufactured in 1440, but only court cards remain from this deck, so it is not known whether it was a Tarot deck or not; the earliest printed trump cards that have survived date from sometime late in the fifteenth century.
11. This image appears in an uncut sheet of six trumps belonging to the collection of the Bibliothèque de l'Ecole Nationale Supérieure des Beaux-Arts in Paris.
12. In 1438, a council attended by many Greek scholars had been convened in Ferrara to explore the possibility of reconciliation between the Greek and Roman churches. It is reasonable to assume that Neoplatonist manuscripts and philosophy may have been part of this exchange. O'Neill remarks that if Michael Dummett's suggestion about the Tarot's origin in the court of Ferrara is correct, there may well be an association with the presence of this council.
13. These suggestions are to be found in Alfred Douglas's book *The Tarot*, in Paul Hudson's *The Devil's Picturebook*, and in Richard Cavendish's *The Tarot*.
14. As to why the men in Cocai's play received five cards and the women six, I can offer no illumination. However, the interested student may form an opinion based on the text itself, which is partially presented in Kaplan's *Encyclopedia of Tarot*, Vol. 2, pp. 8–9.

2.

THE ESOTERIC TAROT

Discoveries and Inventions

W<small>E</small> may know little about the actual origins of the Tarot, but we can trace very clearly the "invention" or "discovery" (depending on how you look at it) of the Tarot as an esoteric instrument. There appears to be no connection at all between these two parts of Tarot history. In fact, the beginning of the second part seems to have been possible only because the first part had been so entirely forgotten.

From the time of its appearance early in the fifteenth century to near the end of the seventeenth century, the game of Tarot had flourished all over Europe; in 1622, a Jesuit commented that Tarot was played more than chess in France. But the popularity of the game declined, and by 1726, though Tarot was still played in some parts of Europe, it was described as "obsolete" in a French book of games. So by 1775, when Antoine Court de Gébelin—a Protestant clergyman, Freemason, and gentleman scholar—came upon the game of Tarot being played by a visitor from "Germany or Switzerland," the traditional background of the cards as a popular game had vanished into virtual oblivion.

Court de Gébelin, describing his first encounter with the cards, explained what happened when his hostess showed him one of the trumps:

Antoine Court de Gébelin, who first suggested—in 1781—that the Tarot cards were an ancient Egyptian book of wisdom, can fairly be called the "Father" of the esoteric Tarot. The Tarot was merely a half-forgotten card game when Court de Gébelin recognized and wrote about its symbolic nature.

I glanced at it and as soon as I did, I recognized the allegory.... Each person showed me another card, and in a quarter of an hour the deck had been gone through, explained, and proclaimed Egyptian. And since this was not a figment of our imagination, but rather the result of selected and sensible knowledge of this game in connection with everything that was known about Egyptian ideas, we promised ourselves to surely make it known to the public one day....

As far as we know, the entire idea of the Tarot as an esoteric and divinatory instrument, so familiar to us now, began at that moment. Court de Gébelin, an avid student of mythology, archaeology, and linguistics, became immediately enthralled with the Tarot, and concluded right away that it was an ancient Egyptian "book" which preserved in symbolic form the fabulous knowledge of that vanished civilization. This book he attributed to the powerful Egyptian god Thoth.

At first glance, this may seem an odd idea for Court de Gébelin to have come up with at a card party. But he was following in a tradition which had thrived among occultists since the Renaissance. Frances Yates, in her fascinating book *Giordano Bruno and the Hermetic Tradition*, explains the background of this whole idea:

The Egyptian God, Thoth, the scribe of the gods and the divinity of wisdom, was identified by the Greeks with their Hermes and sometimes given the epithet of "Thrice Great." The Latins took over this identification of Hermes or Mercurius with Thoth, and Cicero in his *De natura deorum* explains that there were really five Mercuries, the fifth being he who killed Argus and consequently fled in exile to Egypt where he "gave the Egyptians their laws and letters" and took the Egyptian name of Theuth or Thoth. A large literature in Greek developed under the name of Hermes Trismegistus, concerned with astrology and the occult sciences, with the secret virtues of plants and tones and the making of talismans for drawing down the powers of the stars, and so on. Besides these treatises or recipes for the

23

practice of astral magic going under the name of Hermes, there also developed a philosophical literature to which the same revered name was attached. It is not known when the Hermetic framework was first used for philosophy, but the *Asclepius* and the *Corpus Hermeticum*, which have come down to us, are probably to be dated between A.D. 100 and 300.

The Greek writers of this period believed that the distant past was the repository of a "pristine" philosophy and a powerful magic. Accordingly, they often cast their highly imaginative works in the form of writings "by" or dialogues "with" Hermes Trismegistus, who was also supposedly the Egyptian Thoth. When these documents were rediscovered during the Renaissance, the aspiring philosophers and magi of that period quite naturally took them literally and assumed they were the works of an ancient Egyptian god.

By Court de Gébelin's time, this Renaissance misconception had become a cornerstone of the occult philosophy that was passed along by means of secret societies such as the Freemasons and Rosicrucians. Court de Gébelin was steeped in the lore of Greco-Egyptian mysteries, and blissfully unaware that the history (though not necessarily the substance) of these doctrines was entirely fictitious. Moreover, though many works attributed to Hermes/Thoth had been discovered and incorporated into occult lore, there had always been the belief that another work, perhaps the greatest, was still undiscovered. So it is little wonder that Court de Gébelin, on seeing the exotic and obviously symbolic Tarot trumps, immediately believed them to be Egyptian.

He quickly produced an interpretation of the cards that supported his hypothesis. Gertrude Moakley gives this description:

XII.

Prudence, *from the trump designs which accompanied Court de Gébelin's essay on the Tarot. The basic images were taken from the Marseilles deck (which Court de Gébelin mistakenly believed to be the ancient original), but Court de Gébelin made some changes in accordance with his Egyptian interpretations. He believed the Hanged Man was a printer's error, and turned the card upside down to represent the virtue of prudence (the only one of the cardinal virtues missing from the Tarot trumps).*

The trumps, he explained, should be read backwards, beginning from the highest. The first seven trumps represent the Golden Age: XXI Isis (the Universe), XX The Creation (not the last Judgment, as one might ignorantly think), XIX Creation of the Sun, XVIII Creation of the Moon and terrestrial animals, XVII Creation of the stars and fish, XVI the House of God overturned, with man and woman precipitated from the earthly Paradise, XV The Devil, bringing to an end the Golden Age. The next seven cards are for the Silver Age: XIV Temperance, XIII Death, XII Prudence (the cards Court de Gébelin had before him depicted a dancing Prudence instead of the Hanged Man), XI Force coming to the aid of Prudence, X The Wheel, IX Hermit seeking Justice, VIII Justice. The last group is for the Brazen Age: VII War, VI Man fluctuating between vice and virtue, V Jupiter (the Tarot cards of Southern France usually show Jupiter and Juno instead of Pope and Popess), IV King, III Queen, II Pride (Juno and her peacock), I Juggler.[1]

The cards which Court de Gébelin saw were, of course, an example of the Marseilles type, and he had no idea whatsoever that this deck did not represent the "original" images of the Tarot. Thus the whole tradition of the occult Tarot was to be based on the comparatively late Marseilles model, which represents a considerable departure from the earliest known cards. Little is known of how and why certain changes were introduced into the Marseilles images, but one possibility is that among the guilds of cardmakers who produced the many popular Tarot decks of the Marseilles period were members of heretical religious sects or secret societies who added their own symbolism to the design of the cards.[2]

In any event, based on the images he saw, Court de Gébelin formed his ideas about the true nature of the Tarot. He elaborated these ideas in an essay titled "Le Jeu des Cartes," published in 1781 as part of his nine-volume treatise *Le Monde Primitif* (to which the King of France was among the subscribers). The "book" hidden in the Tarot, he believed, contained the Egyptians' "purest beliefs regarding interesting things." He went on to explain:

The trumps which number twenty-two represent in general the temporal and spiritual leaders of society, the physical powers of agriculture, the cardinal virtues, marriage, death, and resurrection or the Creation; the various games of fortune, the sage and the fool, time which consumes all, etc. Thus, we see that all these cards are also allegorical pictures relative to all of life and capable of unlimited combinations.

Court de Gébelin's intuitive grasp of the Tarot images was, in fact, exactly correct—even though he was almost certainly quite wrong about its Egyptian origins. His hypothesis was very persuasive, however, for in Court de Gébelin's day, Egypt was still regarded by romantic occultists as a great repository of esoteric lore—mainly on the strength of the Renaissance inheritance already mentioned, for very little was actually known about the ancient civilization. The hieroglyphics found on Egyptian monuments and papyri were as yet untranslated, leaving room for much rich speculation as to the subjects discussed in this mysterious picture language.

Court de Gébelin himself was a man of serious ideas and good repute, who numbered among his friends the inventive Benjamin Franklin. And his theories about the Tarot, even though based on some false assumptions, were significant; by attempting to apply the anthropological and archaeological knowledge of the time to an analysis of the Tarot, he revealed something of the potent symbolic nature of the cards. But predictably enough, Court de Gébelin's ideas were quickly diluted and popularized, principally through the efforts of a professional fortuneteller who styled himself "Etteilla" (the reverse spelling of his real name, Alliette).

Etteilla had been using an ordinary piquet deck for his cartomancy, but he readily switched to the Tarot. By 1783 he had published a book containing his own interpretation of the Tarot cards and their origin, along with illustrations for his own "rectified" (that is, esoterically renumbered) Tarot deck. The feverish period leading up to the French Revolution was full of potential for the enterprising cartomancer, who is said to have predicted—from his lavish Parisian apartments—the fates met by many at the guillotine.

Etteilla's use of the Tarot was certainly profit-oriented, but even so, he had a distinct influence on the development of the esoteric Tarot. His primary effect was in popularizing the *idea* of Tarot, rather than actually contributing to the theory or design of the cards. The deck he designed, known as "The Grand Etteilla," differed significantly from traditional Tarot cards; the pack included cards, such as "Fire," "Air," "Water," and "Earth," which had no counterparts in the traditional Tarot, and many of the traditional card names were changed radically. The Chariot, for example, became "Dissension," and The Lovers was renamed "Marriage"—which certainly puts a different spin on the images.

Etteilla, a passionate supporter of the Egyptian hypothesis, embellished the story with many new details, including the date of the Tarot's creation (171 years after the Flood), and the circumstances of its creation by seventeen magi working under the direction of Hermes Trismegistus in a temple three leagues from Memphis! But Etteilla was the last Tarot enthusiast to have the luxury of believing that confirmation of his theory would emerge from the ruins of Egypt. In 1799—only eighteen years after Court de Gébelin had published his ideas on the Tarot—the Rosetta Stone was discovered, and soon the hieroglyphic language of Egypt was decoded. As the secrets of exotic Egypt began to be unveiled, however, nothing emerged which revealed any link to the Tarot.

Yet, even though facts did not support the idea of an Egyptian origin for the Tarot, this romantic notion proved peculiarly durable. It was given an imaginative boost when another long-lived Tarot myth was introduced in an 1857 book by J. A. Vaillant about the Romany people. Vaillant was a great student of the Romany, and when he became interested in the Tarot, he immediately fancied a connection between the two.

The mysterious tribes of the Romany were called "Gypsies" in Europe exactly because they were thought to have been descendents of the ancient Egyptians, and so the idea that Gypsies had borne the Tarot with them on their wanderings fit perfectly into the still-popular Egyptian scenario. The Gypsy hypothesis was roundly criticized as early as 1869, when Romain

This nineteenth-century engraving depicts the romantic image of the Gypsy fortune-teller. Note the border of cards on her dress! Gypsies specialized in palm-reading, but they did use cards for divination—generally playing cards rather than Tarot cards, however. Although there is no evidence to suggest that the Gypsies were either the bringers or the keepers of exotic Tarot mysteries, the idea has persisted nonetheless.

Merlin (who also condemned the Egyptian theory as baseless) pointed out that there was reason to believe playing cards had been in Europe *before* the historical date of the Gypsies' arrival. Since the Tarot was, in Merlin's day, thought to have always been a seventy-eight-card deck, composed of both trumps and suit cards, this observation seemed to dispose of the Gypsy influence on the Tarot. Nevertheless, the whole Gypsy idea was so attractive to occultists that it persisted in spite of such historical inconveniences. In 1889, a very influential book on the Tarot was published under the title *The Tarot of the Bohemians*, the "Bohemians" being, in fact, the Gypsies.

Gypsies are, of course, now known to be descended not from the ancient Egyptians, but rather from the ancient Aryan race in India. And, as already mentioned, we know today that (chronologically at least) there is a possibility the Gypsies could have been the agents who brought Tarot trumps into Europe. There is, however, no evidence at all to connect the Gypsies with the Tarot (or with any type of cards) before the eighteenth century; although

27

Gypsies were traditionally spoken of as fortunetellers, their specialty, it seems, was palmistry. When they did begin using cards for divination, they generally used the four-suited playing-card deck.

Perhaps the most interesting thing about the Gypsy hypothesis is the way it was embraced and amplified by the romantic imagination which flourished in the nineteenth century. Like so many other ideas which have come down to us about the Tarot, this one began in the fancy of someone steeped in half-understood or misunderstood lore, and, by a process of enthusiastic embellishment, took on an illusory kind of substance. This kind of elaboration was very characteristic of the times. It was part of a whole cultural style, one which produced not only the lavishness of occult imaginings, but the music of Chopin and Beethoven, the lush poetry of Keats and Baudelaire, the sweeping philosophies of Schopenhauer and Nietzsche. Visual art of the nineteenth century ranged from the epic paintings of David and Delacroix to the dazzling fantasies of Moreau and Redon.

It seems as though, after the long dry spell of Enlightenment rationalism, the human need for a sense of wonder and mystery must have reasserted itself in the nineteenth century, taking many new forms. All sorts of metaphysical interests were once again pursued, with much excitement. Secret societies were formed, magic was studied ardently, great doctrines were proclaimed—and the Tarot, whose potent symbolism and mysterious past were naturally attractive to investigators of the occult, was taken up with enthusiasm. From this swirl of interest, there emerged perhaps the most influential of all Tarot theorists.

Eliphas Lévi Zahed—usually shortened to Eliphas Lévi—was the pseudonym of Alphonse Louis Constant. Reports of Constant's early life differ, but it seems certain that he was born in 1810, that he trained for the Catholic priesthood, and that he turned instead to teaching and journalism, as well as to the serious study of magic and mysticism. When he began to write occult treatises, Constant followed the common practice of adopting a *nomme de plume*, which he derived by translating his own name into Hebrew. (He is now known almost entirely by his pseudonym, and will be referred to as "Lévi" hereafter.)

Like others interested in occultism (a term actually coined by Lévi[3]) during the nineteenth century, Lévi was certain the Tarot trumps must be a very ancient document, containing great esoteric secrets. Indeed, he saw it as connected with many occult traditions, including the Egyptian mysteries. It was Lévi who suggested a connection between the Tarot and the so-called Bembine Tablet of Isis, a large bronze and silver panel covered with Egyptian hieroglyphics which was thought by the Hermetic philosophers of the Renaissance to contain the highest wisdom of the ancient world.[4]

But Lévi's greatest enthusiasm—and his most significant contribution to the lore of the Tarot—was the extensive correlation he developed between Tarot and the great Hebrew system of mysticism, Kabbalah. Although Court de Gébelin had noticed the correspondence between the twenty-two trumps and the twenty-two letters of the Hebrew alphabet, this relationship had not been developed in any detail before Lévi.

28

*Eliphas Lévi (Alphonse Louis Constant),
who created the basic structure of modern
ritual magic, was perhaps the most
influential explicator of the esoteric Tarot.
His linking of Tarot and Kabbalah shaped
the mainstream of Tarot interpretation for
a century, and through his teaching, he
affected leaders of metaphysical movements
in both France and England.*

The profound connection that Lévi saw between the Tarot trumps and the Hebrew alphabet led him to envision a new and different scenario for the origin of the Tarot cards:

When the Sovereign Priesthood ceased in Israel, when all the oracles of the world became silent in presence of the Word which became Man, and speaking by the mouth of the most popular and gentle of sages, when the Ark was lost, the sanctuary profaned, and the Temple destroyed, the mysteries of Ephod and Theraphim, no longer recorded on gold and precious stones, were written or rather figured by certain wise kabbalists first on ivory, parchment, on gilt and silvered leather, and afterwards on simple cards, which were always objects of suspicion to the Official Church as containing a dangerous key to its mysteries. From these have originated those tarots whose antiquity was revealed to the learned Court de Gébelin through the sciences of hieroglyphics and of numbers.[5]

Lévi's insight offered something much more important than simply a new creation myth for the Tarot. He saw the Tarot not just as a fascinating relic of some ancient symbolic system, but as an unparalleled practical tool, a key to the wisdom of the ages:

The universal key of magical works is that of all ancient religious dogmas—the key of the Kabalah and the Bible, the Little Key of Solomon. Now, this Clavicle [Lévi's term for the major arcana of the Tarot] regarded as lost for centuries has been recovered by us, and we have been able to open the sepulchres of the ancient world, to make the dead speak, to behold the monuments of the past in all their splendor, to understand the enigmas of every sphinx and to penetrate all sanctuaries. Among the ancients the use of this key was permitted to none but the high priests, and even so its secret was confided only to the flower of initiates . . . . The Tarot is truly a philosophical machine, which keeps the mind from wandering, while leaving its initiative and liberty; it is mathematics applied to the Absolute, the alliance of the positive and the ideal, a lottery of thoughts as exact as numbers,

29

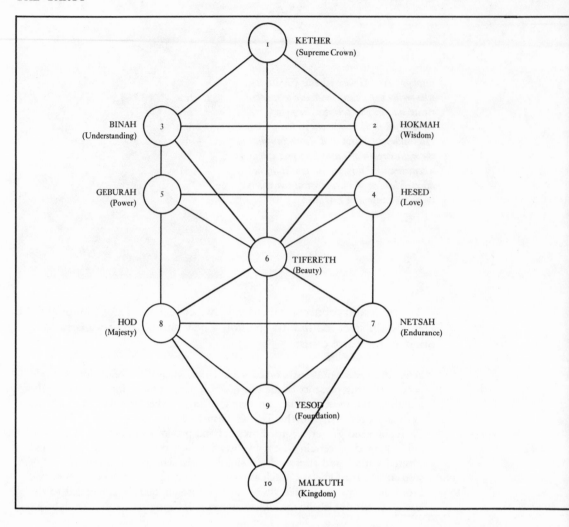

perhaps the simplest and grandest conception of human genius .... An imprisoned person, with no other book than the Tarot, if he knew how to use it, could in a few years acquire universal knowledge and would be able to speak on all subjects with unequalled learning and inexhaustible eloquence.

To understand Lévi's excitement, it is necessary to realize that, from the Kabbalistic point of view, the Hebrew alphabet is not just a system of writing, but rather an expression of all the fundamental facts and forces of creation—which in turn are organized in a complex image called the "Tree of Life." The framework of this tree is made up of ten "*sephiroth*" ("glowing sapphires"), which represent fundamental ideas such as Splendor, Wisdom, Force, and Kingdom. These *sephiroth* are connected by twenty-two wisdom paths, each designated by a letter of the Hebrew alphabet and describing certain psycho-spiritual processes. The twenty-two Tarot trumps, Lévi asserted, are emblematic of these twenty-two paths.

THE TREE OF LIFE

This diagram shows the basic structure of the Kabbalistic Tree of Life. The ten circles are the *sephiroth*, each representing an aspect of God. There are several structures within the Tree. The righthand column is called the "Pillar of Mercy," and it is the male/active/positive side; the lefthand column is the "Pillar of Judgment" and it is feminine/passive/negative. These opposites are reconciled in the "Middle Pillar" or "Pillar of Mildness." There are three groups of *sephiroth*, each forming a triangle, in which two opposing factors are balanced by a third. At the base of the Tree is a single sphere, Malkuth, which represents the whole material world. The meaning of the entire Tree pours through Yesod, the "spout," into Malkuth, where it is made manifest.

The lines running between the *sephiroth* are the twenty-two "paths." The paths form a kind of spiral staircase of spiritual ascent, leading from the Kingdom, or world of man, at the bottom, to the Crown of God at the top. Each path is assigned a Hebrew letter. The paths are numbered from the top down, beginning with Path 1, from Kesser to Hokmah, and ending with Path 22, from Yesod to Malkuth.

The twenty-two paths connecting the *sephiroth* have been assigned variously by different authors to the twenty-two Tarot trumps. Here is a list of the most common attributions:

Path	Trump	Path	Trump
1. (Kether to Hokmah)	The Fool	11. (Hesed to Netsah)	The Wheel of Fortune
2. (Kether to Binah)	The Magician	12. (Geburah to Tifereth)	Justice
3. (Kether to Tifereth)	The High Priestess	13. (Geburah to Hod)	The Hanged Man
4. (Hokmah to Binah)	The Empress	14. (Tifereth to Netsah)	Death
5. (Hokmah to Tifereth)	The Emperor	15. (Netsah to Hod)	Temperance
6. (Hokmah to Hesed)	The Hierophant	16. (Hod to Tifereth)	The Devil
7. (Binah to Tifereth)	The Lovers	17. (Tifereth to Yesod)	The Tower
8. (Binah to Geburah)	The Chariot	18. (Yesod to Netsah)	The Star
9. (Hesed to Geburah)	Strength	19. (Netsah to Malkuth)	The Moon
10. (Hesed to Tifereth)	The Hermit	20. (Yesod to Hod)	The Sun

The best way to develop an understanding of the relationship between the Tarot trumps and the Tree of Life is to draw these paths and their trump assignments on the diagram.

The rest of the Tarot deck has also been linked to this system. Each of the ten *sephiroth* has a number, and these numbers, it is suggested, correlate with those of the ten number cards in the suits of the Tarot. The four suits, in the form of their court cards, relate to the Kabbalah's Four Worlds, or successive emanations of creation, from the highest—the divine or archetypal—through creative and formative dimensions, to the material level of the planetary sphere.

By thus connecting all seventy-eight Tarot cards with the complex structure of the Kabbalah, it seemed possible to form a complete system which interrelates *number*, *word*, and *image*. This sort of grand synthesis had been a compelling goal of esoteric investigation for centuries, so it was no wonder Eliphas Lévi believed that by wedding the Tarot and the Kabbalah, he had discovered a powerful source of knowledge and magic.

Lévi, like Court de Gébelin, had grasped something important about the Tarot, something which has shaped the whole course of Tarot studies. But—

31

also like Court de Gébelin—Lévi let himself be carried away from the heart of the matter by a wave of romantic enthusiasm. It's apparent that the Kabbalah and the Tarot resemble one another in certain respects, but there is no evidence at all to suggest that the Kabbalah and the Tarot were ever linked in any intentional or dependent way. The similarities between the two systems are important not because they indicate a common source, but because they reveal certain basic esoteric concepts embodied in both.

Once one begins to pick up the threads that run between the Kabbalah and the Tarot, it's possible to follow these threads in many different directions—to alchemy, to astrology, to Native American religion. The Greek mystery religions, Hawaiian Kahuna magic, Chinese Taoism, Tibetan Buddhism—*all* of these systems of thought (and many more) have elements in common with those of the Tarot.

It is exactly this wealth of possible associations which encouraged the idea that the Tarot was part of an ancient complex of esoteric knowledge. And as various commentators, each with his own special bit of knowledge, "discovered" new correlations, the mythography of the Tarot was expanded. Next among these contributors was Jean-Baptiste Pitois. Writing under the pen-name of Paul Christian, this prolific French journalist and historian produced, in 1863, *L'homme rouge des Tuileries*, a manuscript which significantly influenced a whole generation of occultists.

The manuscript was alleged to have been copied by an old monk, and although it never mentions the Tarot by name, its allusion to Tarot is quite clear. One of the chief features described is a great circle made of seventy-eight gold leaves which once had been contained in an Egyptian temple at Memphis. On these leaves, according to Christian's story, were images used in the process of initiation into an ancient mystery religion. No factual basis was offered for the tale, but it swiftly became part of the burgeoning background to the occult movement, and helped lay the groundwork for a whole series of secret societies which were to base their practices on the supposed initiatory rites of ancient cults.

Christian was a historian, a professional journalist, and a man of action; there was little about him of the eccentricity which marked so many other occult figures of the time. His interest in occult matters had begun in 1839, when he was appointed (at the age of twenty-eight) a librarian in the Ministry of Public Education. His task was to sort through a huge quantity of books which had been seized during the suppression of the French monasteries in 1790. Among these books were many on magical and philosophical subjects, and Christian began a lifelong study which was to culminate in 1870 with the publication of his *History of Magic*. In the intervening years, Christian was editor-in-chief of the *Moniteur du Soir* and the *Moniteur Catholique*; he wrote a well-respected history of the French Revolution, an account of the French conquest of Morocco, an eight-volume *Heroes of Christianity*; he contributed the introduction to a volume of Helvetius, translated James MacPherson's *Ossian*, and collected a volume of tales called *Stories of the Marvellous from All Times and Lands*. From this partial list of his accomplishments, it's obvious that Christian's abilities and interests were wide-ranging.

Both his eclecticism and his occult interests placed Paul Christian in perfect tune with his times. Among the intellectuals and artists of nineteenth-century France, esoteric ideas were a common coin, and the study of such matters was regarded by many of its participants as a bold counterstroke against the decaying rationalism of mainstream French thought. Victor Hugo, for example, was interested in the Kabbalah, Gerard de Nerval had a considerable acquaintance with alchemy, and Arthur Rimbaud drew on occult literature for some of the symbolism in his poetry.

So it was that in 1870, when Paul Christian published his *History of Magic*, the book was received with quick enthusiasm in France, and was soon known abroad. In this work, Christian gave a full depiction of one of the ceremonies which supposedly took place under the Egyptian pyramids. The aspiring adept was led up a series of seventy-eight steps, and then through a hall containing the images of the Tarot trumps.[6] Christian's trumps were recast a bit to fit into the ambience of his stories, but they are still perfectly recognizable:

I	The Magus
II	The Gate of the Sanctuary
III	Isis Urania
IV	The Cubic Stone
V	Master of the Mysteries of the Arcana
VI	The Two Roads
VII	The Chariot of Osiris
VIII	Themis or the Scales and the Blade
IX	The Veiled Lamp
X	The Sphinx
XI	The Muzzled or Tamed Lion
XII	The Sacrifice
XIII	The Skeleton Reaper or Scythe
XIV	The Two Urns or Genius of the Sun
XV	Typhon
XVI	The Beheaded or Lightning Struck Tower
XVII	The Tower of the Magi
XVIII	The Twilight
XIX	The Blazing Light
XX	The Awakening of the Dead or Genius of the Dead
O	The Crocodile
XXI	The Crown of the Magi

Christian's ordering of the trumps was essentially the same as Lévi's. Indeed, Christian had studied with Lévi briefly, and though he formed a dislike of the man himself, he was undoubtedly influenced by Lévi, as was almost every other occultist of the period.

Lévi had derided the popular fortunetelling decks of his own day, and insisted on the necessity of going back to the "original" Tarot deck (which he thought to be the eighteenth-century Marseilles-type deck that Court de Gébelin had first encountered). While he accepted the order of the Marseilles

Dr. Gérard Encausse, better known as "Papus," was a leading figure in French esoteric circles and the author of The Tarot of the Bohemians—*the first book devoted entirely to the Tarot. This erudite work added much detail, especially regarding numerology, to the growing lore of the esoteric Tarot.*

deck, Lévi asserted that the key to "rectifying" the deck—that is, regaining its esoteric purity—was in the correct placement of The Fool, which he put between Trumps XX and XXI (Judgment and The World). The Fool was designated as 0, rather than XXI, in order to signify its unique character as both beginning and ending the sequence. Christian placed The Crocodile in the same position.

This matter of trump sequence was to become increasingly important as interest in the Tarot grew, for it was generally thought that the secrets of the Tarot trumps were accessible only to those who knew the "correct" order. Many occultists believed that only *true* adepts, those who had been initiated, would know the correct order, and that they would not reveal it to the uninitiated; therefore, went the reasoning, anyone who told the order either didn't know it or was purposefully concealing it! Hence it was later claimed that Lévi and others had purposely concealed the true order of the trumps to preserve the burden of secrecy imposed on them by their occult groups.

The "correct" attribution of Hebrew letters to the trumps was also considered vital to a proper understanding of the Tarot, and every *published* attribution was similarly suspected of being false. It was inevitable that, as these details were being debated, the cards themselves should have to be redesigned, their images esoterically clarified. Lévi himself had announced the necessity of "restoring the twenty-two Arcana of the Tarot to their hieroglyphic purity," but he had never gotten around to it. It was not until 1889 that a deck was produced in accordance with Lévi's system.

The appearance of this limited-edition deck was only one in a cluster of events that took place in the demimonde of French occult enthusiasts during the years 1888 and 1889. The Marquis Stanislaus de Guaita, along with a Spanish-born physician, Dr. Gérard Encausse, founded the Cabalistic Order of the Rosy Cross in 1888; the same year, de Guaita joined forces with amateur artist Oswald Wirth to produce the revised Tarot deck envisioned by Lévi. The trumps of this new deck were published in 1889, and in that year they were also included in the first book devoted exclusively to Tarot—*The Tarot of the Bohemians*, written by Encausse under the name "Papus." (Encausse is known today only as "Papus," and so that is what he will be called hereafter.)

Papus was a follower of Lévi, and his principal contribution was not to introduce revolutionary new insights, but rather to elaborate and refine the ideas which had already become the mainstream of Tarot tradition. These ideas were organized around the Kabbalistic interpretation of the Tarot, and they formed a link between the Tarot deck and the foundations of ceremonial magic. Like virtually all of the Tarot commentators, Papus wrote as much or more on the principles of magical practice as on the Tarot itself. This synthesis of esoteric ideas and esoteric activities was referred to in the period as "occult science."

In the process of further developing Tarot lore, Papus added yet another piece to the myth of Tarot origins which had been gradually taking shape ever since Court de Gébelin. According to Papus, writing in *The Tarot of the Bohemians*, the Egyptian priests had purposefully chosen a game as the repository of their secrets:

> At first [the priests] thought of confiding these secrets to virtuous men secretly recruited by the Initiates themselves, who would transmit them from generation to generation. But one priest, observing that virtue is a most fragile thing, and most difficult to find, at all events in a continuous line, proposed to confide the scientific traditions to vice. The latter, he said, would never fail completely, and through it we are sure of a long and durable preservation of our principles. This opinion was evidently adopted, and the game chosen as a vice was preferred. The small plates were then engraved with the mysterious figures which formerly taught the most important scientific secrets, and since then players have transmitted this Tarot from generation to generation far better than the most virtuous men on earth could have done.

Papus's work on the Tarot—though it was as lavishly romantic in conception as anyone else's—was nevertheless densely argued and carefully supported. Because of the rigor Papus attempted to bring to the subject, *The Tarot of the Bohemians* turned out to be the only work to emerge from the French occult school that has remained of real interest. But others were written. De Guaita himself produced *Le Serpent de la Genêse*, which presented a more mystical approach to the cards, in which, for example, The Hermit signifies the mysteries of solitude, Fortitude the power of will, and The Wheel of Fortune the circle of becoming.

De Guaita was a colorful character, whose relatively short life of thirty-six years was lived with great intensity. Richard Cavendish, in *The Tarot*, gives this provocative description of the young magician:

> He was said to own a familiar spirit, which he kept locked in a cupboard when not in use, and to be able to volatilize poisons and project both them and his own

ROSICRUCIANISM

The symbolic union of the rose and the cross forms both the name and the sign of the Rosicrucians. The legendary origin of Rosicrucianism is said to have been in the fifteenth century (around the same time the Tarot appeared), but in reality, the whole idea was probably created in the early seventeenth century (around the same time the Tarot of Marseilles was becoming standardized), when several pamphlets concerning a mystical "Rosicrucian" order appeared in Germany.

The history of Rosicrucianism is nearly impenetrable, for there is little hard evidence to support the numerous claims and diverse speculations which have grown up around this term. Frances Yates, in *The Rosicrucian Enlightenment*, proposes that Rosicrucianism should be considered *a way of thinking*— exhibited by men like John Dee and Robert Fludd—rather than a doctrine connected with a secret society. The essential fact, according to Yates, is that Rosicrucianism in the later Renaissance was a continuation of the earlier interest in the Hermetic arts, but with the important addition of alchemy. Rosicrucian ideas became incorporated into Freemasonry and other secret societies, and many groups have used the adjective "Rosicrucian" and the symbol of the Rosy Cross to describe their mystical orientation. Most of the major figures in modern magical history have been initiates of self-proclaimed Rosicrucian societies.

In the late nineteenth century, Rosicrucianism enjoyed a vogue among the creative and the eccentric both in England, where the Golden Dawn attracted artists and poets, and in France, where Rosicrucianism influenced the Symbolist movement, chiefly through the salons held by the wildly colorful novelist Joséphin Péladin. In the early twentieth century, manifestations of Rosicrucianism included the somewhat sinister Order of the Temple of the Orient (O.T.O), a German mystical group which emphasized sexual magic, and not one but two American groups, Max Heindel's Rosicrucian Fellowship and Paschal Beverley Randolph's AMORC.

body through space. He lived in rooms hung in scarlet and was accused of constantly dressing up as a cardinal, though his friends said that the truth was merely that he had a favourite red dressing-gown. An aspiring poet and admirer of Baudelaire, Guaita experimented with morphine, cocaine and hashish, and took up occultism with passionate enthusiasm on reading Eliphas Lévi.

Whatever his idiosyncrasies may have been, de Guaita was tireless in his efforts to create a viable occultist order, and together, he, Wirth, and Papus formed the nexus of several esoteric currents. Wirth, a hypnotist, was both a Freemason and a Theosophist, as was Papus; all three men were fascinated by a loosely organized tradition of esoteric teachings called "Rosicrucianism"; and De Guaita and Papus were also involved in the revival of Martinism, a mystical order which had been very powerful in Europe during the late eighteenth and early nineteenth centuries. (Court de Gébelin himself had belonged to a Martinist order, the Elect Order of Cohens.)

The special quality of Martinism was its emphasis on meditation over magical practice. Martinist initiations were not ceremonial, but purely personal, passed along from master to student. This tradition was ideal for De Guaita's purposes, because his involvement in creating a neo-Martinist movement was actually designed to discover and attract promising students who might in turn become adepts in his Rosicrucian group. Like a good many other characters (some of whom we will soon meet), De Guaita was part of an emerging competition—both social and philosophical in nature—for leadership of the occult movement.

This movement was marked by the proliferation of "secret" societies. These groups, many of which sprang up in England and Europe around the same period of time, drew their participants from many different sources. Modern Tarot commentator Mouni Sadhu, in his unique Hermetic textbook *The Tarot*, describes the groups in this way:

> To them came people tired by their long religious search; those disappointed in academic knowledge; those desiring something similar to Masonry, but, as they hoped, in a nobler form; ordinary, curious people of all calibres, and those who were unacceptable to other occult organizations. Finally, there were the really honest men and women who were striving after mystical powers, lovers of talks on occult themes in full salons, and hysterically-minded ladies, who are always keen for membership of societies where there is a taste of mystery.

The fountainhead of all this interest in the occult was a rising, restless dissatisfaction with modern materialism, with the increasing complexity and changefulness of life. There was a strong need to discover—or recover—some sense of continuity, meaning, simplicity; and this need was perfectly addressed by the message that De Guaita's friend Papus presented in his books on the Tarot and the occult sciences. The very first paragraph of *The Tarot of the Bohemians* declared that materialism had failed:

> We are on the eve of a complete transformation of our scientific methods. Materialism has given us all that we can expect from it, and inquirers, though disappointed as a rule, hope for great things from the future, and are unwilling to spend more time in pursuing the path adopted in modern days. Analysis has been carried, in every branch of knowledge, as far as possible, and has only deepened those moats which divide the sciences.

The several streams of esoteric thought which flowed through Papus's mind enabled him to weave a strong fabric of occult associations into his interpretation of the Tarot. He contended that in ancient times, all knowledge had been condensed into a few simple principles. These fundamental laws, Papus believed, could be glimpsed in the Bible, Homer, the Koran, and all the important documents of early civilization; they had been handed along through a chain that included the classical mystery religions and Gnosticism. After being lost to the West in the Dark Ages, these ideas had been passed back to the Renaissance through the discovery of Arabic texts. They were perpetuated by the alchemists, the Knights Templar, Raymond Lull, and the Rosicrucians, and finally preserved by the Masons and the Martinists.

The essential record of that original synthesis, according to Papus, was the

Tarot. However much the primeval knowledge may have been distorted by its passage through many centuries and many voices, the pure form of those fundamental cosmic laws was still to be found in the Tarot. But only those who possessed the *real* key to the Tarot images could know this truth.

Given human nature, a struggle over possession of the real key was inevitable. However, that struggle was to take its most dramatic (or, some might say, melodramatic) form not in France, where the story of the esoteric Tarot had been unfolding for more than a century, but in England. At almost exactly the same time that Stanislaus de Guaita formed his Rosicrucian society, another group of seekers was gathering across the Channel—a group whose aim would become nothing less than the reanimation of the primal imagination.

Notes

1. Moakley's description is from her book *The Tarot Cards Painted by Bonifacio Bembo*. Court de Gébelin's backward ordering of the cards is actually very interesting, and makes a good deal of sense, but it did not catch on among early occultists. It has been revived, however, in a few modern books, such as Stephen Hoeller's *The Royal Road* and Micheline Stuart's *The Tarot Path to Self Development*.

2. This hypothesis might tie in with the work of Harold Bayley, whose overstated but valuable book *The Lost Language of Symbolism* (Rowman and Littlefield, 1968) argued that religious dissidents in the papermaking and printing trades communicated with one another by means of symbolic watermarks. Bayley's book was originally published in 1912, and has attracted the interest of occult theorists ever since. Robert V. O'Neill analyzes the relationship of Tarot symbols and watermarks in his *Tarot Symbolism*, pp. 224–228.

3. In French, *occultisme*. The term was first used in English by the Theosophist A. D. Sinnett in 1881.

4. The Tablet—which surfaced after the sack of Rome in 1527—still has not been deciphered; its hieroglyphics don't seem to correspond with the rest of Egyptian iconography, and it is thought to be from a late, decadent period. Its symbolism, however, does seem to be associated with esoteric ideas.

5. The quotations from Lévi are taken from *The Ritual and Dogma of High Magic*. The quotations given here were translated by different authors, and sometimes differ in style of language; I have chosen the version in each case which seems easiest to understand. The first extract is from Stuart Kaplan's *Tarot Classic*, and it appears to be his own translation. The second is from A. E. Waite's translation (Redway, 1896).

6. This story was the inspiration behind the arrangement of a surrealist art exhibition in 1947, which will be described in part 2.

3.

THE MAKERS OF MODERN TAROT

O N March 1, 1888, an event took place that was to influence greatly the course of esoteric studies and the whole future of the Tarot. This event was the founding of The Hermetic Order of the Golden Dawn, a group which drew into its creative maelstrom not only curious would-be magicians, but also serious scholars, along with many poets and artists interested in symbolism— among them the poet William Butler Yeats (a Nobel laureate),[1] Annie Horniman (founder of the famed Abbey Theatre in Dublin), and painter Gerald Kelly (later president of the Royal Academy).

In Yeats's introduction to *A Vision*, the book in which he explained his complex theory of history and imagination, the poet described his own impressions of the atmosphere within which the Golden Dawn arose:

> We all, so far as I can remember, differed from ordinary students of philosophy or religion through our belief that truth cannot be discovered but may be revealed, and that if a man do not lose faith, and if he go through certain preparations, revelation will find him at the fitting moment . . . . I look back to it [the Golden Dawn period] as a time when we were full of a phantasy that had been handed down for generations, and now an interpretation, now an enlargement of the folk-lore of the villages. That phantasy did not explain the world to our intellects, which were after all very modern, but it recalled certain forgotten methods and chiefly how to so suspend the will that the mind became automatic and a possible vehicle for spiritual beings. . . .

The story of the birth of the Golden Dawn society is legendary in occult circles. It begins in 1887 with the discovery, in a second-hand book stall, of a manuscript written in cipher and appearing to be about seventy-five years old.

The discoverer was the Rev. A.F.A. Woodford, a member of the Societas Rosicruciana in Anglia, a group which affected to integrate the English Masonic tradition with European Rosicrucianism. He passed the manuscript along to two other members of the Soc. Ros. (as it is often written)—a Dr. Woodman, and Dr. Wynn Westcott.

The cipher manuscript turned out to contain a page referring to a continental secret order called "Golden Dawn," and providing information for contacting a German woman, Frau Sprengel, who was among the leaders of that group. According to the traditional account, Dr. Westcott reached Frau Sprengel and received permission to start an English branch of the order as soon as three people were "initiated" so that the requisite ruling group could be formed. Westcott was also given instructions for the organization of the order. In addition to the council of three, the Golden Dawn was to have both inner and outer groups, each composed of several degrees; members would proceed to different levels of the order by passing examinations and participating in initiation ceremonies.

Westcott did as bidden by Frau Sprengel, and soon the Golden Dawn was off to a flourishing start—or so the story goes. But while it is true that the Golden Dawn group thrived almost immediately, attracting a potent clientele, the truth about its origins seems to have been different from the story put forth by Westcott. In the first place, although the cipher manuscript contained some pages watermarked 1809, it seems almost certain the document itself had actually been written sometime in the 1880s, by an unknown continental adept. The manuscript probably *was* found in a bookstall by Rev. Woodford, and it probably was believed by Westcott to be genuine. But all this is largely irrelevant, since the only part of the manuscript that really turned out to be important to the development of the Golden Dawn was the one page concerning the formation of the group—and this page, in fact, seems likely to have been added by Dr. Westcott after the manuscript was received from Rev. Woodford.[2]

Westcott apparently was anxious to form an esoteric group which (unlike the Masons and the Soc. Ros.) would admit women as well as men. He may also have been motivated by the desire to offer a more Western-oriented alternative to Madame Blavatsky's newly formed—and already popular— Theosophical Society.[3] In any event, Westcott presumably felt he needed some kind of charter connecting his new organization with the old esoteric tradition; so, he created an altogether fictitious link to a group which in fact had never existed.

But the bogus beginnings of the Golden Dawn have little to do with the significance of the group in occult history, since the magical order that evolved under the name "Golden Dawn" turned out to be very, very different from the rather picturesque social group Westcott had apparently set out to create.

The reason for this wide and important divergence can be summed up in one name: Mathers. Interestingly, it was the inclusion of the Tarot as an element in the studies of this new group which probably led to Mathers' involvement in the first place. Dr. Westcott had been closely associated with Kenneth MacKenzie, one of the founders of the Soc. Ros.; MacKenzie, in

Samuel Liddell Mathers—who took the name MacGregor to signify his Celtic sympathies—created much of the Golden Dawn ritual, as well as much of the conflict that marked the group's existence. Mathers brought a new eclecticism to occult studies, combining the magical insights and practices of many times and places to produce the distinctive Golden Dawn doctrines.

turn, had been introduced to the Tarot by Eliphas Lévi, who made several trips to England. And it was this Tarot connection that led Westcott and his fellow founders into contact with S. Liddell Mathers, who had already written a short tract on divination with the Tarot.

Mathers soon became the driving force and chief theorist of the Golden Dawn. Eccentric, authoritarian, and—as it turned out—more than a little unwise, Mathers was nevertheless undeniably gifted with exceptional charisma and creative power. Kathleen Raines, in *Yeats, the Tarot, and the Golden Dawn*, tells us that Mathers made an impression on the young poet even before the two had met:

> [Yeats] used to see [Mathers] in the British Museum reading-room where he copied manuscripts on magical ceremonial and doctrine (Yeats must at this time have been working on Blake): "a man of thirty-six or thirty-seven, in a brown velveteen coat, with a gaunt resolute face, and who seemed, before I heard his name, or knew the nature of his studies, a figure of romance." "It was through him mainly," Yeats has written in *The Trembling of the Veil*, "that I began certain studies and experiences that were to convince me that images well up before the mind's eye from a deeper source than conscious or subconscious memory."

Mathers—who soon changed his first name to MacGregor as a gesture of Celtic pride—wrote much of the Golden Dawn's ritual material, along with many of the "Knowledge Papers" which set forth the magical doctrines of the order. And in the process he introduced a new element to traditional occultism. Nevill Drury, a thoughtful commentator on occult matters, describes the innovation this way in his book *Inner Visions*:

> It had been common until Mathers's time for occultists and magicians to work single, specific systems. We can turn to Cornelius Agrippa's alchemical treatises, Edward Kelley's skrying in trance ... Francis Barrett's idiosyncratic magical system, *The Magus, or Celestial Intelligencer* (1801). We find Papus concerned primarily with the origins of Tarot symbolism, Robert Fludd, medieval artist par

41

excellence, infatuated with Rosicrucian imagery, and Thomas Vaughan engaged in a form of tantric alchemy.

Mathers proposed that the Western magician should investigate all the cosmologies of his cultural tradition. In 1887 he published the first English translation of Knorr Von Rosenroth's *Kabbala Denudata* . . . . He was later to preoccupy himself in translating a number of key magical documents which might otherwise have been doomed to obscurity in museum archives.

The significance of this wide range of interests was that the magical rituals of the Golden Dawn, in whose shaping and formation Mathers played a major role, came to draw on every major mythology in Western culture.

Under Mathers's leadership, the Golden Dawn created and implemented a modern magical system which brought together in a coherent way many different systems: Kabbalah, Tarot, alchemy, astrology, and numerology, along with visionary experience and ritual magic. The Golden Dawn was very serious about its purposes, and members were effortful practitioners of the esoteric arts, who worked their way through a series of increasingly complex and mysterious initiations by studying magical lore, taking part in rituals, seeking spiritual visions, keeping elaborate journals—and meditating on the Tarot images.

In the Golden Dawn system, the Tarot was given a complete esoteric context, which it had never had before. It was linked into the whole network of correlations which Mathers had drawn from a variety of traditions, and even more important, it was used in creative ways by the members of the order. Each member had to copy his (or her—nearly half of the three hundred members were women) own deck from a master copy, and as there were no precise instructions about how this was to be done, the result was a wide variety of highly personalized decks. The trumps (also called "keys") were then used as gateways through the imagination, into immaterial realms of being.

The various cards were also assigned to different levels or "grades" in the society, and were used in rituals and initiations. In the fourth level, for example, the symbolic element was water, the Tarot key was The Moon, and the initiatory rite included figures masked in such moon-related guises as the goddess Isis, incanting on the meaning of the Tarot Moon:

> Before you on the Altar is the 18th Key of the Tarot: . . . it represents the Moon . . . . The moon is in its increase . . . and from it proceed sixteen principal and sixteen secondary rays, which together make 32 the number of the Paths of Yetzirah. She is the moon at the feet of the Woman of the Revelation, ruling equally over the cold Natures and the passive Elements of Earth and Water. The four Hebrew yods refer to the four letters of the Holy Name, re-constituting the destroyed world from the waters . . . . The Dogs are the Jackals of the Egyptian Anubis, guarding the Gates of the East and of the West, shown by the two towers, between which lies the path of all the heavenly bodies, ever rising in the East and setting in the West . . . .[4]

This kind of activity—which may well seem a little silly from our contemporary point of view—represented in its time the attempts of some very creative people to actually *enter into* the world of the symbolic imagination. In the late nineteenth and early twentieth centuries, when technology and "modernity" seemed to be draining all the mystery and spiritual potency out of cultural life, many people were looking for some way of restoring connections between the material and immaterial worlds—not just through abstract knowledge, but through *action*. There was experimentation in art, in music, in literature, all of which seemed "crazy" to more ordinary-minded observers; art critics, for example, were horrified by cubism, and a violent demonstration broke out among the audience members at the premiere of Stravinsky's "Rites of Spring."

Occultism was neither more nor less "crazy" than these other forms of experimentation. But all radically creative activities—painting or poetry just as much as mysticism and divination—can be personally dangerous, in the sense that as often as not, they lead to chaotic relationships, emotional imbalances, and excesses of all sorts. These negative consequences of creative experimentation were certainly very evident among the members of the Golden Dawn; for many of these aspiring adepts, the passionate desire to break through into new imaginative realms seems to have overruled common sense entirely.

For the first decade and more of the Golden Dawn, an uneasy truce reigned among its diverse creative personalities, but like most secret societies, the group was always full of intrigue and rife with disagreements over matters of interpretation and emphasis. By 1900, several strong factions had developed, and relations were strained to the breaking point. MacGregor Mathers, living in Paris with his wife Moina (the sister of philosopher Henri Bergson), was attempting to control the members of the London group by means of letters and envoys. Perhaps in an effort to shore up his crumbling power, Mathers announced that Westcott had forged the Golden Dawn page in the cipher manuscript. This revelation began the most violent of the many upheavals that marked the group's existence.

Yeats was heavily involved in these goings-on, and much disturbed by them; he described the penultimate event of this crisis in a letter to his confidante, Lady Gregory:

> I have had a bad time of it lately. I told you that I was putting MacGregor out of the Kabbala. Well last week he sent a mad person—whom we had refused to initiate—to take possession of the rooms and papers of the Society.[5]

The "mad person" was none other than Aleister Crowley, then a young protegé of Mathers. Dressed in Highland regalia, with a black mask over his face, Crowley had attempted to take physical possession of the order's papers and paraphernalia and had had to be ejected by a constable—perhaps justifying Yeats's remark that Crowley had been refused initiation in the first place because "we did not think a mystical society was intended to be a reformatory."

Whatever Crowley's defects of character may have been—and these will be mentioned in more detail shortly—he was nevertheless to become one of the most dynamic "alumni" of the Golden Dawn. (Crowley had, in fact, been a member of the "Outer Order," and had been initiated into the "Inner Order" by Mathers, though this initiation was not recognized by the Yeats camp.) In any event, the tragicomic episode involving Crowley marked the splintering of the Golden Dawn—and, ironically, began a period of considerable productivity surrounding the Tarot. From the ruins of the Hermetic Order of the

Golden Dawn there arose several new esoteric societies. And since the Tarot had been among the most important and carefully studied subjects of the Golden Dawn's magical system, it was not surprising that each faction of the fragmented order eventually produced its own "rectified" and "perfected" Tarot deck, complete with a book of interpretations.

By far the most influential of these new Tarots was created by A. E. Waite. Waite had begun his work with the Tarot late in the nineteenth century, when he translated the works of Papus and Eliphas Lévi into English. He joined the Golden Dawn in 1891, and seems to have played little part in the dramatic events which led up to the 1900 schism. But in 1903—after the group had been under Yeats's leadership for a short period—Waite took over control of the London temple, changed the name of the order from "Hermetic" to "Holy," and replaced the magical emphasis of Mathers with an agenda that focused on mysticism. Yeats and the majority of Golden Dawn members chose to remain with the magical path, and founded another order, the Stella Matutina.

Although rather puffed-up, and considered by some (principally Crowley and his followers) a bit comical, Waite was a thoughtful scholar, determined to correct the misunderstandings and fanciful speculations which had grown up around the Tarot. His very important book, *The Pictorial Key to the Tarot*, was published in 1910, and in it he effectively denounced—in a characteristically dry style—the notion of Tarot's Egyptian origin, together with other popular pseudo-historical scenarios. This profile of Eliphas Lévi is a good example of the way in which Waite placed the by-then almost mystical past of Tarot interpretation in a new, more realistic light:

In 1860 there arose Eliphas Lévi, a brilliant and profound *illuminé* whom it is impossible to accept, and with whom it is impossible to dispense . . . . After all, he was only Etteilla a second time in the flesh, endowed in his transmutation with a mouth of gold and a wider casual knowledge. That notwithstanding, he has written the most comprehensive, brilliant, enchanting *History of Magic* which has ever been drawn into writing in any language. The Tarot and the de Gébelin hypothesis he took into his heart of hearts, and all occult France and all esoteric Britain, Martinists, half-instructed Kabalists, schools of *soi disant* theosophy— there, here, and everywhere—have accepted his judgment about it with the same confidence as his interpretations of those great classics of Kabalism which he had skimmed rather than read.

It could fairly be said that Waite's own approach to the Tarot set the tone for much of what has been thought and written about the subject in the twentieth century. The Tarot, asserted Waite, "has no history prior to the fourteenth century," and he gave this view of its nature:

The Tarot embodies symbolical presentations of universal ideas, behind which lie all the implicits of the human mind, and it is in this sense that they contain secret doctrine, which is the realization by the few of truths imbedded in the consciousness of all, though they have not passed into express recognition by ordinary men. The theory is that this doctrine has always existed—that is to say, has been excogitated in the consciousness of an elect minority; that it has been perpetuated in secrecy from one to another and has been recorded in secret literatures, like those of Alchemy and Kabalism; that it is contained also in those Instituted

Arthur Edward Waite designed the most popular of all modern Tarot packs, the Rider-Waite deck, and explained it in the still-popular book A Pictorial Key to the Tarot. *Waite also wrote books on alchemy and Rosicrucianism which are today considered classics.*

Mysteries of which Rosicrucianism offers an example near to our hand in the past, and Craft Masonry a living summary, or general memorial, for those who can interpret its real meaning.

One of Waite's especially significant contributions to the interpretation of the Tarot was his recognition of the importance of alchemy, in addition to the Kabbalah, as a means of understanding the symbolism of the Tarot. Both the Rosicrucian tradition and the Golden Dawn rituals made much use of the symbolism of alchemy, which revolves around the nature of the elements and the fusion of male and female polarities.

Alchemical work—which has been practiced in various cultures for many centuries—can be viewed in two ways. On the one hand, it concerns the physical process of transmuting base metals into higher ones: lead into gold. This aspect of alchemy contributed a great deal to the development of modern chemistry. But alchemy can also be seen as a psycho-spiritual process, in which the adept aims to purify the inner self and attain higher levels of consciousness. Waite, in keeping with his general inclination toward mysticism, viewed alchemy in this way, as a spiritual undertaking. Although Waite did not present the "alchemical Tarot" in explicit detail, his knowledge of alchemy (he translated a number of Renaissance alchemical texts and wrote several books on the subject which are now regarded as classics) certainly influenced strongly the development of his Tarot interpretations.

Waite's book was illustrated with a new set of Tarot images, designed by

45

him and executed by Pamela Colman Smith, an American artist. These images, published as a deck by Rider and Company in 1910, featured an innovation that was to influence most subsequently designed decks: the use of storylike pictures on the minor arcana pip cards, illustrating their divinatory meanings. Partly for this reason, and partly because of its colorful, accessible style, the Rider-Waite deck is still the most popular Tarot in existence, and Waite's book sells briskly even today.

But though Waite is well-known today among those interested in Tarot, a far more famous (or infamous) alumnus of the Golden Dawn was the self-styled "Great Beast," Aleister Crowley, a man as different as could be from the serious and mystical A. E. Waite. Although arguably a little mad—he pursued "sex-magick," engaged his detractors in long-distance battles carried out by sorcery, and claimed to have been Eliphas Lévi in a former life[6]—Crowley was nevertheless a perceptive and imaginative student of the esoteric. Together with artist Lady Frieda Harris, he created one of the most beautiful and unusual of all Tarot decks. The "Thoth deck" was published—in a limited edition of two hundred copies—as part of Crowley's masterwork on the Tarot, *The Book of Thoth*.

In titling his Tarot commentary *The Book of Thoth*, Crowley probably intended to be ironic, for it seems likely that he viewed himself not as explicating a centuries-old work, but rather as actually writing—for the first time—the long-promised "book" of Thoth/Hermes. Crowley's approach didn't assume that any historical relationship existed between the Egyptians and the Tarot deck; in fact, he stated clearly that "the origin of the Tarot is quite irrelevant, even if it were certain."

According to Crowley, the Tarot was to be understood as "a pictorial representation of the Forces of Nature as conceived by the Ancients according to a conventional symbolism." This "ancient scheme of the Elements, Planets and Zodiacal Signs, was summarized by the Qabalists in their Tree of Life," Crowley wrote, and so the Tarot was "beyond doubt a deliberate attempt to represent, in pictorial form, the doctrines of the Qabalah." Based on this hypothesis, Crowley developed an expanded—and somewhat idiosyncratic—blend of Kabbalism, Eastern mysticism, and Western mythology to illuminate the Tarot. This synthetic vision he expounded in *The Book of Thoth*, a work which is, if by no means trustworthy, nevertheless provocative and rich with associations.

Waite's and Crowley's approaches to the Tarot were alike in one respect: They were both concerned with the Tarot as a symbolical tool, and they studied it in a practical rather than a theoretical way, believing that the use of the Tarot images could be a path to knowledge and transformation. Their two decks, however, were as different as could be. The Waite deck is rendered in primary colors, with a cheerful, open, almost naive style, while Crowley's Thoth deck is haunting, swirling, colored in beautifully eerie shades, filled with barely veiled sexuality. Waite's pictures are crowded from border to border with traditional symbols, and everything from the pattern on a dress to the color of a flower is intended to be highly meaningful; Crowley's pictures, on the other hand, depend not on conventional symbolism but on an

Aleister Crowley, the self-described "Great Beast," combined an acute intelligence with an extremely eccentric character. His "Thoth" Tarot deck, and the Book of Thoth *which accompanied it, added a new aesthetic and scientific dimension to the study of Tarot, but he is better known for his use of sex and drugs in magical pursuits than for his genuine contributions to magical theory.*

atmosphere of strangeness, which makes it seem as if each card were a peephole into another world.

Crowley's reputation for extremities of thought and behavior is so fully developed that it is something of a surprise to read his *Book of Thoth*. There he gives a very restrained account of the Golden Dawn and its misadventures, in addition to a literate, informative, and very readable exploration of all the Tarot cards. The theories he presents are far from being bizarre (at least from our contemporary point of view), and if they had been attributed to someone other than the notorious character described in British tabloids as "the wickedest man in the world," they would probably have been viewed quite differently.

The originality of Crowley's approach is especially visible in his use of the "new science" to elaborate his ideas. By the time of Crowley's later writings, the theories of Einstein, Planck, and Heisenberg were already well-known, and *The Book of Thoth* was the first work in which the Tarot was approached in a post-Newtonian framework. The following passage demonstrates that Crowley had quickly understood what was to dawn only slowly upon others:

> The essence of Science today is far more mysterious than the cloudiest speculations of Leibnitz, Spinoza or Hegel; the modern definition of Matter reminds one irresistibly of the definition of Spirit given by such mystics as Ruysbroek, Boehme and Molinos. The idea of the Universe in the mind of a modern mathematician is singularly reminiscent of the ravings of William Blake.[7]

Left: The Lovers, from the Rider-Waite deck. Right: Lust, Crowley's version of The Lovers, from the Thoth deck. These two classic decks are the most famous of the twentieth century, but they could scarcely be more different. Waite's is brightly colored and filled with traditional symbolism, while Crowley's is a muted swirl of strange shapes and hues. Both decks were drawn by women. Waite's collaborator was set designer Pamela Colman Smith, Crowley's, talented painter Lady Frieda Harris.

Traces of Crowley's distinctive scientific interest are to be found throughout *The Book of Thoth* and in the designs of the Thoth deck. The twenty-first trump, for example, which Crowley calls "The Universe," includes among its symbols "the skeleton plan of the building of the house of Matter. It shows the ninety-two known chemical elements, arranged according to their rank in the hierarchy." Crowley adds that "the design is due to the genius of the late J.W.N. Sullivan," and refers the reader to Sullivan's book *The Bases of Modern Science*.

Though most of his ideas on the Tarot were developed during the Golden Dawn period, Crowley's deck and book were not published until 1944, a year before his death. By that time, their appearance was little more than a belated finale to occultism's golden age. The creative spirit of occult inquiry that flourished early in the century had, like so much else, been dimmed by the social and political tensions of the world between the two great wars. As A. E. Waite expressed it years later:

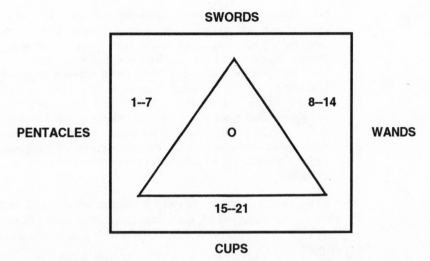

Ouspensky offered an alternative to the prevailing Kabbalistic interpretation of the Tarot's structures. Ouspensky's scheme, shown in this diagram, places man's soul (a dimensionless point) in the center of the spiritual world (the triangle, which is God in Trinity). Both are encompassed by the square, representing the material world. The Fool, or zero card, equals man's soul; the remaining trumps are divided into three equal groups of seven, forming the triangle; and the four suits make up the aspects of the phenomenal world.

The War of 1914 engulfed all the Schools and all their brave imaginings; and when it was in fine suspended by the figurative peace of Versailles, the Schools emerged but slowly from the weltering chaos and were shorn of their chief personalities, their adornments and appeal.

Waite made this observation in 1930, in the introduction to a new work by French occultist A. E. Thierens, titled *The General Book of the Tarot*.[8] Its publication marked a return of the French influence in Tarot studies, already evidenced by the appearance in 1927 of a new deck and book, *Le Tarot des Imagiers du Moyen Age*, by none other than Oswald Wirth, one-time associate of Stanislaus De Guaita. But although these works were "new" in the sense of being published for the first time, there was little innovative about them. Both Wirth and Thierens were squarely in the French tradition, as descended from Eliphas Lévi. Like Crowley, they continued to rework the same ideas, as the momentum of the occult revival steadily diminished.

The Golden Dawn method certainly dominated Tarot thought in the early twentieth century, just as Lévi's approach had dominated the late nineteenth century. But there were other developments taking place as well. In 1910—the same year that Waite's *Pictorial Key* was published—a young Russian produced an unusual pamphlet on the Tarot. P. D. Ouspensky, the best-known follower of the mystic Gurdjieff, departed significantly from the usual emphasis on Kabbalah, replacing the Tree of Life with this more Christian metaphysical schema:

Now, if we imagine twenty-one cards disposed in the shape of a triangle, seven cards on each side, a point in the center of the triangle represented by the zero card, and a square round the triangle (the square consisting of fifty-six cards, fourteen on each side), we shall have a representation of the relation between God, Man and the Universe, or the relation between the world of ideas, the consciousness of man and the physical world.

The triangle is God (the Trinity) or the world of ideas, or the noumenal world. The point is man's soul. The square is the visible, physical or phenomenal world. Potentially, the point is equal to the square, which means that all the visible world is contained in man's consciousness, is created in man's soul. And the soul itself is a point having no dimension in the world of the spirit, symbolized by the triangle.

Ouspensky went on to offer a cycle of meditations based on the trumps. His ideas on the Tarot, which show considerable influence from Oswald Wirth, were expanded in his book *A New Model of the Universe*, published in England in 1930.

Meanwhile, a quite different line of Tarot inquiry had been given new impetus in England by Jesse L. Weston's influential 1920 study of the Grail legends, *From Ritual to Romance*. Weston's work is best known as the inspiration for T. S. Eliot's epic poem, "The Waste Land," but for students of the Tarot, it is of interest for another reason as well. In it, Weston takes up A. E. Waite's notion that the four suits of the Tarot minor arcana are analogues of the four Grail Hallows.[9]

Weston uses this Tarot connection in support of her argument that the symbolic objects—cup (or dish), lance, sword, and stone—represented in the Medieval Grail romances are similar to the four treasures of Celtic lore—cauldron, spear, sword, and stone—because both are fragmentary records of the secret rituals of an ancient fertility cult. Weston contends:

We have . . . evidence that these four objects do, in fact, form a special group entirely independent of any appearance in Folk-lore or Romance. They exist to-day as the four suits of the Tarot.

To reinforce this idea, Weston quotes from a private correspondence with Yeats, in which he wrote:

(1) Cup, Lance, Dish, Sword, in slightly varying forms, have never lost their mystic significance, and are to-day a part of magical operations. (2) The memory kept by the four suits of the Tarot, Cup, Lance, Sword, Pentangle (Dish), is an esoterical notation for fortune-telling purposes.

The details of Weston's theory about the origins of the Grail lore have not proven too durable in the light of later scholarship, but her general approach was very provocative. By combining anthropological scholarship with literary criticism, Weston opened up new territory which has been richly developed by scholars in recent years. Moreover, by treating the Tarot as a symbol system, rather than as an occult instrument, Weston widened the context of Tarot inquiry.

The connection of the Tarot with the Grail material has suggested some

THE TAROT SUITS	THE GRAIL HALLOWS	THE TREASURES OF IRELAND
Cups	The Grail , chalice from which Christ drank	The Cauldron of The Dagda, father of all
Swords	The sword of King David	The sword of Nuada, king of the Irish Celts
Wands	The sacred lance which pierced Christ's side	The spear of Lug, "many-skilled" god
Pentacles	The platter from which Christ ate the Paschal Lamb	The stone of Fal, or Sovereignty

Jesse Weston followed A. E. Waite in linking the four Tarot suits to the four Grail Hallows, and she also suggested a connection with the Four Treasures of Celtic Ireland. The pursuit of the Grail Hollows, chronicled in numerous stories and poems of the Middle Ages, is an allegory of man's search for spiritual perfection. Like the alchemical process of transmutation, the Grail Quest is an outward symbol of an inward process.

interesting ideas—such as Tarot scholar George Wald's explanation of the mysterious Tower card, which was originally called The House of God:

> The card portrays one of the most striking incidents in the legends surrounding King Arthur and his knights and the Holy Grail . . . the "dolorous" stroke struck in the Grail Castle—the House of God—by one of Arthur's knights, the luckless Sir Balin.[10]

According to Sir Thomas Malory's account of the incident in *Le Morte d'Arthur*, when Sir Balin smote King Pellam with the Grail spear, which he had discovered in the Castle Tower, "therewith the castle roof and walls broke and fell to the earth." The wound received by King Pellam would not heal, and he became the Fisher King, whose illness and impotence brought disaster to his people and turned his realm into the Waste Land. (The Emperor and The Hanged Man have been associated with the Fisher King, before and after his wound.)

"Although the Arthurian cycle of legends concerned Britain," Wald points out, "it was read by Italians and French as well, and, indeed, was known throughout Europe as a subject of art." There seems good reason to see some influence of the Grail legends at work in the Tarot, and nothing contradicts the idea. The influence may go back even further, to connections with the Celtic treasures, as Weston proposed, and to other pagan motifs as well. (In recent years, the pagan background of the Tarot has been developed by a whole group of theorists who will be discussed a bit later.)

All in all, the Tarot books published in England and France between the two World Wars added virtually nothing new to Tarot theory. All were

51

elaborations of ideas which had been formulated during the fertile Golden Dawn period, and though the authors sometimes gave new twists to these old ideas, the creativity of the European approach to Tarot was fading. In its place came new energy, from a surprising source. For the first half of this century, much of the innovation and animation of the occult movement was to be found not in London or Paris, but in—Los Angeles! So our account of Tarot history must now turn to different shores.

Notes

1. Yeats's involvement with the Golden Dawn was especially important, for he saved—often with annotations—all the notebooks, letters, and other memorabilia which he gathered in his association with the group. These materials provide some excellent insights into the workings of the group and its influences on the creative imagination. And although Yeats rarely spoke openly of the order or its practices, and made few references to the Tarot, it is known that he and his wife, a medium whose automatic writing became an important source in the development of Yeats's philosophy, made use of the Tarot in their occult researches.

2. See Ellic Howe's article on the Golden Dawn in the *Encyclopedia of the Unexplained*. Howe used some Golden Dawn papers and members' correspondence to deduce the probable truth about Westcott's deception. Israel Regardie, a member of the Golden Dawn in its later days, wrote extensively about the order, and though he did not feel that Howe's interpretation was necessarily correct, he agreed there was much evidence to support it.

3. The Theosophical Society, founded in 1875 by Helena Blavatsky and Henry Steele Olcott, exercised a tremendous influence over the growth and dissemination of occult and metaphysical ideas until well into the 1920s. In spite of much internal strife and many schisms, as well as numerous instances of fraudulent and/or ridiculous behavior by its leaders, the T.S. attracted the interest of intellectuals and progressives searching for a new source of spiritual direction. The most lasting accomplishment of the Theosophical Society (which continues its activities today) was the introduction of Eastern philosophy and occultism into Western metaphysical speculation. More will be said about the T.S. in part 2.

4. Quoted in Nevill Drury's book *Inner Visions*, p. 18.

5. Quoted in George Mills Harper's book, *Yeats's Golden Dawn*, p. 29.

6. Crowley was born on the day of Lévi's death.

7. This comment of Crowley's, written before 1944, clearly prefigures the line of thought which was popularized by Fritjof Capra and others in the 1970s.

8. Thieren's book—reissued in a 1975 American edition under the title *Astrology and the Tarot*—is still interesting today in that it juxtaposes the interpretations of Papus, Mathers, and Waite.

9. Waite published a large volume entitled *The Hidden Church of the Holy*

Graal: Its Legends and Symbolism in 1909; it contained a chapter describing "The Hallows of the Graal Mystery Rediscovered in the Talismans of the Tarot." This chapter was included as an appendix in Waite's 1933 book *The Holy Grail*.

10. Quoted by Stuart Kaplan in his *Encyclopedia of the Tarot*, Vol. 2, p. 174.

4.

THE TRANSFORMATION OF TAROT

BETWEEN the Tarot of the Visconti-Sforzas and the Tarot as we know it today, there is certainly a world of difference. So far, we have seen two of the stages through which Tarot interpretation has passed. The first of these, from Court de Gébelin to Papus, produced the whole idea of an "esoteric" Tarot and put in place the major elements of traditional Tarot interpretation; the second, which centered around the Golden Dawn, refined and advanced those basic elements, providing a detailed structure for the magical and divinatory uses of Tarot.

The third stage in the development of today's Tarot was marked by a change of scenery and a fresh influx of colorful characters. The new American venue offered an exuberant and much more public setting for Tarot research. Absent were the ostentatiously "secret" societies, the veiled references, and the aristocratic eccentrics; in their place were businesslike organizations that pursued occult ideas with the same practical attitude General Motors brought to the matter of transportation.

The result of the American influence on Tarot can be seen now in the diversity, the eclecticism, and the individualism of contemporary Tarot interpretation—as well as in the increasing commercialization of Tarot. Over the last two decades, the Tarot has become both a subject of serious scholarship and a lucrative business enterprise. The pivotal player in this transformation was actually a Swiss psychoanalyst who wrote only a single sentence about the Tarot, but as we shall see, the foundation for his influence was laid by an assortment of esoteric adventurers who made their way West in the early part of this century.

California, of course, has long been a mecca for seekers of all sorts, so it should not be surprising that a chapter in the history of the esoteric Tarot unfolded there in the 1920s and 1930s. In those decades, an energetic assortment of occult groups arrived or arose in the City of Angels, and from this apparently unorganized confluence of events, there developed a thriving center of Tarot studies. Though little attention has been paid to this period in Tarot history—perhaps because it did not boast such larger-than-life figures as Mathers and Crowley—there was, nevertheless, something important happening.

Paul Foster Case is perhaps the best-known figure of the Los Angeles group, and he was the closest in spirit to the original ideas of the Golden Dawn. As a teenager, Case was interested in stage magic, and he worked with playing cards. A chance question about the origin of playing cards started him on a course of research that led to the Tarot, and from there to a Golden Dawn chapter in New York, where he was initiated in 1910. When the leader of the chapter died a few months later, Case succeeded him, but his relationship with the group deteriorated, and in 1920, Case founded a group of his own called Builders of the Adytum (generally referred to as B.O.T.A.).[1]

Case published his book *The Tarot* in 1927, and a B.O.T.A. deck in 1931. The deck used slightly modernized versions of the Waite designs, but gave them in black outline so that the user could color in the cards personally. This idea, of course, was a streamlined version of the original Golden Dawn practice, in which each adept had to draw his or her own cards. In 1933, B.O.T.A. moved to Los Angeles, and established a colorfully decorated Temple of Tarot and Holy Qabalah, from which the group's correspondence course is still distributed today, along with Case's books and the B.O.T.A. deck.

Case was responsible for if not inventing, then at least popularizing yet another now-well-known myth of the origins of the Tarot. In his book *The Tarot*, Case gave this account:

> According to an occult tradition, in which I am inclined to place confidence, the actual date of [the Tarot's] invention was about the year 1200 A.D. The inventors, this tradition avers, were a group of adepts who met at stated intervals in the city of Fez, in Morocco. After the destruction of Alexandria, Fez became the literary and scientific capital of the world. Thither, from all parts of the globe, came wise men of all nations, speaking all tongues. Their conferences were made difficult by differences in language and philosophical terminology. So they hit upon the device of embodying the most important of their doctrines in a book of pictures, whose combinations should depend on the occult harmony of numbers.

Case's approach to the Tarot was forward-looking in its day, and quite refreshing, for though he develops thoroughly the Kabbalistic associations of the trumps, he also discusses the psychological dimensions of the cards— bringing to bear both Freudian and Jungian insights—and introduces an

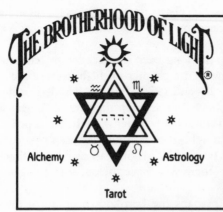
The esoteric schools and organizations which sprung up in California during the 1920s and 30s were distinguished from the traditional European secret societies by their energetic self-promotion. Recognizing the potential of mass marketing, they reached out to metaphysical seekers across the country through ads like these, which have been appearing in the backs of magazines for more than half a century.

open, personal approach to the cards that might be seen as especially "American" in nature. "Study the picture," he suggests in his description of one trump, "and find words to express its meaning in a formula of auto-suggestion. Your own words are best, and have the most power."[2]

Two other Americans, not associated with the Golden Dawn, emerged in Los Angeles esoteric circles around the same time as Case. Manly Palmer Hall, who founded the Philosophic Research Society, wrote prolifically on a wide range of occult subjects, and his work generally displayed qualities of common sense and critical thinking which are not always found in occult research. He included the Tarot in his central work, published in 1928 as *An Encyclopaedic*

Outline of Masonic, Hermetic, Qabbalistic and Rosicrucian Symbolical Philosophy. (This book is today known as *The Secret Teachings of All Ages.*) In 1929, Hall issued a deck drawn by J. A. Knapp and based on the designs of Oswald Wirth; then, in 1930, Knapp published his own deck, with a commentary written by Hall.

Hall revised and expanded this commentary, and it was published as a booklet in 1978, together with illustrations of the Knapp deck, then long out of print. But Hall still did not offer any explanation of perhaps the most interesting feature of the Knapp deck: the "meditation symbols" Hall had added to each card. Every trump card has a small crest bearing one of these symbols (a swan, for example, in the upper left corner of Strength); for each of the minor arcana suits a different shape (the ankh for Swords, the mandorla for Cups, the triangle for Batons, and the cube for Coins) is used to frame the symbols. On the Queen of Cups, a lotus appears in the mandorla; on the Seven of Batons, the triangle contains a single feather; and so on.

It is fascinating, and quite provocative, to try puzzling out the relationship between the symbols chosen and the cards that bear them. Very likely, this was Hall's way of encouraging an experiential approach to the Tarot. Hall believed in the necessity of personal interaction with the Tarot images, as he explained in *The Tarot: An Essay*:

> The cards can never be explained solely by the study of the hieroglyphics themselves, for the symbols have passed through many stages of modification. Each succeeding generation has redrawn the Tarots, until frequently only the roughest outline of the original idea remains. The student must look behind the cards for the psychology which produced them. . . . Like all other forms of symbolism, the Tarot unfailingly reflects the viewpoint of the interpreter himself. This does not detract from its value, however, for symbolism is one of the most useful instruments of instruction in the spiritual arts, because it continually draws from the subjective resources of the seeker the substance of his own erudition.

In 1936, another American Tarot deck appeared, this one from the Church of Light. The founder of this group was Elbert Benjamine, an initiate of the mystical Brotherhood of Light, which claims to receive its teachings from discarnate "Masters." In 1909, the twenty-seven-year-old Benjamine—who had been studying on the "Inner Plane" with these Masters for nine years—felt he had been instructed to prepare a complete course of occult instruction. He began this task after moving to Los Angeles in 1915, and finished in 1934, two years after he founded the Church of Light.

The material was published in twenty-two volumes as a correspondence course, organized chiefly around astrology and employing a distinctive system of Kabbalistic correspondences; *Sacred Tarot* is one volume in that series. Benjamine, who published under the name C. C. Zain for numerological reasons, created a Tarot deck which was meant to be Egyptian, though the drawing style often seems more Greek or Roman; the deck—still distributed by the Church of Light—actually resembles a French deck issued in 1896 by Falconnier.

Zain's Church of Light materials were out of the mainstream of Tarot development in that they continued and added to the idea of the Tarot's Egyptian origin. Zain elaborated on the story of initiations under the Pyramid, and offered a new background for the old tale, tracing it back to the remote civilizations of Atlantis and Mu. But since his account of the Tarot's nature and origins was based on "revealed" teachings, the value of Zain's contribution to our understanding of Tarot must depend on one's belief in the Brotherhood of Light and the information given by its Masters.

Zain did, however, add something of general importance to the development of Tarot interpretation by stressing the connections between Tarot and astrology. Although correlations between the two occult studies had already been drawn in the Golden Dawn and other systems, Zain added much practical detail. The Church of Light Tarot designs include astrological symbols on each card, for use both in meditation and in divination.

Not long after Zain's work on the Tarot appeared, another Los Angeles resident began doing something quite startling, from the occultist point of view. Israel Regardie, a member of the Golden Dawn and one-time disciple of Aleister Crowley, had come to America after his split with Crowley in 1934. Starting in 1937, Regardie published four volumes of the papers of the Golden Dawn, revealing for the first time to an open audience their complete magical system, along with details of the order's rituals and practices. His material is of great interest, but since Regardie came into the Golden Dawn in the 1920s, well after its creative period was finished, we probably cannot get an entirely satisfactory picture of the group through his eyes.[3]

Regardie discontinued his occult activities for some time after the publication of the Golden Dawn materials. He served in the Army during World War II, and afterward devoted himself to practicing a system of mind-body therapy based on the work of Wilhelm Reich. But in the mid-1950s, angered by what he considered an unfair depiction of Crowley in John Symonds's biography *The Great Beast*, Regardie began to issue—through the up-and-coming occultist publishing house Llewellyn—new, annotated editions of Crowley's works, along with works of his own on alchemy, magic, and the Golden Dawn. In his later years, he became well-known as an observer and analyst of the contemporary occult scene.

Paul Foster Case and C. C. Zain died in the early 1950s, but the groups they founded are still active; both Manly P. Hall and Israel Regardie lived—and continued to publish—into the late 1980s. All four of these adventurous Americans were wide-ranging in their influence on the development of the esoteric Tarot. C. C. Zain provided a generous helping of the romantic mystery that had fueled secret societies for centuries, while Manley Palmer Hall introduced a clearheaded and more rigorous attitude. Paul Foster Case brought Tarot and depth psychology to the table together, while Israel Regardie formed a link between the past and the present of Tarot studies. Case and Zain, moreover, strengthened the connections between the Tarot and two other occult systems, numerology and astrology.

Perhaps most important, these four figures laid the groundwork for an increasingly "technical" attitude toward the Tarot. Though Tarot studies today take many forms, the best contemporary approaches have in common a framework of carefully worked-out ideas and activities that draw on a wide variety of traditions, ranging from Tantrism to Native American religions. The common characteristic of these varied influences is their emphasis on a "sacred technology" by means of which the ordinary range of human experience can be expanded. Among serious students, the Tarot is now widely seen as a technical instrument of this type.

This recognition has been made possible in large part by a new kind of scholarship which has taken shape in the second half of the century, and which has given renewed energy to esoteric interests. Mircea Eliade, a distinguished historian of religions, has pointed out in his essay "The Occult and the Modern World" that in the nineteenth century, occultism had been chiefly the property of the creative imagination—of poets and painters and composers; historians and other scholars had taken very little interest. But in the twentieth century, Eliade continues, the situation has been almost reversed:

> As a matter of fact, one can almost say that the fantastic popularity of the occult which started in the middle sixties was anticipated by a series of fundamental scientific books on esoteric doctrines and secret practices published between 1940 and 1960 . . . . First of all, there are the splendid monographs of Gershom Scholem on the Kabbalah and Jewish Gnosticism and mystical systems . . . . Or the publications of René de Forestier on the eighteenth-century occult Freemasons; Alice Joly and Gerard van Rijnback on Martines de Pasqually and the secret lodges of Lyon . . . . Also . . . we have witnessed a more correct and comprehensive appraisal of the Chinese, Indian, and Western alchemies.

The late-blooming legitimacy of occult scholarship was made possible, to a large extent, by the work of psychologist Carl Gustav Jung. Jung provided a foundation for the serious study of occult traditions by establishing a rational position from which to take seriously the irrational. Although Jung was not a part of the "esoteric establishment," his work on the nature of the archetypal imagination has probably been more important than any other factor in advancing the cause of serious esoteric studies.

Jung was an extraordinary scholar, with a formidable command of sources ranging from ancient Greek and Hebrew texts to Renaissance alchemical treatises to Chinese philosophy; he studied the myths and art of virtually every culture, from American Indians to Tibetan Buddhists; he investigated all forms of imaginative expression, from dreams to schizophrenic hallucinations. Through a lifetime spent both in scholarship and in the practice of psychoanalysis, Jung commanded respect in many circles.

Jung's redefinition of the structure of psychological life was extremely important to those interested in esoteric ideas, because Jung established a rigorous, believable explanation of the powerful role that images play in our lives. He brought a highly trained mind and a vast capacity for research to bear upon ideas which had previously been dismissed as "superstition," "primitivism," and the like, demonstrating that the principles of imaginative life are fundamentally the same in all times and places. Jung established that imaginative life is not some accidental luxury, but rather the driving force of all human experience, and he proved, with convincing detail, that there are patterns underlying the apparent chaos of the unconscious—patterns that can be discovered through the study of myths, folktales, dreams, and occult idea/image structures such as alchemy and the *I Ching*.

During the second half of the twentieth century, Carl Jung has been the central influence on occultism in general, and certainly on the study of Tarot. His theory of the "archetypal unconscious"—a reservoir of imaginative knowledge shared by all humankind, and expressing itself in recognizable ways through the imagery of art, dream, and vision—has become the basis for a new, and, in many respects, more sound, approach to the nature and symbolism of the Tarot. Almost any Tarot book published in the last twenty years includes some references to Jung, to archetypes, to the psyche, or to myth, dreamwork, transformation, active imagination, or any one of a number of other concepts developed in Jung's vision of depth psychology.

Jung himself wrote almost nothing specifically about the Tarot cards, though he does say quite clearly that in his view, "the image series of the Tarot cards were descendants of the archetypes of transformation."[4] This observation, brief as it is, has sparked a considerable amount of Tarot commentary, and has produced an almost prevailing conceptualization of the trump sequence as a depiction of the stages in a process of psychological deepening and maturation which Jung called "individuation."

Psychologist Ralph Metzner discusses the Tarot in his excellent book *Maps of Consciousness*, and provides this concise explanation of the Tarot's nature, based on Jung's insights:

> Myths and tales may make the valuable teachings of transformation more accessible to the common understanding, and they may communicate to those who would be unable to comprehend the teachings directly. However, they are still culture bound and limited by the linguistic and literary media of the age and time. So it is not surprising that an attempt should have been made to express the archetypes of psychic transformation in direct, visual form; a form that would resonate in the mind and feelings of the perceiver without the intermediary of language or code. To show in images the steps that must be taken, the many phases of the inner work, and thus to ensure the teachings a universality that transcends cultural and linguistic conventions. This is the Tarot.

Building on a Jungian foundation (whether consciously or not), the Tarot writers of today have created diverse and fascinating new approaches to the cards, incorporating mythology, mysticism, psychotherapy, imaginal work, and self-analysis. These new directions were already apparent in several books in the 1970s, books which rekindled interest in the Tarot after a long period during which Tarot cards were almost impossible to find in America, except through association with one of the California correspondence courses. After World War II, Americans were focused on family-building and material success, rather than spiritual exploration. It was not until the revolutionary 60s that Tarot was rediscovered by the "underground" during the general upsurge of occult pursuits.

In 1971, Eden Gray's very clear fortune-telling text, *The Complete Guide to the Tarot,* was published, and though Gray made no pretense at serious or mystical interpretations of the cards, her sensible, easy-to-use approach attracted a whole new audience to Tarot. The popularity of Gray's books, which remain bookstore staples today, brought stacks of Rider-Waite decks back into the marketplace, and encouraged the publication of other, more thoughtful Tarot books. During the 70s, the main lines of a new, psychospiritual style of Tarot inquiry began to be laid out by writers such as Richard Gardner, Richard Roberts, Stephan Hoeller, Joseph D'Agostino, Arland Ussher, and Micheline Stuart.

Also in the 70s, a more objective type of Tarot scholarship got underway. Alfred Douglas's excellent introduction, *The Tarot,* appeared in 1972, and in 1975, Richard Cavendish's lavishly illustrated book of Tarot history an symbolism. Then, in 1978, Stuart Kaplan, owner of U.S. Games Systems, Inc., published his formidable *Encyclopedia of Tarot,* containing not only the first thorough survey of Tarot history, but also illustrations of over 3,200 different cards, from 250 Tarot and tarock decks. Kaplan's fascination with Tarot has made him the foremost collector and publisher of Tarot cards, and he has since published two more volumes of the *Encyclopedia,* each larger than the last. A fortunate by-product of Kaplan's romance with the Tarot has been the reproduction of many historical Tarot decks, such as the Visconti-Sforza and the beautiful Tarocchi de Mantegna. Today, the interested student of Tarot can enjoy working with decks which were for hundreds of years merely museum items.

New Tarot designs began to appear in the 1970s, and they have continued to arrive at an ever-accelerating pace. Peter Balin's exotic Xultún deck, based on Mayan glyphs, was the first venture outside the accepted European conceptualization of the cards, and it was but the beginning of a tide of cross-cultural perspectives on Tarot. Juliet Sharman-Burke's Mythic Tarot, which unites the Tarot with Greek mythology and popular psychology, was an outstanding success in the late 1980s, and recently, Native American interpretations of the Tarot have become extremely popular.

Another line of development was opened by Sally Gearhart's 1977 book, *A Feminist Tarot.* A steadily growing stream of revisionist Tarot literature followed, and with it came a completely new style of Tarot deck—round cards rather than square, featuring predominantly female figures, and goddess-related themes. Vicki Noble's Motherpeace deck and Ffiona Morgan's Daughters of the Moon Tarot are popular examples of this approach. Other woman who have significantly influenced contemporary Tarot interpretation include Mary K. Greer and Gail Fairfield, both of whom have given substance to the use of Tarot as a tool for personal growth.

These new directions will all be discussed in more detail in part 2, as we look at recent developments in the occult tradition; part 3 will offer an overview of the many Tarot books and decks which give expression to contemporary esoteric interests. But first we will be exploring in more depth the array of complex ideas which form a background to the Tarot, as part 2 turns from the known history of the cards to the many mysteries that are evoked and revealed by this marvelous assortment of images.

This image of The Lovers is taken from the book Flight of the Feathered Serpent, *written by Peter Balin to accompany his Xultún Tarot. When this deck was published in the early 1970s, its Mayan images were a spectacular departure from the predominately French/Italian Tarot tradition. Since then, an increasing number of other-cultural Tarots has appeared, including decks based on Native American, Greek, Celtic, and even Japanese imagery.*

Notes

1. *"Adytum"* is the Greek word for an inner temple or sanctuary.
2. Although the use of repeated phrases is common in magical practice, Case's reference to auto-suggestion probably reflects the popularity of Couéism in America during the 1920s. This self-improvement method, advocated by French psychotherapist Emile Coué, required the practitioner to repeat the sentence "Day by day, in every way, I am getting better and better." Saying something positive over and over to oneself was thought to have a salutary effect on the unconscious.
3. Regardie had copied his own set of Tarot cards as a teenager in 1923, by which time significant changes had been made in the design of the cards, and in the doctrines and practices of the order. But he later attempted to reconstruct, as closely as possible, the original Golden Dawn symbolism, and a deck based on these images was published in 1977 as the Golden Dawn Tarot, drawn by Robert Wang. The style of the drawings in this deck is rather slick, however, and doesn't reflect the highly personalized, sketch-like quality of the drawings found in the original notebooks of Golden Dawn members.
4. This remark is found in *The Integration of Personality*, p. 89.

INTERLUDE

One Tale of Tarot

IN spite of all the thought and effort which has been given to the Tarot in the last two centuries, we remain today as far as ever from a definitive answer to the question, "Where did the Tarot come from?" Perhaps it is not necessary to have an answer. It may be enough, after all, to know the Tarot contains archetypal images and structures which are a vivid, continuing part of human psychological life.

Still, it seems to me that one needs a myth of the Tarot, a story which gives it the weight of a past. So after surveying all the information we have about the history of the Tarot, and assessing the various theories about its possible origins, I've come up with a story that gives me satisfaction, and I will close part 1 by telling it.

The story begins in the "Dark Ages," in some esoteric context we know nothing about. In those ravaged centuries just after the fall of the Roman Empire, society was disrupted by waves of barbarian invasions on the one hand, and by violent religious ferment on the other. As a result, groups possessing esoteric knowledge may well have gone underground to preserve their lives and lore; the Tarot images could have been created as memory aids or meditational devices by one of these groups.

It seems probable to me that the Tarot images were codified over a period of time, just as the books of the Bible or the hexagrams of the *I Ching* were, and that they incorporated ideas and symbolism from many different sources. But in any case, there came to be a body of twenty-two images, and for some reason—probably so they could be placed in different orders—they were drawn or painted on separate cards. By and by, the group that had created these cards fell into disarray and the Tarot images became separated from their original esoteric purpose—but they retained their intrinsic fascination, which attracts even people who haven't the least concern with metaphysical matters.

And so the collection of images was kept intact somewhere because of its odd, interesting nature.

Then card games came along. The playing-card deck had probably developed—like chess pieces or mah jong tiles—by a process of casual invention, spontaneous modification, and gradual standardization. Sometime after card-playing reached Italy in the fourteenth century, someone (perhaps a printer?) had the idea of using the curious old collection of twenty-two image cards as "trumps" to make this new kind of game more complex and exciting—and thus *cartes di trionfi* was born.

At first the images may have been crude renderings, perhaps based on sketches such as those made by Golden Dawn students. But perhaps the nobles desired a more elegant version of this new game, and a court painter was commissioned to create beautiful new versions of the odd old images; he of course added some bits here and there to flatter the patron and his family, as was the usual custom. The idea of these luxuriously personalized cards quickly caught on, and soon other painters in other courts were copying and embellishing the same pictures. Meanwhile, printers were stamping out popular woodblock versions, and soon the game was being played up and down the social scale.

Initially, the Church opposed the use of the Tarot trumps because it recognized in those images the reflection of something heretical or magical; sermons were preached against the cards, and intermittent (unsuccessful) attempts were made to forbid them. But people were interested in the *game*, not in the symbolism of the cards, so after a while, the Church abandoned its opposition, and everyone forgot about any esoteric aspects of the Tarot. The many Renaissance mystics and occultists, like Giordano Bruno and John Dee, had more than enough ideas to engage them, so they ignored the lowly card game.

Of course the potent symbolism of the Tarot trumps seems obvious to us now, but for hundreds of years, the power of the images was, like Poe's purloined letter, hidden in a very obvious place. Eventually, the popularity of Tarot games waned and seventy-eight card decks became less common, while fifty-six (or fifty-two) card decks became standard. In the fashionable cities, Tarot was passé—and it was precisely this fact that allowed Court de Gébelin to recognize the esoteric nature of the trump cards when he saw them: The moment someone knowledgeable about occult matters encountered the cards *without* knowing them as a popular game, their significance was obvious.

The theory articulated (if not invented) by Papus holds that the originators of the Tarot images had purposefully chosen a game to hold their secrets because they knew that frivolous mankind would not always be concerned with esoteric wisdom, but could be counted on to have a lively interest in gaming. Personally, however, I find it more credible that the Tarot images "accidentally" became part of a game after their esoteric properties had fallen into disuse. This conjecture is supported, I think, by the fact that the dissemination of esoteric lore often follows just such a pattern: Secret knowledge is accumulated by small groups and closely held among "initiates" for a period of time; then, for reasons of internal dissent, or persecution, or simply the falling away of interest, the secret society fails and its lore gradually becomes public property.

In any case, as long as the Tarot trumps were part of a game, their symbolic significance was effectively concealed. But as soon as Court de Gébelin rediscovered the esoteric possibilities of Tarot, other people started to look at the Tarot images from this point of view. They began to search for esoteric structures and correspondences in the Tarot, and they found more than they could assimilate. The Tarot is so exceptionally full of symbolism that it has elements in common with practically every other symbol system that has ever existed—and so it may easily seem to be a fragment of some great, coherent, lost *supersystem* of esoteric knowledge. Lévi, Papus, and other nineteenth-century commentators jumped to this conclusion, and, recognizing the superb symbolic facility of the Tarot, believed it to be a key relic of some ancient golden age.

Then, in the process of trying to restore the Tarot to what they believed was its "pristine" glory, these theorists unwittingly collaborated in the creation of an entirely *new* esoteric instrument. Because they had discovered the Tarot trumps already melded to the four-suited deck, they assumed that the whole seventy-eight-card deck was a symbolic unit, and they came up with inventive interpretations that gave esoteric meaning to the four suits, the court cards, and the number cards; the trumps became the "major arcana" and the lesser cards the "minor arcana." (It may very well be that the suit cards do have an occult background, and therefore have properties in common with the trumps; but historical evidence suggests that the fifty-six-card deck developed independently of the trump cards, and so the seventy-eight-card deck was probably not, in reality, "created" as a single unit.)

So—at least according to my story—the Tarot as we know it today is the product of two factors: first, the powerful symbolism which somehow, for some reason, was given form in the trump images, and second, the fertile inventions written down and passed along by generations of students who fell in love with those images. The resulting tradition may not be as clear, organized, and accurate as we would like, but it is full of passion and imagination, and, best of all, it has plenty of room for new ideas. I find it most pleasing to think of the Tarot in this way—not as some hoary fragment of ancient "wisdom," but as a living tradition of imagination and inquiry.

Part 2
MYSTERY

PROLOGUE

So many things have been said about the Tarot, by so many people, speaking from so many points of view, that it is very hard to know where to begin in considering the mystery of Tarot. I have no expectation of solving the mystery, nor am I sure that a solution is possible, or even desirable. My intention is mainly to analyze the mystery itself.

A mystery is, in fact, something of much deeper import than we normally think of when using the word. Today, the term "mystery" is used almost exclusively in one of two rather superficial ways—either to describe a story in which significant pieces of information (such as the identity of a murderer) are withheld from the audience, or to designate something (how migrating birds know where to go, or why men and women can't communicate with each other) which can't be explained satisfactorily on the basis of what we presently know.

These senses of the word "mystery" are at least distantly in keeping, however, with its old, deeper meaning. The word derives originally from a Greek word meaning "to initiate," which came in turn from the root "to keep silent." During the initiation process, certain things were revealed to the initiate— things which could be known *only* by going through an initiation process carefully designed to bring about an altered state of consciousness or awareness in the initiate. Initiates were forbidden to reveal their new-found knowledge to those who had not been prepared by undergoing the ritual experience, and so the groups that have placed themselves in the mystery tradition over the centuries (Rosicrucians, Freemasons, and so on) have come to be called "secret societies."

The vow of secrecy worked so well that we have no reliable descriptions of what actually happened in the original mystery initiations, but we do know that they were practiced all over the ancient world, and generally featured several different stages, marked by ritual fasting and bathing, nighttime processions, and the viewing of sacred objects or images. Most of the initiation ceremonies were reenactments of mythic events, such as the death and dismemberment of the Egyptian god Osiris, or the rape of Persephone by the Greek god Pluto. The chief features of the initiation imagery were related to fertility, either sexual or agricultural (erect phalluses, sheaves of corn, and the like), but the underlying theme seems always to have been concerned with overcoming death. It's easy to see how a good many of these mystery elements could be discovered in the Tarot images by an imaginative mind.

In the initiation process, mysteries—secrets of life, death, power, and eternity—were revealed, just as the murderer is exposed at the end of a mystery novel. Mysteries such as these are *knowable*, though not in the ordinary way. But there is yet another sense of the word "mystery," in which something is called a mystery because it is inherently *not* knowable. This use of the term is found today mainly in Christian theology, where it is used to denote something—the Eucharist, for example—which may be understood on some level by the intellect, but which can never be fully grasped because it is, by its very nature, beyond the scope of human knowing. One of the reasons this sort of mystery cannot be known is that its meaning is inexhaustible; we can never compass all of its nature.

It would be extreme at the least to say the Tarot is this second sort of mystery—so manifold in its meanings that it surpasses human understanding. But it *would* be true to say that there are so many possible levels of understanding which may be brought to Tarot (or found through Tarot) that it would tax the patience and resources of most people to exhaust them.

Several commentators, as we saw in part 1, have claimed an *initiated* (or "revealed") knowledge of the Tarot, gained through participation in some secret ancient tradition, or by communication from some other-worldly source. Paul Foster Case, for example, spoke of an "occult tradition" that the cards were "invented" at a gathering of sages in Fez, Morocco, around A.D. 1200; yet nowhere in the history of Tarot is any such story told publicly by anyone else, leaving us to wonder where and how Case learned of this tradition. A. E. Waite referred to "the Secret Tradition concerning the Tarot, as well as a Secret Doctrine contained therein"; he explained that in his own writing, he "followed some part of it without exceeding the limits which are drawn about matters of this kind and belong to the laws of honour."

Among the authors who lay claim to special knowledge, each is careful to distinguish himself from those "others" who lay false claim to the truth, or who know only a portion of the *real* truth. The secret nature of their claimed knowledge, meanwhile, has automatically exempted them from the necessity of proving or supporting their stories. So, in the final analysis, there is not one whit of a reason to believe any of these claims, though at the same time, there is not necessarily reason to doubt the sincerity of their authors. Suffice it to say that every new seeker after the "truth" of Tarot will be starting from scratch, because the mystery of the cards, if knowable, is not yet known.

I hope that part 1 sufficiently covered what *is* known about the historical Tarot, its antecedents and its early uses, and how it came to us in the form we see today. But now that we've surveyed what has been established about the Tarot as an historical object, we must consider the next question: Is the Tarot *only* an historical object, or is there more? Is there any valid reason to think the Tarot is more meaningful, or meaningful in more ways, than any "ordinary" historical object—say, an Etruscan fresco, or Benjamin Franklin's bifocals?

For many people, the very fact that Tarot continues to seduce the imagination is enough to justify further study. The Tarot has not withered away, nor has it simply remained frozen in time, an antique. Rather, it has flowered into successive patterns of interest, generating new uses and interpretations. And after all—how many other artifacts of the early Renaissance still excite such widespread and lively interest today?

The least this can mean is that the Tarot expresses and excites something significant in the imagination. But opinions about just what this "something" is, and how it is expressed, are diverse and often divergent. The purpose of part 2 will be to sort out the many ideas that are today associated with the Tarot. I will try to select for consideration those ideas which are serious and sensible (in the broadest meaning of that word), and to explain just how they are related to the Tarot and to each other. I will also try to go beyond what is commonly written about the Tarot, to produce information and ideas which will offer a new—and perhaps more satisfying—framework for consideration.

I've chosen five viewpoints from which to examine the Tarot. The first and most obvious of these is its long affiliation with metaphysics and the occult. Second, and increasingly dominant, is the more recent association of Tarot with Jungian psychology and the creative imagination. The third and fourth vantages are both concerned with the use of Tarot as a tool for discovery; one undertakes an analysis of divination, the other offers some amplifying ideas from the world of science. Finally, the fifth point of view—perhaps the least familiar—is that of cultural criticism; from this angle we will see how the images and themes of Tarot have been used in modern art and literature to explore the nature of the spirit.

Though there are many different ways today of looking at the Tarot, much of its identity is still tied up with the whole stream of theories and practices we call the "occult tradition." So we begin with that aspect of Tarot, which has dominated its history since Court de Gébelin liberated the Tarot images from their long captivity in the guise of a card game.

5.

TAROT AND THE OCCULT TRADITION

THE term "occult" has been with us for a surprisingly long time. According to the distinguished historian of religions Mircea Eliade, "occult" was first included in the *Oxford Dictionary* in 1545, defined as that which is "not apprehended, or not of ordinary knowledge." Less than a century later, it was given this added meaning: the subject of "those ancient and medieval reputed sciences, held to involve the knowledge or use of agencies of a secret and mysterious nature (as magic, alchemy, astrology . . .)."[1]

In recent years, "occult" has become something of a portmanteau word, taking on several uses beyond the traditional. It is employed by skeptics to indict anything outside of or opposed to conventional science, and by the uninformed to describe anything weird, abnormal, or frightening. Among those who have a casual interest in occult matters, the word "occult" is today commonly used as if it were interchangeable with the terms "esoteric" and "metaphysical." And some contemporary scholars use the word "occult" to mean "occluded" or "hidden," with reference to significant aspects of scientific and social history which have been obscured by the dominance of rationalism.

This last use of the term is closest to the sense which governs the present chapter, since my intent in what follows is to describe the context in which Tarot has developed, and to explore the whole history and range of ideas which bear on our understanding of Tarot. But in order to maintain a basic distinction among several related terms, I will in general use the term to refer to the activities and interests which have made up the long tradition of Western magic, and the term "esoteric" to refer to the theories which underlie occult practices,[2] I will use "metaphysical" (meaning simply "beyond the physical") as a more general term which can take in both of the others.

There is no way, of course, to compress into a neat, brief presentation the rich variety of metaphysical concepts which have evolved around the world and throughout history. The best I will be able to do is to begin at the beginning, and try to summarize the basic chain of ideas which seems to have associations with the Tarot. As to where the "beginning" might be—I'm not sure if there is a single assumption that would be agreed upon by *all* metaphysical schools, but I believe most would subscribe to the statement that *a single, simple set of universal principles is the source of everything that exists.*

This basic concept, expressed in many different forms, can be found woven through the whole history of thought, from ancient Egypt, India, and China, through Pythagoras and Plato, through the Gnostic Christians, through the Renaissance alchemists, and right up to a present-day form which physicists call the "grand unified theory" (GUT) or "theory of everything" (TOE). But while the theorists and practitioners of many different esoteric (and religious, and even scientific) schools of thought might agree on this proposition, they would differ widely on several corollary questions: Just what is the source of these supposed universal principles? Is it possible to know the principles—and if so, how? What should anyone who gains such knowledge do with it?

Diverging answers to these questions split metaphysical groups into several different streams, and each of these streams has its own esoteric doctrine, and its own occult practices. Perhaps the chief division is between the categories of *magic* and *mysticism*. Speaking in very general terms, magic has as its aim certain *achievements*—creation, transformation, the enhancement of the will, the enrichment of the imagination, the acquisition of power. Mysticism, on the other hand, seeks certain *experiences*—principally, the feeling of oneness with creation or with a supreme being. Though magical and mystical pursuits sometimes overlap, and though the words are often used in similar ways, there are real differences in these two approaches, and in the attitudes of those who follow them.

It might be said that both groups really share one ultimate goal— knowledge of the Divine—but the nature of "knowledge" would be defined quite differently by the magician and by the mystic. From the magical view, the saying "knowledge is power" rings very true (though not necessarily in any evil or selfish sense), while from the mystical vantage point, the Biblical sense of the term "knowledge" is much closer to the mark. Mystical knowing is a kind of union, an incorporation of the self into the Absolute.

For quite a large number of people, the mystical experience happens spontaneously, once or twice in a lifetime. William James described, in his classic book *The Varieties of Religious Experience*, such an event in his own life:

> I remember the night, and almost the very spot on the hillside, where my soul opened out, as it were, into the Infinite, and there was a rushing together of the two worlds, the inner and the outer . . . . The ordinary sense of things around me

73

faded. For the moment nothing but an ineffable joy and exaltation remained . . . .
It was like the effect of some great orchestra when all the separate notes have
melted into one swelling harmony that leaves the listener conscious of nothing
save that his soul is being wafted upwards, and almost bursting with its own
emotion . . . . I have stood upon the Mount of Vision since, and felt the Eternal
round about me. But never since has there come quite the same stirring of the
heart.

The occasional or situational experience of mystic union seems to be a
natural part of the inner creative process, and it generally comes to people who
have been struggling, intellectually or artistically, consciously or unconsciously, with the questions of existence. There are a few brave souls, however,
who devote their lives to the search for a sustained experience of this mystical
state, and they have left behind records of their own experiences. Richard of
St. Victor, Meister Eckart, St. Teresa of Avila, St. John of the Cross, William
Blake, Pierre Teilhard de Chardin, and Thomas Merton are among the most
famous of these seekers. Much has been written, too, about different categories and styles of mysticism, and theories have been propounded about how
mystical "superconsciousness" can be achieved. But in the final analysis, there
are no reliable "instructions" to be followed, no certain map of the mystical
way; each must find his own route, with only a few guideposts, for mystical
experience is unique and personal. The mystical "path" is one of opening and
invitation, concerned with preparing the ground of consciousness to *receive*
the experience of union.

Since the highest types of magic have as their goal an expanded consciousness capable of participation in the most sublime levels of being, their aim is
not different in kind from that of mysticism, but there is a good deal of
difference in style. While it may be true that Tarot images are used by some for
the transformation of consciousness, the nature of this transformation is rarely
mystical, in the strict sense of that word. Tarot is associated principally with
the magical path, and for this reason, its associations are complex and diverse.

The magical path, unlike the mystical, has many maps, all carefully detailed
and each claiming to be the best map, or even the only "true" map. This
profusion (or, perhaps confusion) of instructions is one of the main problems
encountered in trying to make sense of the realm of occult activities, and
before we go any further with the exploration of Tarot in the occult context,
I'd like to consider for a moment some of the procedural difficulties. Sociolo-
gist Randall Collins, in his essay "Toward a Modern Science of the Occult,"
makes what I think is a very good suggestion concerning the study of occult
systems:

Our guiding principle should be: *trust the experiences, not the interpretations.*
Explorers of the occult have experienced realms of consciousness and aspects of
existence that have been all but obliterated for the Western scientific establishment. They are guides who can enlarge our worlds. But the verbal systems that
they have built to explain them, and the human organizations they have constructed around them, ought to be treated with the same skepticism and detached

analysis as everything else in the mundane world. These ideas are theories and ought to be subject to continuous consideration—tested against other aspects of occult (and mundane) experience, discarded, revised, and developed as need be. The great obstacles to avoid are dogmatism and scholasticism, and there is plenty of both in almost all of the occult traditions.[3]

Collins goes on to point out that the many overly complex and convoluted occult systems are testimony to lifetimes spent by occult intellectuals playing the game of "esoteric one-upmanship."

The situation for anyone who wants to make sense of the occult tradition is made even more difficult today, because so many historically separate strands have been drawn together—sometimes carelessly and illogically—to form new syntheses which may or may not have any real value. Occult writers freely mix terms and ideas from Eastern philosophy, classical mystery religions, the Kabbalah, the Hermetic arts of the Renaissance, the theories of self-styled modern magicians, the doctrines of quasi-religions, the mythologies of tribal cultures, messages from supposedly discarnate entities, teachings of gurus, and so on, often taking out of context whatever features of these systems happen to fit the needs of the moment.

Certainly the synthetic process is not in itself a bad thing. But it's all too easy to create seemingly rich and significant explanations of occult systems by building up layers of reference and allusion—without actually having sorted the worthwhile information from the worthless, and without ever showing whether the bits and pieces really do fit together in a meaningful way. This kind of thinking is frequently found in contemporary occult writing, and it has the unfortunate result of dazzling (or baffling) the neophyte on the one hand, while offending the knowledgeable on the other. Tarot is particularly afflicted by such "synthesism" because it can be related, by even the moderately re-sourceful, to practically everything under the sun.

Relationships alone, however, do not make meaningful systems. Manly P. Hall warned, in his essay on the Tarot, against taking too seriously the "happy coincidence that the Hebrew alphabet contained 22 letters . . . . It is inevitable that this apparently supporting fact should excite a wide field of speculation, but we must not jump to conclusions. Almost any number can be fitted into some system of philosophy." Similarly, many systems of philosophy can be fitted to almost any phenomenon, without much having been accomplished. The fact that two things (or any number of things) have something in common does not mean they are related to each other in any direct way; in the case of the Tarot and the Hebrew alphabet, there is no reason at all to think that an historical or causal or theoretical or any other relationship exists between these two phenomena.

A significant relationship is one in which it can be demonstrated (*a*) that the two things related in some way illuminate one another, and/or (*b*) that the fact of the relationship itself establishes something of interest. If the "twenty-two-ness" of the Tarot trumps tells us something about the Hebrew alphabet, or vice versa, that's great; if the fact that the trumps and the alphabet both number twenty-two tells us something about "twenty-two-ness," so much the better. But only at such a level of analysis do relationships begin to become satisfying; on a superficial level, they are merely tantalizing.

There are many tantalizing suggestions about the Tarot, but few satisfying connections. And it's difficult to sort out the tangle of occult associations that has grown up around the subject. The newcomer must certainly wonder how it is that books about Tarot take so many different approaches, and refer to so many different ideas. One book is talking about the Kabbalah, another about shamanism, another about the Greek gods—and everything from numerology and astrology to aromatherapy and herbology may be brought into the discussion. Can all these things possibly apply? And if so, what sense can be made of it all?

The purpose of this chapter is to provide—in a very limited and basic way—some background for the many ideas which are frequently found to be "fellow travelers" of Tarot in occult literature. In recent years, with the serious study of cross-cultural metaphysics, many new twists and turns have been added to the Tarot maze, and these interesting developments will be looked at in some detail. But for a long while, from the time of Court de Gébelin through the late 1960s, the interpretation of Tarot mysteries ran very much along the lines of the Western magical tradition, so this seems the fitting place to begin.

EARLY WESTERN MAGIC: FROM PLATO TO PICO

The word "magic," like so many words in the occult vocabulary, derives from the Greek—in this case, the Greek word for "seer" or "wizard." The root meaning contains references to the two main activities popularly associated with magic: divination of future events and manipulation of natural and supernatural forces. Both these activities have, over a long period of time, become very much degraded in the public imagination, the one into "fortunetelling," the other into association with demonism. The best that is thought of magic by most people today is that it's a product of unsophisticated minds, a kind of crude forerunner to "real" science. Very few realize the majestic sweep of magical philosophy in its highest form—or the true power (of certain sorts) that can be achieved through magical practice.

The popular opinion of magic is not actually wrong, just incomplete. There have always been two tiers to magic: an unenlightened level of superstitious spell-casting and the like, running parallel with an intensely imaginative level, where elegant structures of cosmic order are created and momentous questions are explored. This is as true of legendary Tibet—where the great monasteries of the Lamas coexisted with the magical animism of ancient Bon Po—as of Renaissance Europe—where "puffers" were derided by the serious, spiritual alchemists for ignorantly trying to bake lead into gold in their ovens.

Because there are two levels of magical practice, it is always possible—merely by selecting what is and what is not to be considered—to construct either a negative and ridiculous picture of magic or a positive and persuasive one. But the truth is actually somewhere in between—and this very quality of ambiguity says something important about magic's close alliance with the always-ambiguous human imagination.

The beginnings of what we think of as Western magic go back—like the word "magic" itself—to ancient Greece. There was certainly plenty of magical activity before that; for as far back as we have any records of human beings at all, we have indications of magic. But the particular set of ideas which form the basis of the Western magical tradition began with Pythagoras (ca. 582–507 B.C.) and Plato (ca. 427–347 B.C.). Plato is thought to have studied with the Pythagoreans, and learned from them the theory that all relationships in the universe can be expressed in terms of numbers; he is also believed by occultists to have been initiated into Egyptian mysteries of some kind. (There is no proof one way or another concerning Plato and Egypt, though there are some suggestions that a connection may have existed.[4]) In his many philosophical commentaries, Plato introduced or elaborated concepts, such as the "archetype" and the "world soul," which have been of great importance to magical theorists ever since. This passage from the *Timaeus* is one of many which provides the ground of later metaphysical ideas:

> Again into the same cup in which he had blended and mixed the soul of the Universe the Creator poured what was left of the elements, mingling them in much the same manner, yet no longer so pure as before, but one or two degrees less pure. And when he had the whole compound, he divided it into souls equal in number to the stars, and assigned each soul to a star, and placing them in the stars as in a chariot, he showed them the nature of the Universe, and told them the laws of Fate—how that their first birth would be ordained the same for all, lest any should suffer wrong at his hands; and how, after being sown into the instruments of time, each into that appropriate to it, they must be born the most God-fearing of animals.[5]

It was five hundred years later, in the third century of our own era, that the philosophical implications of certain of Plato's concepts began to be worked out in detail by Plotinus and his pupil Porphyry, who came to be called "Neoplatonists." Seeking to explain just *how* matter was derived from the realm of pure ideas, Neoplatonism developed a whole hierarchy of "emanations": From the undivided One derived the *Nous*, or "Mind," and from the *Nous* proceeded *Anima Mundi*, the "Soul" or "World-Soul," an immaterial link between *Nous* and the material world. The World-Soul was subdivided several times along the way, into "layers" that accounted for higher and lower levels of the human soul and of natural phenomena. This Neoplatonist philosophy, with its emphasis on the spirit, influenced the early Church fathers (especially St. Augustine), and shaped some of the basic ideas of Christian theology; it was also the guiding force of the Scholastic philosophy which dominated the Middle Ages until the late twelfth century. The Ptolemaic earth-centered universe of concentric heavenly shells, the medieval feudal society, and the hierarchies of angels and saints were all inspired by the Neoplatonist doctrine of emanations.

Also influential in the early formation of Christianity was Gnosticism.

This detail from Robert Fludd's Utriusque Cosmi Historia *(1617) depicts the* Anima Mundi *or "World Soul" believed by the Neoplatonists to link the mind of God and the material world. The concentric rings depict the many layers into which Neoplatonist theory divided the universe—encompassing every imaginable phenomenon, from the spheres beyond the planets to the mineral crust of the earth.*

The term "Gnostic"—derived from the Greek word "*gnosis*," meaning "knowledge"—is used very loosely to describe a number of groups whose philosophies had in common some degree of dualism (a belief in the radical separation between spirit and matter) and a conviction that salvation must be achieved by means of knowledge. *Gnosis* was one of three kinds of knowledge differentiated by the Greeks, and its special quality was that it was gained through meditation or intuitive perception; the two other types were *mathesis* (knowledge gained by the ordinary means of conscious learning) and *pathesis* (felt or suffered knowledge). The Greek mystery religions tried to incorporate all three kinds of knowledge, but placed the most emphasis on "pathetic"— that is, experienced—learning. The Gnostics, on the other hand, stressed inwardness and self-knowing as the path to higher awareness.

Gnosticism probably pre-dated the birth of Christ. When Christianity appeared, the Gnostics, in part because of their belief in interior illumination, adopted an approach to the new religion which was very different from the orthodox interpretations we know today. For example, Gnostics did not agree that humans were fallen from a perfect world created by a perfect God, suggesting instead that the material world might be inherently *imperfect*, designed to entrap the soul. Some Gnostics (the "pessimists") believed that the whole purpose of life was to escape from this imprisonment in matter, while others (the "optimists," of course) believed that the material world partakes of the Divine. The Gnostic interpretation of Christianity also differed from orthodoxy in referring to God as both Father *and* Mother (women were equal participants in Gnostic religion), in believing that Jesus gave secret teachings to his apostles, and in denying the importance of the Old Testament.

Gnostics believed the individual quest for self-knowledge was more important than Church teachings, and that fact made the conservative interpreters of Christianity quite fearful of them. The orthodox type of Christianity was oriented mainly toward *mathesis*, or conscious knowledge, and did not generally encourage mysticism. Though Gnostic ideas were influential in the early formative stages of Christian theology, by the third century the "other side" had established an organized Church structure that rejected Gnosticism, and had created an official version of the New Testament that excluded a number of existing Gospels (such as the Gnostic "Gospel of Thomas" and "Gospel of Truth")[6] which were in circulation at the same time as the orthodox Gospels of Matthew, Mark, Luke, and John.

The Gnostic writings gave a very different picture of Jesus and his teachings, as, for example, in these passages from the Gospel of Thomas:

Jesus said, "I am not your master. Because you have drunk, you have become drunk from the bubbling stream which I have measured out . . . . He who will drink from my mouth will become as I am: I myself shall become he, and the things that are hidden will be revealed to him."

Jesus said, "Let him who seeks continue seeking until he finds. When he finds, he will become troubled. When he becomes troubled, he will be astonished, and he will rule over all things."

79

These passages, with their references to hidden truths and to the power which may be gained from *gnosis*, must certainly have been troubling to the orthodox faction; the suggestion that Jesus gave special teachings to some was bound to make those who had not received any such "hidden" tradition feel defensive. But although a good deal of the orthodox resentment against the Gnostics can be explained in political and theological terms, it was also true from the beginning that the charges against the Gnostics included their involvement with magic.

The general suspicion of things magical also posed problems for another body of ideas circulating in the early centuries of the Christian era, those contained in the writings known as the *Hermetica*. As we saw in part 1, these works, though they were attributed in the Renaissance to the ancient Egyptian magus Hermes Trismegistus, were really written by an assortment of unknown authors in the second and third centuries A.D. There were many popular Hermetic writings concerned with magical practice, and even the more lofty philosophical works attributed to Hermes had much in them pertaining to magical doctrines.[7] But because the *Hermetica* were not at all directed toward changing or refuting Christianity—in fact, they purported to have been written in an age long before Christ—some of the Church Fathers were not concerned with censoring them, but rather with trying to discover signs that they predicted the coming of Christ. Lactantius, writing in the third century, was already completely convinced of the antiquity of the *Hermetica*, and he found it very meaningful that Hermes—"a man of great antiquity and fully imbued with every kind of learning"—not only recognized "God" but referred to the "Son of God" in his writings.[8] Thus the *Hermetica*, unlike the Gnostic texts, were not condemned as heretical, in spite of their magical taint.

The story of "serious" magic now takes a millennial leap, to the Renaissance rediscovery of the *Corpus Hermetica*.[9] Believing these writings (on authority of the Church Fathers, no less) to be very ancient documents, the magi of the Italian Renaissance began building on the ideas they contained, and so the foundations of modern magic were laid. The Hermetic documents themselves had little coherence, having actually been written by different people at different times, but they all used the same astrological framework for their cosmology, which depicted a material world ruled by the stars. The universal principles of being were thought to be "filtered" through the constellations and planets, and each of these astrological symbols served as the focal point for a group of correspondences on the material plane.

This doctrine of correspondences—economically expressed in the famous Hermetic dictum, "As above, so below"—is the foundation of the whole of Renaissance *magia*. The Renaissance magician believed that the sensible world around us reflects, down to its smallest detail, the workings of the higher spheres. Thus each star and each constellation were connected "sympathetically" to special, appropriate parts of the natural world; each had its own gems, colors, plants, sounds, and animals. In addition, the idea of correspondences continued at the level of the human body, which was said esoterically to be a "microcosm" or "little world" reflecting the "macrocosm" or great structure of the universe. Each part of the body was linked with an astrological ruler

Hermes portrayed as a mystagogue, from Achille Bocchi's Symbolicae Quaestiones, *1574. The Greek god Hermes, also considered to be the Egyptian god Thoth, was called "Hermes Trismegistus" ("Thrice-great Hermes") by the Renaissance magi, who believed he was the author of great and ancient metaphysical documents such as the Emerald Tablet. However, the* Hermetica, *works attrituted to the great magician, were actually created in the early centuries of our own era by Neoplatonist philosophers.*

(Mars, for example, rules the muscular system and certain glands), while human temperaments were divided into four classifications and related to the four elements (choleric/fire, phlegmatic/water, sanguine/air, and melancholic/earth); the four elements, of course, had their own elaborate correspondences. So by tracing the correspondences, it could be determined which gem was connected with which part of the body, for example, or which colors and plants were related to a certain temperament.

The belief in an ordered universe composed of endless interconnections governed all aspects of medieval and early Renaissance thinking. But it was largely a static concept, with influences coming *down* from the stars, controlling the fates of those below. The rediscovery of Hermetic magic opened up a whole new realm of activity, for it brought with it the idea of magically *altering* the influences of the stars by using their correspondences on the material plane. The most common way of accomplishing this was the creation of magical objects called *talismans* to "draw down" the power of desired astral influences. The typical talisman was made of a metal sympathetic to the star in question, engraved with an appropriate image and perhaps set with a corresponding stone. The more correspondences the better, so the magician might also expose himself to appropriate scents, colors, plants, and so on.

These were the main activities of the "astral magic" which was taught in the

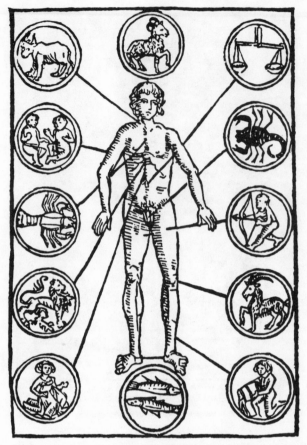

This fifteenth-century woodcut shows the correspondences between zodiacal influences and parts of the human body. For hundreds of years, the doctrine of correspondences was not merely an occult conceit, but a common assumption about the way the universe was organized. Microcosmic man was believed to reflect in every detail the great macrocosmic order.

Hermetica. But the Renaissance magicians were ultimately to go well beyond this relatively simple level of practice. The first architect of Renaissance magical theory was Marsilio Ficino (1433–1499), who is best known for having translated Plato's works. More important for our purposes, however, is the fact that—at the request of his powerful patron, Cosimo d'Medici—Ficino first translated the *Corpus Hermetica*. The dying Cosimo was more anxious to read the words of the immortal Trismegistus than those of Plato, because the Hermetic writings were thought to be older than Plato's, and to the Renaissance mind, the oldest ideas were the most "pristine"—unspoiled messages from a time when man was closer to God. So Ficino's scholarship brought him into contact with a type of magic which seemed much loftier than the crude practices that had passed among the medieval magicians. Moreover, this Hermetic magic was *natural* magic, quite divorced from the world of evil spirits and demonic influences which corrupted the illicit magic condemned by the Church.

Drawing upon the Hermetic writings, Plotinus's Neoplatonism, and a book (by an unknown Arabic author) called the *Picatrix*, Ficino began—in a very gingerly way—to explore the potentials of magical activity. An important purpose of "natural" or "astral" magic was healing, of both a physical and a spiritual kind. For example, Ficino addressed some of his magical work to overcoming the melancholic effects of Saturn by attracting other astral influences. Frances Yates, in her marvelous book *Giordano Bruno and the Hermetic Tradition*, explains Ficino's advice for attracting non-Saturnian astral influences, pointing out the elegant approach which distinguished Ficinian magic from that of the old "hole-in-corner" sorcerer:

> Gold is a metal full of Solar and Jovial spirit and therefore beneficial in combating melancholy. Green is a health-giving and life-giving colour, and the reader is urged to come to "Alma Venus" and to walk in the green fields with her, plucking her flowers, such as roses, or the crocus, the golden flower of Jupiter. Ficino also gives advice on how to choose a non-Saturnian diet, and thinks that the use of pleasant odours and scents is beneficial. We might be in the consulting room of a rather expensive psychiatrist who knows that his patients can afford plenty of gold and holidays in the country, and flowers out of season.

Along with his "lifestyle" suggestions, Ficino also gives recipes for creating talismans. For example, a long and happy life may be invited by making, on a clear, white stone, an image of Jupiter as "a crowned man on an eagle or a dragon, clad in a yellow garment."

Today there are reasons (as I shall try to show in chapter 8, "Tarot in the Light of Science") to think these innocuous-sounding activities can actually be effective—though not for the reasons that Ficino and his contemporaries imagined. The basis for believing in astral influences changed when we stopped living in Ptolemy's earth-centered cosmos and started inhabiting the Copernican heliocentric universe. But although some parts of Renaissance magical theory have since been replaced by more sophisticated constructions, much of it continues even now to provide the basis for most occult activities. Magic today still subscribes to the underlying esoteric doctrine that the fundamental principles of being are expressed in a kind of *original language*, which is made up of only a small number of what we could call "primary units of meaning," or perhaps, like Plato, "pure ideas." These idea-units are continuous and undifferentiated on the highest level of being—the *astral plane*—but each has a variety of manifestations on the *material plane* which reflect (at the "local" level of our human experience) the unseen, immaterial principles of being.

The system of correspondences worked out carefully by Renaissance magicians was lost in the glare of a new scientific light shining on the seventeenth, eighteenth and nineteenth centuries. But after hundreds of years, it was retrieved and elaborated by MacGregor Mathers and the members of the Golden Dawn group. In the Golden Dawn system, the planet Mars, for example, would have as its color scarlet-red, its musical note C, its gemstone ruby, its animals bear and wolf, its plants absinthe and rue, and its fragrance pepper. But the Golden Dawn system also added the Tarot trumps to its correspondences, specifying The Tower as the "key" of Mars.

The magic which came down to the Golden Dawn from the Renaissance was more than just sympathetic or natural magic, however. Ficino's pious and

THE EMERALD TABLET

The best-known of the so-called Hermetic documents is the Emerald Tablet, which is the source of the famous dictum "As above, so below". The Emerald Tablet, which was revered in the Renaissance as the essential alchemical doctrine, contains references to a number of things which may correspond to images found in the Tarot; for example—the sun and moon, the father (Emperor?), the nurse (Empress?), the world, strength, meditation (Hermit?). Though there is probably no direct connection between the two, similarities such as these make it easy to see how Court de Gébelin and others discerned an "Egyptian" flavor in the Tarot.

This is the complete text of the Emerald Tablet:

It is true without lie, certain and most veritable, that what is below is like what is above and that what is above is like what is below, to perpetrate the miracles of one thing.

And as all things have been, and come from one by the meditation of One; thus all things have been born from this single thing by adaptation.

The Sun is its father and the Moon its mother.

The Wind has carried it in his belly and the Earth is its nurse. The father of all the perfection of all the world is here.

Its force or power is entire if it is turned into earth.

Thou shalt separate the Earth from the Fire, the subtle from the gross, softly, with great ingenuity.

It rises from the Earth to the sky and again descends into the Earth, and receives the force of things superior and inferior.

Thou shalt have by this means the glory of all the world. And therefore all obscurity shall flee from thee.

And this is the strength strong of all strength. For it shall vanquish any thing subtle and anything solid penetrate.

Thus the world is created.

From this shall be and shall proceed admirable adaptations, of which the means is here.

And in this connection I am called Hermes Trismegistus, having the three parts of the philosophy of all the world.

It is finished, what I have said of the operation of the sun.

---

elegant exploration of magical practice had soon been supplemented by exotic, complex, new elements. A student of Ficino's, Giovanni Pico della Mirandola (1463–94), added a crucial dimension to the magical edifice by claiming that natural magic was too weak to be successful without the addition of Kabbalistic magic. Kabbalah, like the *Hermetica*, was thought to be of very ancient origin, though in fact the formative book of Kabbalism, the *Sefer Yetzirah*, was written between A.D. 300 and A.D. 600, later than even the *real* dates of the Hermetic writings. The detailed version of this Jewish mystical philosophy was developed in medieval Spain, and was expressed in the second great Kabbalistic text, the *Zohar*. The *Zohar* contained the version of Kabbalah

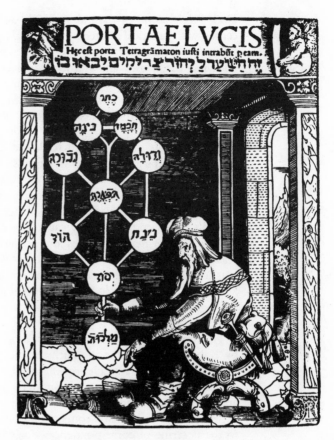

This illustration from Paulus Riccius's 1516 manuscript, Porta Lucis *("Gate of Light"), captures the atmosphere of Renaissance magic and suggests the importance of Kabbalah, as symbolized by the sephirotic tree, or Tree of Life. For Renaissance magi, the twenty-two Hebrew letters and ten numbers associated with the Tree were "thirty-two marvellous ways of wisdom," revealing—and in a sense, creating—the essential form of all that is.*

known to Pico and the other Renaissance magicians, and it amplified the whole doctrine of correspondences, as in this passage:

> When the Holy One who created the Universe wished to reveal its hidden aspect, the light within darkness, He showed how things were intermingled. Thus out of darkness comes light and from the concealed comes the revealed. In the same manner does good emerge from evil and Mercy from Justice, since they too are intertwined.

This statement, with its pairs of opposites and its talk of the "hidden" and the "revealed," is obviously reminiscent of Gnosticism. In plain fact, all the traditions rediscovered and adopted by the Renaissance magicians were versions of Gnostic doctrine bobbing back to the surface after centuries of obscurity beneath the weight of Christian orthodoxy.

Nonetheless, Neoplatonism, the *Hermetica*, and Kabbalah all added something new and more daring to the development of magical philosophy. The magic which derived from Kabbalism went substantially further than the aims of Ficino's natural magic, because it actually sought to tap into the power *beyond* astral influences—the power of the angels, archangels, and, ultimately,

85

God. Pico's blend of natural and Kabbalistic magic was not so much concerned with practical matters such as healing; rather, it was a creative process by which the imagination was developed to higher levels of abstraction. By knowing the names and numbers (derived by a Kabbalistic form of numerology called "gematria") of various angels, and using these in invocations and in contemplation, the Kabbalist might approach knowledge of the *Sephiroth*—that is, the names or powers of God, represented on the Tree of Life.

The addition of Kabbalism took the esoteric foundations of magic to another level. It supplemented the expression of the universal principles on the material plane with corresponding expressions on the *mental plane*, in the form of numbers and letters. This was a simple but powerful development. If numbers and letters participate in the original or primal state of being, as the Kabbalists contend, then they can be used for occult purposes, such as the construction of magical spaces and powerful invocations. By means of this reasoning, the twenty-two-letter Hebrew alphabet came to play an important part in occult activities, as did the theory of numbers. The occult science we know today as "numerology" is a blend of Kabbalistic number theory and the Pythagorean concept of a "vibrational" universe based on mathematical principles.

The modern interpretation of the Tarot has been influenced tremendously by Kabbalistic ideas for the fairly simple reason that there are twenty-two trumps and twenty-two Hebrew letters. Other than that correlation, there is nothing to tie the two together. But in the magical universe, correspondences are all-important, and so this one has been enough to inspire much thought. Moreover, the Kabbalistic connection is very important in relating the Tarot to the doctrine of correspondences, for while the *minor* arcana has obvious natural affinities (the four suits correspond with the four elements, the four humors, the four classes of society, and so on), the *major* arcana is absolutely devoid of any apparent order that would "plug in" to the magical universe. Thus the "happy coincidence" of twenty-two-ness, as Hall called it, is vital because it brings the trump cards into the fold.

But even though their work in the development of magical thought and practice laid a major part of the foundation for the magical interpretation of the Tarot, Ficino and Pico della Mirandola—so far as we know—regarded the Tarot, if they regarded it at all, as nothing more than a popular card game. This is, as already discussed, one of the great puzzles concerning the esoteric Tarot: Since the cards were almost certainly known at the time by these Renaissance magicians, it is very striking that the trump images are never mentioned in their magical treatises. It may be that Renaissance Italy was so awash with magical/mystical/spiritual endeavors that Tarot was simply a minor expression of the fervor of the times, overshadowed by other more dramatic developments. And it also seems likely that the Tarot cards would have been considered too new to compete with the gloriously "ancient" *Hermetica* and Kabbalah.

Furthermore, the important Renaissance magicians were considered serious philosophers and theologians, not mere occult dabblers. They hoped to elevate their work to the status of an adjunct to religion, and the Tarot images may have been thought too vulgar or too pagan to fit comfortably into this magico-religious alliance. (The magicians had to be quite careful, for the winds of favor blew unpredictably; Pico was first attacked by the Church for some of his magical views, and spent some time in confinement before gaining the support of the new pope, Alexander VI, who was very interested in magical matters.)

Whatever the reasons may have been, the practice of magic in the Renaissance went well beyond the works of Ficino and Pico, and beyond Italy, with no mention of the Tarot. But the structure of magical theory continued to become more elaborate, more complex—and more ambitious.

ELEMENTS AND TYPES OF MAGIC

An overview of magical activity in Europe was offered by German physician Heinrich Cornelius Agrippa von Nettesheim (1486–1535) in his early–sixteenth-century compendium *De occulta philosophia*. Agrippa divided magical activity into three levels. First came *natural* magic (similar to Ficino's), then what Agrippa called *celestial* magic. Frances Yates, in *Giordano Bruno and the Hermitic Tradition*, paraphrases Agrippa's description of celestial magic this way:

> When a magician follows natural philosophy and mathematics and knows the middle sciences which come from them—arithmetic, music, geometry, optics, astronomy, mechanics—he can do marvellous things. We see to-day remains of ancient works, columns, pyramids, huge artificial mounds. Such things were done by mathematical magic. As one acquires natural virtue by natural things, so by abstract things—mathematical and celestial things—one acquires celestial virtue.

The practice of celestial magic was concerned with the making of talismans bearing efficacious images, the arrangement of numbers and letters in magic squares, and the enactment by speech and gesture of appropriate incantations. Using these methods, Agrippa claimed, the magus could bring forth the power of the celestial realm and actually infuse that power into inanimate matter, creating in this manner structures and devices—such as flying mechanical birds and talking bronze heads—which were beyond the power of "ordinary" mechanics.[10]

In Agrippa's third category, *ceremonial* or *religious* magic (an intensified version of Pico's Kabbalistic approach), the magus works his way up to actual contact with angelic spirits. To reach this level, he must first undergo a process of physical and spiritual purification. Once the magician has prepared himself, the activities of ceremonial magic include elaborate rituals, utilizing many familiar religious elements, such as music, candles, bells, altars, etc. This "ceremonial" approach to magic is the culmination of the other approaches, and it is from this type of magic that the ritual magic popular in the late nineteenth and early twentieth centuries derived much of its theory and practice.

Another magical approach which was to influence the development of ritual magic was the Enochian magic derived from the work of the Elizabethan magus John Dee (1527–1608). Having read and admired Agrippa's work, Dee—an accomplished astrologer, mathematician, and mapmaker—became determined to find answers to the riddles of alchemy by consulting with spirits. He had no natural psychic talent himself, and he became allied with a talented but half-charlatan "scryer," Edward Kelley, who purportedly received from his spirit contacts a complete magical language, called "Enochian," which could be used for invocations. Whatever its origins, Enochian is not merely gibberish; it has the properties of a language, and has been periodically revived by magicians as a means of making contact with spirits.[11]

Tools such as Enochian invocation became increasingly vital to the magus, for the highest levels of Hermetic magic, from the Renaissance practice to the present, go far beyond merely drawing *down* celestial favor, as Ficino's natural magic was intended to do. "High" magic promises that whoever can fully understand the system of correspondences and use it properly will be able to work back *up* the chain and make contact with sources of power and knowledge which exist on higher levels. In modern occult parlance, this process is generally called "rising on the planes" or something similar. (A contemporary Kabbalist approach to magic uses the term "pathworking" in much the same way, to denote working one's way upward along the paths between the Sephiroth on the Tree of Life.) The practice of this type of magic is considered to be very risky because the magician actually travels out of our worldly plane and into astral regions which are fraught with psychical—and even physical—dangers. The lower astral planes are alleged to be populated with soul-destroying demons, and the traveler will meet terrifying tests of courage and spiritual strength along the way.

The fearsome aspect of astral travel is a theme found in many magical traditions. The Tibetan Book of the Dead, for example, which tells (in what is probably a psychological rather than a literal way) of the states passed through by the soul after death, describes hellish torments on the plane of "karmic illusion":

> Then the Lord of Death will place round thy neck a rope and drag thee along; he will cut off thy head, tear out thy heart, pull out thy intestines, lick up thy brain, drink thy blood, eat thy flesh, and gnaw thy bones; but thou wilt be incapable of dying. Even when thy body is hacked to pieces, it will revive again.

This experience is very like that which the shaman undergoes on his soul journey to the realms beyond (a voyage which will be discussed later in this chapter).

It is precisely because the aspiring magician needs to be carefully and thoroughly prepared for these difficult astral encounters that many magical societies employ a system of *initiations*. The student-adept is allowed to take only one step at a time. First he or she must learn the signs and associations that will be used in meditation to reach a particular path or astral region; the student is tested, and then must practice to a level of mastery before going on to the next step. Knowledge of the correspondences is vital, for if a magician goes astray in the astral regions, only images will serve as guideposts—for example, if you are supposed to be in the realm of Venus and you meet a horse, something is wrong, for the horse belongs to Mars. It is generally thought that magical progress requires supervision on a personal basis, so most magical traditions insist on the necessity of a teacher, often refusing to put doctrines and practices in writing so that they will not reach the attention of the "immature."

One of the most effective methods of magical training is the use of symbolic images to train the imagination. The process of meditating on the images, retaining them, and visualizing them builds the precision and stamina of the imaginal faculty and leads the imagination toward the states of being that correspond with the images. Obviously, this is another place where the Tarot may come in. From the magical point of view, the colors and symbols on the Tarot cards take on great importance, as do the numerical structures of the cards and their connections with the Hebrew letters; all of these factors can combine to make the Tarot images potent aids to the magical imagination.

But the Tarot images were almost certainly never used by early Hermeticists for the purpose of rising on the planes; this connection was introduced, for practical purposes, by the Golden Dawn system. Renaissance magicians used a very wide variety of complex images (such as, for Saturn, a man with a stag's head, camel's feet, on a throne or on a dragon, with a sickle in the right hand, an arrow in the left) to awaken the imagination and focus it on the desired astral destination. In order to remember all these images and their associations—along with a great number of other useful items—many Renaissance magicians used a system of "artificial memory."

The *ars memoria*, or Art of Memory, was devised in classical times, and was widely used in the Middle Ages by scholars as well as by magicians, for in the days before printing, much information had to be committed to memory. The original method of artificial memory was to create in the imagination a vivid picture of a memory structure—a house, a temple, even a city. This structure was then furnished with images, each image having "attached" to it a fact or idea. The images were not supposed to be symbolic of the things they represented, but rather were required to be as striking as possible, whether unusually beautiful or unusually ugly or simply very strange. In this way, the images engaged the imagination and so were easy to recall, bringing the "attached" facts along with them.

The memory art was basically, of course, just a way of arranging the imagination for more efficient use, much as we arrange our kitchens and offices so that things needed will be ready at hand. But in the magical milieu of the Renaissance, artificial memory was carried to a higher level by Giordano Bruno (1548–1600),[12] and the memory images themselves became part of a magical system. Instead of creating a physical talisman to contain magical power, the magician might project that power into an image which could be mentally manipulated. If these images were organized to represent the divine order of the universe, Bruno believed, they would actually take on a participation in the divine power. And if, ultimately, the magician could encompass all these images in mind *simultaneously*, he would experience fusion with the mind of God.

The Tarot images have been linked with the memory arts by several theorists. Robert O'Neill explains the connection this way in his *Tarot Symbolism*:

> If the set of images being used for meditation represent all the ideas of the cosmos, then holding all of them simultaneously in the mind unites the magus with all of the cosmic powers. The critical concept is clearly stated in the Divine Pymander, attributed to Hermes Trismegistus. If you can embrace all things at once in thought, including time, place, substance, quantity, quality, you can understand God! . . . Dante or Camillo may have captured all of the Divine Ideas in their works. But their works were too complex to be grasped all at once in the mind. The fifty symbols of the Tarocchi of Mantegna or even the thirty-five symbols of the Minchiate are clearly philosophical classifications of the sciences, but have simply too many images. Fifty symbols cannot be imagined all at once. The Tarot designers chose a smaller number, twenty-two, as the perfect compromise between representing all of reality and being able to hold the images simultaneously in mind.

O'Neill believes the Tarot trumps were specifically designed for this purpose, based on the early mystical memory system of Ramon Lull (1232–1316). But if the cards were actually, as evidence seems to suggest, designed at least a century later (well after Lull, but well before Bruno), it may have been that the trumps were merely general expressions of the magical revival and the Renaissance craze for images.

The power of images was also recognized in another of the Hermetic arts of the Renaissance—alchemy. The tradition of alchemy goes all the way back to the roots of metallurgy, but its incorporation into the magical arts of the West seems to have taken place mainly in the same period of Hellenistic syncretism (from around 300 B.C. to A.D. 300) that produced Gnosticism, Neoplatonism, and the *Hermetica*; in fact, the *Hermetica* included alchemical treatises. Some of the most important early development of alchemical ideas took place in the Islamic world, and the word "alchemy" itself comes to us from the Arabic, but the practice of alchemy is believed to have begun in Egypt and China. Alchemy entered Europe with the Islamic influence in Spain, and alchemical texts translated from the Arabic were the staple tools of the medieval alchemists. The ancient Greek texts were unknown until the Renaissance, when their rediscovery fueled a new wave of interest in the "royal art."

The popular impression that alchemy was a pseudo-science practiced by credulous fools or greedy charlatans has long been challenged, on the one hand by historians of science, who have shown that physical alchemy was an intelligent scientific pursuit which provided a foundation for modern chemistry, and on the other hand by historians of the imagination (like Carl Jung and Mircea Eliade), who have demonstrated that alchemy was used as a means of achieving deep psychological transformation. Alchemical work was based on the same doctrine of correspondences that animated magical work, but it was practiced in a different way.

Broadly speaking, the goal of alchemy was the resolution of opposites, by first dissolving the material (*solve*) and then regenerating it (*coagula*) in a new, perfected form. The alchemical process involved transcendence of fundamental dualities (male/female, good/evil, matter/spirit), and it unfolded in a series of stages marked by changes in color. First came the blackening (*nigredo*) or decomposition of the material; then the whitening (*albedo*) or bleaching, which produced a silver elixir; next there appeared a rainbow or iridescent vapor; and finally, the reddening (*rubedo*), which yielded a red liquid or powder, often referred to—in the characteristically mysterious language of alchemy—as the "Philosopher's Stone."[13] The final product was said to be the "elixir of life," key to immortality; it was also believed to serve as a catalyst for the transmutation of other materials (e.g., turning lead into gold).

Alchemical work took place both outwardly, through actual experiments on matter, and inwardly, through the imaginal processes of the alchemist, and it is seldom quite clear which of these aspects is being referred to in alchemical texts. The texts which describe alchemical theories and activities are very confusing, for at least two reasons. First, the alchemical writers frequently *intended* to puzzle rather than enlighten the aspiring alchemist, both to test his resolve and to keep the secrets of alchemical work from passing into the possession of the unworthy; crucial steps and ingredients of the physical alchemical process were left out or misrepresented. Second, the inner or psychic dimension of alchemy could not be explained straightforwardly, but could only be presented through allegorical stories and symbolic illustrations. And so alchemical treatises are strange indeed, filled with passages like these:

> That universal thing, the greatest treasure of earthly wisdom, is one thing, and the principles of three things are found in one . . . . The three things are the true spirit of mercury, and the soul of sulphur, united to a spiritual salt, and dwelling in one body . . . .

> We also spoke of the "fire of the sages" as being one of the chief agents in our chemical process, and said that it was an essential, preternatural and Divine fire, that it lay hid in our substance, and that it was stirred into action by the influence and aid of the outward, material fire.[14]

Despite its often maddening difficulties, alchemy occupies a crucial place in the structure of occult practices. Alchemical ideas and images played a particularly important role in the formation of Rosicrucianism. The Rosicrucian movement began very early in the seventeenth century with the publication in Germany of two pamphlets proclaiming the existence of a secret society, the Fraternity of the Rosy Cross, devoted to "magia" and "cabala," the two great Hermetic sciences. Modern research into the origins of Rosicrucianism suggest that this group probably never actually existed, but the program presented in the pamphlets was so attractive that very soon there were groups calling themselves "Rosicrucian" and claiming to have received the secret knowledge of that fraternity.[15] The Rosicrucian manifestos promised a fusion of occult and scientific activities, good works (the self-proclaimed Rosicrucians professed to freely heal the sick, using the medical secrets of the renowned occult physician Paracelsus), and a utopian ideal of brotherhood and shared esoteric knowledge.

A third Rosicrucian pamphlet—*The Chemical Wedding of Christian*

The lion in this drawing from the Rosarium Philosophorum, *1550, is green, and probably represents natural matter. Devouring the Sun (sulphur), it produces "the blood of the Green Lion," or mercury. The allegorical use of images to represent processes is a common feature of alchemical literature. Though there is a rich vein of speculation concerning links between Tarot and alchemy, the lion and the sun are among the few alchemical images directly shown in the Tarot.*

Rosenkreutz—introduced the alchemical allegory which was to become the foundation of all subsequent Rosicrucianism. The phrase "chemical wedding" refers to the alchemical union of male and female, symbolized by the King and Queen, and by the Sun (sulphur) and Moon (mercury). These members of the wedding party are just a few of the symbolic cast of characters found in alchemical imagery. Others include the Green Lion (representing the *prima materia* or starting matter), the Red Dragon (another term for the Stone), the Phoenix (which rises from its own ashes), the Androgyne or Hermaphrodite (embodying both male and female), and the Homunculus (a tiny man who may appear in the distilling vessel at a certain stage of the work). These characters are frequently represented in the many drawings which alchemists used to symbolize the stages of their work.

It is here, in the imagery of alchemical art, that some commentators see a possible connection with the imagery of Tarot. The style of the Tarot images is quite different from the style of alchemical art, however, and there are few direct parallels between the contents of the Tarot images and alchemical illustrations. But it is possible to see a reflection of the alchemical process in the concepts of the major arcana cards. A very simplified version of these relationships would place The Fool as the *prima materia* and The Magician as the alchemist. The Papess and The Empress would be the spiritual and material versions of the feminine principle. The Pope and The Emperor would fill the same roles for the masculine principle, and The Lovers would be the "chemical marriage." Death, The Devil, and The Tower may all be associated with aspects of the *nigredo*, and The Star and The Moon with the *albedo*. Judgment, then, would represent the final transformation, and The World would appear as the Great Stone itself. (The "middle" cards which I have left out—The Chariot, Justice, The Hermit, The Wheel of Fortune, Strength, and The Hanged Man—can all be associated with technical phases of the work, but that requires much more detail about the alchemical process than can be given here.)[16]

Though the Rosicrucian groups of the seventeenth century never, so far as we know, had any involvement with the Tarot, their general approach to occult practice—which combined all the Hermetic arts and tried to present them in a "scientific" framework suitable to the dawning Age of Enlightenment—was to prove very instrumental in transforming the Tarot from a popular game into an occult instrument. As we saw in part 1, the originators of the esoteric Tarot (Court de Gébelin, Lévi, Papus, Mathers) were all involved in fraternal organizations that defined themselves as part of the "Rosicrucian" tradition.

Indeed, it was the network of such secret societies—the Freemasons, the Martinists, and so on—which kept vestiges of Hermetic philosophy alive as the Renaissance world of magic was slowly but certainly eclipsed by the Enlightenment and the rise of natural science. The magical world view was not publicly revived until the beginning of the nineteenth century, with the publication of Francis Barrett's *The Magus, or Celestial Intelligencer*. This account of Hermetic magic became quite popular, and inspired the work of Eliphas Lévi, which led in turn to the development of the tradition now called "ritual magic."

It was Lévi who added a crucial element to the magical mix: the human will. Though he certainly did not invent this concept, he did bring to it the prominence it has enjoyed in magical theory since his time. The magical will was thought by Lévi to be a real, *material* force—something like the "galvanic stream," which was proposed by some theorists of mesmerism to account for the influence one person could exert over another. Most occultists now think of the will as something psychological, akin to the power of concentration, but still consider it to be a primary and potent force in magical procedures. The various implements of ritual magic—the candles, incense, images, incantations, and the like—are seen as aids to concentration, assisting the magician in focusing his or her will on the desired goal.

The *law of will* was one of three proposed by Lévi. The others were the *law of astral light*—an invisible substance, said to permeate all of space, which could be used by the magician to act at a distance—and the *law of correspondences*, which offered an updated version of the old Renaissance doctrine. These ideas, again, were not unique to Lévi; the astral light is similar to the "ether" which was supposed by nineteenth-century scientists to carry light waves. But Lévi put all this in such a dramatic way that, in spite of the fact that he undertook hardly any real magical practice at all, he was able to give his ideas a great aura of potency. Lévi's approach was carried on by MacGregor Mathers, right into the formation of the Golden Dawn.[17]

MODERN MAGIC: WEST MEETS EAST

It was in the Hermetic Order of the Golden Dawn that the last element of modern ritual magic was put in place. The avant-garde magicians of that group added the *law of imagination*, concerning the power to produce and sustain mental imagery, which could then be directed in its effects by the will. Of course this idea was not new either. It was reminiscent of alchemical operations and of the magical memory arts. But in the Golden Dawn, imagination was seen in a newly psychological light, and it was integrated into a magical system more complete than any created before.

Tarot and the imagination will be the focus of the next chapter, so I'll say little more on the subject here. But it's worth pausing for a moment to consider the timing of all this activity. The advance in magical ideas achieved by the Golden Dawn took place at about the same time that Freud was evolving his theories concerning the unconscious, and Einstein his new formulations of space and time. Looking back, we see that the Hermetic revival of the Renaissance, too, had accompanied a profound shift in world views—as had the eruption of Gnostic, Neoplatonic, and Hermetic writings in the early Christian period. These synchronous occurrences remind us that magic is always with us, and that it reflects the mind of its time. When the cultural imagination is strongly at work, breaking out of an old paradigm into a new one, the attraction of magic is intensified and its creative power contributes to the changes taking place.

As we saw in part 1, the Golden Dawn—in spite of its follies and its excesses—had a profound and lasting effect on occult studies. But there were those, exemplified by Aleister Crowley, who believed the "magic" of the Golden Dawn was merely a diluted and Christianized version of the powerful and dangerous original. They claimed that the revival of ritual magic had overlooked the most substantive element of magical practice, one which had been misunderstood or concealed by the Hermetic magicians of the Renaissance. That element was sex.

The doctrine of correspondences inevitably suggests a special understanding of sexuality. If the human body is the microcosmic reflection of the universal order, then human sexual energy may be seen as the correlate of divine creative energy, and human sexual intercourse as a reenactment of the process by which immaterial and undifferentiated being projects itself into matter, thus "creating" the material world. So the act of sexual union may be a celebration of the generative power at the heart of creation; and it may also be used *in reverse* by the adept as a means of returning imaginally to the ground of being. By this reasoning, sexuality may be used to "raise" consciousness, but only if it is practiced in a ritual or ceremonial manner, utilizing the network of correspondences which links our physical experience with the organizing principles of the universe.

This was the basic idea of Aleister Crowley's "sex magick," but the theory was little understood by others and the practice was largely unsuccessful as carried out by Crowley and his disciples. Crowley's intemperateness and his drug addiction undermined entirely whatever serious content there may have been in his approach to magic—which was, in any event, too extreme to appeal to most occultists. But the legacy of Crowleyan magic has been to reintroduce elements of magic which were for a long time obscured in the West by the anti-sexual bias of Christianity. One effect of this reconsideration has been to direct attention to Eastern forms of magic, especially the ancient discipline of Tantrism.

Although Crowley's sex magic was by no means as elegantly conceptualized or as elaborately ritualized as the Tantric practices of India, the goals were similar.[18] Tantrism employs sexual metaphors to represent the nature of creation, and a very specialized form of sexual activity is undertaken by Tantric practitioners as a means of reenacting the primal process of reality. But Tantrism is not merely a sexual discipline by any means; there is a great deal of emphasis on meditation, utilizing complex and highly symbolic visual images called *yantras* to focus the imagination. The use of the Tarot images as yantras was a feature of Golden Dawn practice, and was part of Crowley's magical undertaking.[19]

Eastern occult philosophies have, of course, been known in the West to some degree for centuries, though during certain parts of history that degree has been very small. But the tremendous impact of Eastern ideas on Western occultism in the twentieth century is very largely due to the influence of the Theosophical Society, which was founded in 1875[20] and continues in operation today. There was, as far as I know, no official interest among Theosophists in the Tarot, at least not during the society's most influential period, but the Theosophical Society contributed a great many of the ideas employed by today's occultists and frequently applied to the Tarot. These ideas are often complementary to those of Western magic, but they use a very different vocabulary and conceptual background.

Like the Golden Dawn, the Theosophical Society included many talented

Yantras *are meditative diagrams, used by Tantrists to focus concentration and to organize perception into an awareness of the divine. The most important of these is the Sri Yantra, shown here. It is composed of nine interpenetrating triangles, symbolizing male and female. These in turn generate circuits of other triangles, and the whole becomes a condensed image of all creation. The Tarot images are often characterized as the Western equivalent of the yantra.*

people, underwent numerous schisms, and achieved a wide influence among occultists. Unlike the Golden Dawn, which was never very large and always known mostly among artists and intellectuals, the Theosophical Society attracted substantial numbers of people and generated a terrific amount of publicity—which meant that its effect on the popular perception of esoteric matters was quite potent. But the Theosophical Society was certainly not the best source of information about Eastern philosophies, tending to be selective and sensational in what was presented, and this led to the introduction of a number of diluted and distorted ideas into the occultist repertoire.

So many ideas poured from the Theosophist fountainhead that it is very difficult to capsulize the Theosophical Society doctrines or their effects. The society's founder, Madame Blavatsky, created huge tomes ("I write, write, write," she told Yeats, "as the Wandering Jew walks, walks, walks") filled with what can only be described as idiosyncratic theories. Annie Besant and C. W. Leadbeater, eventual leaders of the Theosophical Society, produced works with more objectively serious content, including Leadbeater's classic works on the subtle body and the chakras. Much of the material in these various works was claimed to have been received clairvoyantly—frequently from Tibetan "Masters" who were said by Blavatsky to be interested in the course of human events, but there are also quite a lot of references to Hindu and Buddhist texts, yogic practice, Taoism, esoteric Christianity, Hermeticism, and other metaphysical systems.

Perhaps the chief accomplishment of the Theosophical Society was popularizing the idea of comparative religion. In the process, two important areas of investigation—reincarnation and esoteric anatomy—were opened up. Generally speaking, reincarnation—like spiritualism—does not have a strong Tarot connection, and I have left both of these areas out in this account of the occult tradition.[21] But the doctrine of the subtle (or "etheric") body is very relevant to our study of Tarot. The idea of a nonmaterial body is found in many sources, both Eastern and Western. The sixteenth-century occult physician Paracelsus called it the "sidereal body," and described it this way:

> Hence man has also an animal body and a sidereal body; and both are one, and not separated. The relation between the two is as follows. The animal body, the body of flesh and blood, is in itself always dead. Only through the action of the sidereal body does the motion of life come into the other body. The sidereal body is fire and air, but it is also bound to the animal life of man. Thus mortal man consists of water, earth, fire and air.

The *subtle* body is generally considered to exist between the *material* body and the *astral* body; the subtle body is an energy network which coincides with the physical body and remains attached to it, whereas the astral body is "detachable" and can be used for traveling out of the physical body on the astral planes. The subtle body maintains the life of the physical body while the soul is inhabiting the astral body.[22]

The idea of the astral body can be taken as metaphorical—that is, as a body-sense formed by the imagination to retain orientation and coherence during imaginal work—but the existence of the subtle body is felt by most occultists to be "literally" true. Even medical science today admits that energy fields, magnetic resonances, and electrical impulses are a vital part of human physiology, though in orthodox medicine this knowledge is (somewhat oddly) used mostly in diagnostic techniques, and rarely for therapeutic purposes. Alternative therapies such as chiropractic, acupuncture, and even the "laying-on of hands" do use the energy body in a demonstrably effective way to heal the physical body by improving its relationship to the energy body.

The three bodies must, we would think, be connected to one another at some points in order both to maintain their "coincidence" (that is, to continue occupying exactly the same volume of space under normal circumstances) and to intermingle their effects so as to create what we think of as a living, soul-inhabited person. These connecting points are called the *chakras*—from the Sanskrit for "wheel"[23]—and they serve as centers of consciousness (in the sense that "consciousness" is the interface between the material and immaterial aspects of being). The number of chakras is generally fixed at seven, and these are aligned vertically in the body from the "root" chakra at the base of the spine to the chakra known as the "thousand-petalled lotus" on the top of the head. In between are chakras located near the sexual organs, the navel, the heart, the throat, and the eyes. (The chakra located between the eyebrows is the famous "third eye.")

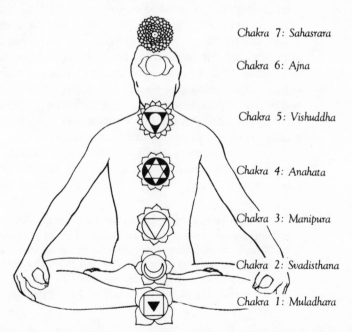

Chakra 7: Sahasrara

Chakra 6: Ajna

Chakra 5: Vishuddha

Chakra 4: Anahata

Chakra 3: Manipura

Chakra 2: Svadisthana

Chakra 1: Muladhara

The Eastern schema of seven chakras, or energy centers, connecting the "subtle" or "astral" body with the material body has for a long time been integrated into Western metaphysics. Each chakra has its own symbolic mandala, and each is thought to be associated with certain functions of the body and with specific aspects of consciousness. Some theorists have connected the Tarot with the raising of the Kundalini, or "serpent power"—a path to the highest level of consciousness, symbolized by the crown chakra.

An account given in certain branches of yoga and in Tantrism as the "raising of the serpent-power" (*kundalini*) expresses, in what could be thought of as a poetic or mythic way, the nature of the process. The female, or *Shakti* energy, coiled (like a snake) at the base of the spine, is awakened—usually by elaborate exercises and long discipline, but sometimes spontaneously—and rises through the body, piercing or "opening" the chakras. Since the chakras are centers of consciousness, the result of this process is an alteration in consciousness, the increase of consciousness to a new level. If the kundalini is raised all the way to the lotus chakra, where *Shiva*, the masculine principle of energy, dwells, the culmination is complete absorption in the divine bliss; this is thought to be a very rare achievement, not attainable by "ordinary" yogic means. Like the magical process of rising on the planes, raising the kundalini has traditionally been viewed as a dangerous undertaking, to be done only with the most careful and expert supervision.[24]

It doesn't take a great deal of acuity to notice that in the above description, on one level at least, the process taking place is the union of male and female—and so we have returned to the subject of sex. The blending of masculine and feminine elements within the psyche is one of the most frequent and fundamental themes of magical/mystical practice in all cultures. In Eastern traditions, the symbolism is more clearly revealed, and some practitioners, such as the Tantrists, use physical sexual acts to create this union *objectively*, as an aid to internalizing the process and creating a *subjective* union.

In the Western occult tradition, the "chemical marriage" or "mystical union" of masculine and feminine is an explicit theme in alchemy, and also an implicit element in many other types of magical practice. As we have already seen, sexuality is an important aspect of magical philosophy, both because human sexual union may be a mythic reenactment of the primal creative act, and because the experience of sexuality may be a psychic tool for the achievement of altered states of consciousness. So it is not surprising that magical imagery is saturated with sexual connotations.

Sexual symbolism is an observable aspect of the Tarot, one which has provoked much comment and speculation. Almost all of the trumps can be given a sexual interpretation, as Richard Cavendish points out in *The Tarot*:

> To take only one example at this point, the trump called Justice shows a woman holding a sword in one hand and a pair of scales in the other. The symbol is a traditional one and seems quite obvious and straightforward. But in most Tarot interpretations the sword is a phallus and the scales are testicles. This explains Papus's otherwise mystifying description of the woman as the Mother, who is "nature performing the function of Eve." Crowley simply called her the Woman Satisfied.

Cavendish seems to be overstating the case when he says "most" Tarot interpretations take this line, but it is true that the Tarot has always invited just such imaginative interest. Not only do the individual trumps have sexually suggestive aspects, the whole of the trump sequence can be seen as a path of sexual

The "Chemical Marriage" was an important theme of alchemy, symbolizing the union of male and female. Like all the elements of alchemy, the chemical marriage was presented allegorically, and it is difficult to say whether the alchemical union of Sun and Moon (sulphur and mercury) was an allegory of sexual union—or vice versa. Among the Tarot trumps, The Sun, The Moon, and The Lovers seem to have obvious parallels with the Chemical Marriage. (This drawing is from the Rosarium Philosophorum, *1550.)*

integration which passes through many aspects of male/female duality (Emperor/Empress, High Priestess/Heirophant, Chariot/Justice, Sun/Moon, and so on), with partial unions (The Lovers, Temperance, The Star) and separations (The Hermit, The Devil, The Tower) along the way, culminating in the ultimate mystical union of the "androgyne," or unisex figure, who dances in the center of the World card. The suits, too, are charged with sexual significance, the Wands and Swords being the projective male symbols, the Cups and Pentacles the receptive female symbols.

The sexual symbolism of the Tarot is probably at least part of the reason why Tarot has become an especially important part of the revitalization of magic which has taken place over the past two decades. The largely masculine and European tradition of ritual magic has been undergoing a transformation, as the magical practices of women and of other cultures have begun to be rediscovered.

THE NEW MAGIC: FEMINISM AND THE SHAMANIC WAY

Although the integration of masculine and feminine energies is a continuing esoteric theme, and although the feminine has been given more emphasis by far in the occult tradition than in the mainstream of Western culture, neverthe-less, occult activity in the West has been dominated by male practitioners and masculine structures. Women were active in the spiritual and political lives of most Gnostic groups, and it is recorded that a few women practiced alchemy and magic; but beyond those distant generalities, little is known (if, indeed, there is anything to know) about the history of women's participation in Western occultism. Today's movement to recover feminine spirituality contends that because the feminine carries great archetypal power, patriarchal societies have systematically excluded women from religious as well as from political power, using a variety of means to suppress the traditional expressions of feminine spirituality. From the Middle Ages to the twentieth century, women's participation in spiritual life—whether in conventional religion or in occult studies—has been very limited.

But a shift toward feminine influence in Western occultism began to occur—not coincidentally—at about the same time women began their crusades for birth control, suffrage, and other forms of empowerment. It's interesting in this regard to recall that the formation of the Golden Dawn society seems to have been motivated, at least in part, by a desire to rival the popular new Theosophical Society, which was the first metaphysical group to include women. The Theosophical Society not only had women among its adepts, but was actually led, to a great degree, by women (first Madame Blavatsky, then Annie Besant, and later "the Purple Mother," Katherine Tingley). The Golden Dawn, however, though it held women among its members (and some of these had considerable influence), proved staunchly masculinist in most respects. Women served chiefly as tools of the men; for example, both of the well-known Tarot decks—Rider-Waite and Thoth—which emerged from the Golden Dawn were conceived by men, with women serving as their "illustrators" and receiving little or no credit for their creative roles. Similarly, MacGregor Mathers and W. B. Yeats both married women who received, through clairaudience and automatic writing, much of the material their husbands used in creating their respective magical/mystical writings.

In recent years, however, feminine sexuality has emerged strongly in the development of a magical style that poses an alternative to the ritual magic of the Golden Dawn and its offshoots, and a renewed interest in feminine modes of spirituality has encouraged the growth of what might broadly be called "feminist magic." This process began, perhaps ironically, with the renewed interest in witchcraft. Witchcraft, as virtually everyone knows, was a crime persecuted by the Christian Church in varying degrees from the Middle Ages until well into the eighteenth century, and the principal victims of this persecution were women.

The historical fear of witches—who were thought to be in league with the Devil, and to have ways of manipulating and even injuring people—has been seen by later generations first as a particularly exaggerated form of superstition, and then as a misunderstanding of mental illness. "Witch hunts," it was felt, may have had political motivations, and may also have been examples of mass hysteria. But in 1921, anthropologist Margaret Murray's influential book *The Witch-Cult in Western Europe* argued that the Christian crusade

100

against witchcraft was not the product of politics, superstition, or misunderstanding, but rather an attempt to stamp out very real remnants of a pagan
nature religion.

Murray's book was incorrect in most of its specifics, but the general idea
that a form of nature-worship persisted in Europe and the British Isles seems
true. Though this early work attracted interest, it was not until the 1940s that
the idea of a popular revival of pagan witchcraft took hold, fostered by Gerald
Gardner, an amateur folklorist. Gardner secured the help of Aleister Crowley
in writing a manual of rituals to be used in witch groups called "covens," so it's
not surprising to find that Gardnerian witchcraft emphasized nudity and, in
many covens, included ritual sexual activity.

Interest in this approach to witchcraft has waxed and waned in the intervening years; more recently, so-called "robed covens" have moved away from the
sex-magic component of witchcraft, some toward Hermetic magic, some toward a greater emphasis on nature-worship, and some toward a more general
form of Goddess-worship. Though many of these contemporary adherents still
prefer to call their activities "witchcraft," or simply "the craft," the Anglo-
Saxon word "wicca" (which actually referred to a sorcerer[25]) is now widely
considered to be the most acceptable term, and it is used frequently to describe
feminist spiritual practice, as are the terms "Dianic religion" and "Goddess-
worship" (though not all Goddess-worship is associated with wicca).

Goddess-worship has gained a great deal of momentum in recent years,
attracting many women (and some men) who may have had little interest in
occultism *per se*, but who are seeking a more meaningful approach to living.
Guiding figures in this movement—Merlin Stone, Carol Christ, Zsuzsanna
Budapest, Starhawk, and others—have turned to a variety of cultural traditions in search of the roots of women's spiritual identity. Chief among these
sources has been the pre-Christian culture of Europe, as journalist Margot
Adler explains in her survey of contemporary neopaganism called *Drawing
Down the Moon*.

> Followers of Wicca seek their inspiration in pre-Christian sources, European
> folklore, and mythology. They consider themselves priests and priestesses of an
> ancient European shamanistic nature religion that worships a goddess who is
> related to the ancient Mother Goddess in her three aspects of Maiden, Mother and
> Crone. Many Craft traditions also worship a god, related to the ancient horned
> lord of the animals, the god of the hunt, the god of death and lord of the forests.
> Many . . . see themselves as modern-day heirs to the ancient mystery traditions of
> Egypt, Crete, Eleusis, and so on, as well as to the more popular peasant traditions
> of celebratory festivals and seasonal rites.

But the rituals and influences of other traditions—Native American, Asian,
African—have been drawn in as well. And in addition to the "pagan" manifestations of Goddess-worship, there are flourishing efforts to recover the
feminine elements in traditional religions—Christianity, Judaism, and even
Buddhism.

The driving force of the Goddess-worship movement is the recovery of

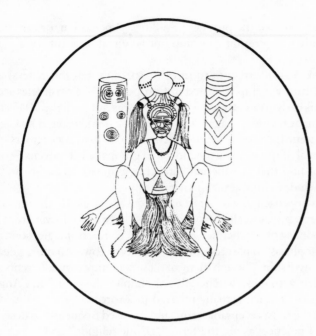

This ink drawing of the Motherpeace card for the High Priestess depicts a powerful medicine woman, rather than the nun-like lady shown in most decks. The Motherpeace Round Tarot—painted in a wash of bright colors—turned all the time-honored Tarot conventions upside down when it appeared in 1981, introducing a whole mix of races, reversing genders, and depicting a vital communal life, filled with play and set in jungles, desserts, and mountains.

feminine spirituality and a way of culture which is based on feminine, rather than masculine principles. Elinor Gado, in her lovely book *The Once and Future Goddess*, describes it this way:

> In our own time, in our own culture, the Goddess once again is becoming a symbol of empowerment for women; a catalyst for an emerging spirituality that is earth-centered; a metaphor for the earth as a living organism; an archetype for feminine consciousness; a mentor for healers; the emblem of a new political movement; an inspiration for artists; and a model for resacralizing woman's body and the mystery of human sexuality.

Of course there have been many different goddesses, worshipped by many different cultures; the "Goddess" of the feminist spirituality movement is a composite of all these, representing the principle itself rather than some particular cultural expression. The ideas and practices of Goddess-worship have much in common with the theories and methods of ritual magic which we've already been considering, but with this important difference: In the male-dominated tradition of ritual magic, magical operations are considered as distinct events, whereas Goddess-centered life is completely saturated with magical thinking. Magic is integrated into the daily rituals of life.

Wiccan magic is centered around the importance of observing seasons and cycles, with ritual celebrations of events such as the solstice and equinox. Here the doctrine of correspondences is employed in terms of relationship with the earth and its rhythms, so that each month has its appropriate color, flower, tree, creature, and so on. There is more than one scheme of these associations, of course, but all are concerned with creating an intense and magical focus on moments in time. The following example for the month of April is taken from Zsuzsanna Budapest's book *Grandmother of Time*.

> *Full moon aspect: Seed moon, budding trees moon*
> *Universal event: Nesting of the birds . . .*
> *Communal event: May eve, ushering in summer . . .*
> *Color: Crimson, green, brown*
> *Tree: Alder, fern, willow*
> *Flower: Sweetpea, daisy*
> *Creature: Hawk*
> *Gem: Diamond*

Budapest also explains which particular health matters (balancing the nerves, cleansing and strengthening), types of activity ("to bend, to aim"), areas of personal growth ("to develop, to know, to enrich, to pleasure") and magical pursuits ("passion spells and devotions to the dead") are especially receptive to attention at this time of year.

Feminism, and, in particular, feminist-oriented Wicca, has exerted a major influence on recent trends in Tarot. One of the strong components of women's role in the spiritual life of a society has traditionally been the power of divination, and it is this connection which has drawn the Tarot into the center of the feminist spiritual movement. So far, little has been said in this section about divination, because although divination occupies a place in the occult tradition, its place is relatively insignificant. Divination, though widely practiced in almost all times, has always attracted so many charlatans that few serious magicians wanted to be associated with it. In chapter 7, "Tarot As a Way of Knowing," I will try to develop more fully a theoretical and historical background for divination, but for the time being, let's continue with the feminist interest in Tarot.

This interest has produced several evocative Tarot decks—including the Motherpeace Round Tarot and the Barbara Walker deck—and some interesting books on Tarot. The feminist interest in Tarot focuses on its imaginal quality, rather than on its connections with abstract occult sciences such as astrology and numerology, and in this way differs from the long-prevailing magical/Kabbalistic approach. In turning away from such conventional constructions, the feminist influence on contemporary Tarot has served to broaden significantly the associations of the cards. Healing, for example, is seen as an important part of the feminine spiritual role in society, and this conjunction has produced some intriguing ideas about the use of Tarot images in healing—both for divining health matters, and for use in healing visualizations.

Divination, healing, magical practices, and mystical alterations of consciousness are all aspects of *shamanism*, a phenomenon which has recently inspired great interest not only among feminist spiritual groups, but among occultists in general. The figure of the shaman was first brought to popular attention in the early 1970s by Carlos Casteneda's accounts of the Yaqui sorceror Don Juan, but the shamanic way had already begun to receive serious

103

The shaman or "wizard" performs important sacred functions. The shamanic path usually begins with an initiation that involves symbolic death and rebirth; while in the "other world," the initiate's outer form may be devoured by spirits. The importance of this process is captured in the skeletonized representation of the shaman which frequently appears in drawings and on ceremonial costumes. This illustration is of a rock painting from a Salish site in British Columbia.

study among scholars well before that. Historian of religions Mircea Eliade published his classic text on the subject, *Shamanism: Archaic Techniques of Ecstasy*, in 1951, and *From Medicine Men to Muhammad*, a sourcebook of readings in spiritual technology and mysticism, appeared in 1967.

Eliade points out, in *Shamanism*, that while shamanic activity is a type of magic, it is a very particular type; and while it is a means of healing, again, it has a specific and distinctive "style." The shaman is:

> medicine man, priest, and psychopompos; that is to say, he cures the sickness, he directs the communal sacrifices, and he escorts the souls of the dead to the other world. He is able to do all this by virtue of his techniques of ecstasy, i.e., by his power to leave his body at will. In Siberia and in northeast Asia a person becomes a shaman by hereditary transmission of the shamanistic profession or by spontaneous vocation or "election" .... In North America, on the other hand, the voluntary "quest" for the powers constitutes the principal method. No matter how the selection takes place, a shaman is recognized as such only following a series of initiatory trials after receiving instruction from qualified masters.

The story of the shaman is dramatic. He (or she) is selected—either by another shaman or by the "spirits" themselves or by a compelling inner impulse—to receive the knowledge of certain techniques. The shamanic candidate must prove his fitness by undergoing a profound spiritual crisis; this involves going into a trance (which often takes the form of falling "ill"), traveling to "other worlds," encountering horrific challenges, and finally being rent to pieces (or something similar). He must heal himself by conquering the fear of death. During the journey he makes contact with spirits, from whom he will be able to enlist help on later journeys. Thus the shaman shows his ability to make contact with the spirit powers and at the same time, gains a unique understanding of illness and death. After this experience, he is a new *kind* of person, with extraordinary powers; he is able to fly, to heal, and to travel in the other world as an intermediary between the community and the gods.

Many of the Tarot trump images can be seen as evoking stages of the shamanic journey and aspects of the shaman's role in the community. The Fool, for example, may represent the neophyte, The Magician the initiated shaman. The Hanged Man can be related to the theme of crucifixion that is often found in the visions of the shaman's initiatory journey, while The Devil is remindful of the demons encountered by the shaman as he makes his way through the destruction of the self symbolized by Death, and toward the regeneration symbolized by The World. The Hermit is very like the shaman in his periods of self-imposed exile, and The Tower may be seen as an image of the sudden spiritual crises which mark the shaman's passages from this realm to the other.

There are many more associations which can be drawn. For example, Vicki Noble, creator of the Motherpeace Round Tarot, describes the Strength card this way:

> Like the most ancient women with their bone calendars and their awesome menstrual potency, the central character of the Strength card is practicing the art of bending energy to her will . . . . She represents the part of every woman that is magical and open to what one author has called the "unseen Real," able to converse with animals, and even—as in the traditional decks of Tarot cards—to tame the wild beasts through her divine compassion and deep feminine focus.

It's interesting to note that Strength is one of the cards which traditional interpreters have had the most trouble with, precisely because Strength is usually represented by a woman.[26] The proper position of the Strength card has been hotly debated (Waite switched its traditional position with that of Justice, others switch the two back); the name of the card has been changed (Crowley made this card "Lust"); and commentators have proposed many associations for the lion (the alchemical symbol of the sun, the lion of St. Mark, the lion in the Androcles legend, and so on), but—none for the woman!

The feminist and the shamanic perspectives often overlap, and both have significantly influenced contemporary thinking about Tarot. They represent the kind of creative rethinking of magical ideas which is continually enriching the occult tradition. Even more important, however, is the widening effect of these ideas beyond the boundaries of occult precincts. Goddess-worship and shamanism are emerging as significant cultural phenomena, challenging our old ways of thinking about many topics—health, the environment, relationships, ethnicity, and personal responsibility. Through this process, magic may once again become a vital part of our everyday lives.

It seems very unlikely that the Tarot cards as we know them today were created by shamans or Goddess-worshippers or even magicians of any kind. Yet as we have seen in this brief review of the occult tradition, there are resonances between the Tarot images and almost every aspect of magical/mystical endeavor. This network of correspondences has led to many trips down the garden path, taken by Tarot enthusiasts who, thrilled by their discovery of the Tarot's similarities to some phenomenon or another, have gone on to create elaborate theories based on their imagined connection. As we have seen, there are those who would believe the Tarot is a veiled record of secret teachings from the Egyptian Book of Thoth, or from the Greek mysteries of Eleusis, or from the mystical sects of early Christianity; others would link the Tarot with the Kabbalistic Tree of Life, with the alchemical stages of transmutation, or with the elemental rites of pagan Goddess-worship. From the standpoint of what we know today, we have to feel that none of these ideas is true. But we also have to ask—does it matter?

Let's assume, for the sake of simplicity, that these theories are not "actually" accurate, but that they contain some kind of "higher" truth. From that position, it becomes possible to see through the confusion, and to recognize some much more important and fundamental questions: What do all these ideas, beneath their seeming diversity, have in common? And what does their variety tell us about the human psyche, about the imagination, about the nature of spiritual life? Why has the Tarot attracted so much speculation, and encouraged so much creative development? Perhaps most important: Is there anything real, identifiable, and supportable to be said about the Tarot?

If these questions cannot actually be answered, they can at least be illuminated, and I will try to shed some light on these continuing concerns in the following chapters of part 2.

Notes

1. This information is taken from Mircea Eliade's essay "The Occult and the Modern World," included in Eliade's book *Occultism, Witchcraft, and Cultural Fashions*.
2. Edward A. Tiryakian offers this distinction in his paper "Toward a Sociology of Esoteric Culture." He defines "occult" as referring to *activities*, and "esoteric" as referring to the *ideas* upon which those activities are based. I think this constitutes a good differentiation. The paper is included in Tiryakian's excellent (though out-of-print) 1974 anthology *On the Margin of the Visible: Sociology, the Esoteric, and the Occult*.
3. This essay is contained in *Consciousness and Creativity*, edited by John-Raphael Staude.
4. It is widely accepted, based on the earliest biographies of Plato (which date from several centuries after his death), that Plato did travel to Egypt. But there is no record of what he did there, nor are there any references to initiations.
5. It is interesting to note that several of the themes and images from the Tarot occur in this passage: Cups, The Chariot, The Star, Time (an early name for The Hermit), Fate (another traditional name for The Wheel of Fortune), and The Universe, (Crowley's name for The World).
6. Fifty-two Gnostic texts were discovered in Egypt in 1945, among them the Gospels of Thomas and Philip, and two texts entitled the Gospel of Truth and the Gospel to the Egyptians. This group, often referred to as the Nag Hammadi "library," also includes a number of other texts attrib-

uted to followers of Jesus. The Nag Hammadi texts are copies, dating from around the fourth century A.D. Though scholars disagree on the dates of the original materials, they are generally thought to have been second-century at the latest, and it is possible that some were actually written before the orthodox Gospels.

7. Of the many texts which comprised the *Corpus Hermetica*, the best-known today are the philosophical works *Pimander* (also written *Pymander* and *Poimandres*) and *Asclepius*, and the alchemical text called the *Emerald Tablet*.

8. Augustine, on the other hand, rejected the *Hermetica* because of their magical element, even while embracing (to a certain extent) some very similar but nonmagical ideas of the Neoplatonists. (It's likely that the Neoplatonists were in fact themselves influenced by the *Hermetica*, but of course Saint Augustine had no way of knowing that!) There were several uses of the term "Son of God" in the Hermetic texts; one that Lactantius referred to specifically is found in the *Asclepius*:

> The Lord and Creator of all things, whom we have thought right to call God, since He made the second God visible and sensible . . . . Since, therefore, He made Him first, and alone, and one only, He appeared to Him beautiful, and most full of all good things; and he hallowed Him, and altogether loved Him as His own Son.

9. There was plenty of magical practice in the Middle Ages, and the name of Hermes Trismegistus was well-known. But as magic was roundly discouraged by the Church, which dominated all aspects of society, medieval magic was generally of a low sort. Exceptions were the speculative works of Albertus Magnus (1193–1280) and Roger Bacon (1214–94), both of whom styled their activities as scientific or philosophical, rather than magical, but who were, we can see in retrospect, firmly in the Hermetic tradition.

10. Agrippa's remarks regarding "ancient works" and "artificial mounds" having been built by mathematical magic refer in part to accounts recorded in the Hermetic writings. References of this sort contribute to the present-day idea of a magical background to Stonehenge, the Pyramids, and other early monuments and earthworks.

11. Dee also developed a theory of symbolism, which he described in his best-known work, *The Hieroglyphic Monad*, thought to have been used as the philosophical basis for the Rosicrucian manifestos.

12. Bruno was an advanced thinker for his times. He accepted the Copernican idea of the universe, believed that there were many worlds, and spoke out widely for a true Hermetic reform of Christianity, by which he apparently meant abandoning the "pedantry" of the established Church in favor of a more vital and magical "Egyptian" form of religion. He was put to death by the Inquisition for heresy, and though it is not known exactly what the fatal charges were, they seem to have been concerned chiefly with his criticism of the Church, rather than with the practice of magic.

13. Some accounts of the procedure have many more steps, or different ones, or a different order of operations. There is no absolute version of the alchemical process, but the description given here outlines the most typical procedure. The Latin words given in parenthesis were the terms typically employed by medieval and Renaissance alchemists.

14. Both of these passages are taken from alchemical works contained in a seventeenth-century collection called *The Hermetic Museum*, translated and introduced in a modern edition by A. E. Waite in 1893.

15. The Rosicrucian manifestos appear to have been more political than philosophical or esoteric in purpose, but among idealists of the period, these two areas of interest were closely intertwined. The fascinating origins of the Rosicrucian movement are detailed in Frances Yates's *The Rosicrucian Enlightenment*.

16. This account of alchemical/Tarot relationships owes much to the ideas in Robert O'Neill's *Tarot Symbolism*. O'Neill also gives a detailed account of such parallels as there are between the Tarot images and specific alchemical illustrations.

17. Mathers was also responsible for the popularization of "Abramelin magic," through his translation of a manuscript which was reputed to date from the fifteenth century, but which was almost certainly of eighteenth-century origin. Abramelin magic is quite different from ritual magic in that it depends very much on the internal processes of the magician; the work is conducted in a natural, rather than a ceremonial setting, and the magician's great task is to make contact with his personal guardian angel, who will instruct him in the use of powerful magical talismans.

18. I would like to note briefly that Tantrism and Tantric sexual practices have been very much romanticized by Western occultism, which frequently and erroneously attributes to Tantric sex an interpersonal character. To quote from a lecture at the Naropa Institute by Agehananda Bharati, author of *The Tantric Tradition*, "The sex of Tantra is hard-hitting, object-using, manipulative ritual without any consideration for the person involved . . . . The notion that Tantrics have some privileged information about the essence of male and female *à la* Jung is nonsense." Authentic Tantrism employs sex as a psycho-physical technology, and the role of both men and women is traditionally very depersonalized; in this respect, Crowley was perhaps closer to actual Tantric practice than many "nicer" Westerners have been.

19. Mandalas—symmetrical patterns organized around a definite center—are the best-known type of yantra. The mandala pattern is found in several of the Tarot trumps, particularly The World and The Wheel of Fortune. Much more on the mandala and its symbolism may be found in José and Miriam Arguelles's book, *Mandala*.

20. In this same year, Eliphas Lévi died, and both Aleister Crowley and Carl Jung were born.

21. There are some recent attempts to link the practice of Tarot with the

exploration of past lives and karmic influences. See, for example, W. C. Lammey's book *Karmic Tarot*.

22. Different esoteric systems include different numbers of "bodies"—some just two, some four or more. But the division into three described here is by far the most frequently encountered scenario.

23. The chakras are said to be visible to some clairvoyants as turning wheels. In this connection, it's interesting to note some references in the Western mystical tradition, such as Ezekial's vision of "wheels within wheels," or the description by sixteenth-century visionary Jacob Boehme—who almost certainly knew nothing of yoga or kundalini—of seven wheels, one within another, turning on the "hub" of God.

24. The "activation" of the chakras may be seen as one description of the process of internal magic. Ralph Metzner, in *Maps of Consciousness*, makes a very interesting case for the idea that alchemy is a psycho-physical process, with the goal of raising the kundalini.

25. Many women feel that Anglo-Saxon culture, with its orientation toward nature worship, is closer to the feminine in spirit than the more abstract Greek culture. There seems to have been some tacit recognition of this fact throughout the development of our language, since the Anglo-Saxon derivatives "witch" and "witchcraft" have always been associated primarily with women, while "magician" and "magic," from the Greek root *mag*, have traditionally been associated with men. (Although "wizard" sounds as if it is related to "witch" or "wicca", it is actually from a German root meaning "wise". However, "warlock," sometimes used as the masculine equivalent of "witch," is from the Anglo-Saxon word meaning "oath-breaker.")

26. Some early decks show Strength as a "wild-man" character (sometimes Hercules), also subduing a lion, but with a club. Most decks show a woman, however, either with a lion, or standing near a broken pillar. Paul Foster Case, in *The Tarot*, gave one of the few original interpretations of Strength, associating it with the kundalini; Vicki Noble takes the same approach in the article quoted in the text, "When Kundalini Rises: Motherpeace Strength and Tower Cards," in *Snake Power*, Candlemas 1990.

Bibliographic Note:

The Art and Imagination series from Thames and Hudson contains beautifully illustrated and very affordable volumes on aspects of the occult tradition. Titles of special relevance to the topics introduced in this section are *Alchemy: The Secret Art* by Stanislas Klossowsky de Rola, *Kabbalah: Tradition of Hidden Knowledge* by Z'ev ben Shimon Halevi, *Magic: The Western Tradition* by Francis King, *Tantra: The Indian Cult of Ecstasy* by Philip Rawson, and *Subtle Body: Essence and Shadow* by David V. Tansley. A similar series from Crossroad is called The Illustrated Library of Sacred Imagination. Titles of special interest include *Shaman: The Wounded Healer* by Joan Halifax, and *The Androgyne: Reconciliation of Male and Female* by Elémire Zolla.

On occult history in general, there are no books which I feel are really excellent, unfortunately; but Kurt Seligman's *Magic, Supernaturalism and Religion* is a well-known text, along with Colin Wilson's *The Occult* and Richard Cavendish's *History of Magic*. (I personally feel that all three favor sensationalism and gossip over a deep analysis of occult phenomena, but they all contain some interesting materials.) Manly P. Hall's *Secret Teachings of All Ages* presents a motherlode of occult information with a balanced point of view, but it's overwhelming in size and scope. *The Encyclopedia of the Unexplained*, edited by Richard Cavendish, is a good reference book in this category, along with J. E. Cirlot's *A Dictionary of Symbols*; both are discussed in more detail in part 3.

F. C. Happold's *Mysticism: A Study and an Anthology* and Evelyn Underhill's *Mysticism* are the standards in this field. On early Greek philosophy, try *Plato for Beginners* by Robert Cavalier. In the field of Gnostic studies, Hans Jonas's *The Gnostic Religion* is the classic text, but also see the works of Elaine Pagels (*The Gnostic Gospels* and *Adam, Eve, and the Serpent*) for an updated view.

On all aspects of Hermeticism and Renaissance magic, Frances Yates is the acknowledged authority. See *Giordano Bruno and the Hermetic Tradition*, *The Art of Memory*, and *The Rosicrucian Enlightenment*. (Though they may include more historical and political detail than one always wants, Yates's books are fascinating and very readable; Joseph Campbell describes her *Giordano Bruno* as "about as clear and sound an introduction to the subject [of Hermeticism] as I have discovered anywhere.")

Popular books on magical Kabbalism are numerous, and the best among them are probably those by Gareth Knight and Israel Regardie; for a more scholarly view of Kabballah, the works of Gershom Scholem are standards. For three different views of alchemy, see Titus Burckhardt's *Alchemy*, Mircea Eliade's *The Forge and the Crucible*, and C. G. Jung's *Alchemical Studies*. The Theosophical Society suggests Robert Ellwood's *Theosophy: A Modern Expression of the Wisdom of the Ages* as a good introduction to Theosophy. On Tantrism, John Blofeld's *The Tantric Mysticism of Tibet* is a classic text; there is also a new book that provides an excellent introduction to practical aspects of Tantric meditation—*Tools for Tantra* by Johari Harish.

So many good books are available on Goddess-worship, wicca, shamanism, and related topics that it is difficult to make a selection, but these will provide a good start: Elinor W. Gado's *The Once and Future Goddess*, Margot Adler's *Drawing Down the Moon*, Starhawk's *Spiral Dance: A Rebirth of the Ancient Religion of the Great Goddess*, Mircea Eliade's *Shamanism*, Holger Kalweit's *Dreamtime and Inner Space: The World of the Shaman*, and *Shaman's Path: Healing, Personal Growth, and Empowerment*, edited by Gary Dorre.

A periodical which covers topics of interest in occult studies with a fair degree of seriousness is *Gnosis*.

6.

TAROT AND THE IMAGINATION

Subconsciousness always directs the activities of the
subhuman forces of nature. This is true whether the action of
those forces be hostile or friendly to man. Subconsciousness, in
turn, is always amenable to impressions originating at the
self-conscious level of mentation.

> PAUL FOSTER CASE,
> *The Tarot* (1927)

Psychology is not everything, it is merely a subjective
analogue of a greater objective reality. Thus the term
"collective unconscious" is sometimes used, although we
would prefer to forget psychologically based terminology
altogether and go back to good old-fashioned occult terms
such as the astral plane.

> GARETH KNIGHT,
> *The Treasure House of Images* (1986)

Is the modern unconscious actually the astral plane of the occultists? Or (and this is *not* the same question) is the astral plane really the unconscious? Today, most writers on the Tarot invoke Jung rather than Eliphas Lévi, and talk about imagination rather than magic. So it's interesting to consider whether they are just putting new labels on old occult concepts, or whether our contemporary understanding has revealed occult ideas as merely immature versions of psychology. *Or* whether, perhaps, these different "languages" reveal parts of being that flow together.

With so much emphasis in Tarot literature being placed on the unconscious and its processes, it seems important to consider where these ideas come from and what they mean. To begin with, just what *is* this "unconscious" we speak of so casually? The idea of an unconscious—a part of the self that one is not actually aware of most of the time—is today accepted without thought or question by most people. It's not a new concept; as Lancelot Law Whyte explains in *The Unconscious before Freud*, "the idea of unconscious mental processes was, in many of its aspects, conceivable around 1700, topical around 1800, and became effective around 1900." It was in 1900, with Freud and psychoanalysis, that the exploration of the *structure* of the unconscious began, revealing the considerable impact of the unconscious on our lives, our behavior, our mental and physical health. There emerged from Freud's work a realization that the "ego", the part of ourselves we are consciously aware of, is not the vast, solid continent which it usually seems to be; it's more like the cone of a volcano—merely the visible tip of a structure which reaches down to a dark, molten center.

In the deep recesses of the unconscious, according to Freud, is a realm of primitive, instinctual drives—the "id"—where the death instinct (*thanatos*) and the sexual drive (*libido*) are in continual conflict; this realm is dominated by the "pleasure principle," a need for immediate gratification of needs. As children, we learn that many of our impulses and desires are unacceptable, so a "super-ego," or internal censor forms to keep up with a growing list of "shoulds" and "shouldn'ts." A personality structure—the "ego"—develops to mediate among the impulses of the id, the demands of reality, and the rules of the super-ego.[1] One of the techniques of mediation used by the ego is the repression of unacceptable material (sexual and aggressive urges, for example) into an unconscious reservoir of fears and memories and desires unknown to our daylight, reasoning, conscious minds. When too much material is repressed, the result is a "neurosis"—a distortion of the conscious mind by unconscious influences.

This whole construction of Freud's was so persuasive that it became an assumed part of our thinking. Just about everyone refers, without so much as a pause, to this or that being "unconscious" or "repressed" or "neurotic." But where did the image of a multilayered consciousness really come from? Is it a "true," *literal* description of psychological life? Or is it a poetic fiction?

Julian Jaynes, in a fascinating book called *The Origin of Consciousness in the Breakdown of the Bicameral Mind*, points out how each age describes consciousness in terms of its own themes and concerns.[2] The first half of the nineteenth century, he observes,

> was the age of the great geological discoveries in which the record of the past was written in layers of the earth's crust. And this led to the popularization of the idea of consciousness as being in layers which recorded the past of the individual, there being deeper and deeper layers until the record could no longer be read.

And the Freudian unconscious (originally called the *sub*conscious—the level below the conscious level) was not only geological, it was mechanical; Jaynes points out that in the later nineteenth century, the model of the steam engine pervaded the popular imagination, and in turn provided an imagery of consciousness in which the boiling subconscious accumulates energy to power conscious life. This energy, when repressed, would force its way explosively into consciousness, expressing itself as pathology.

It was this imagining of psychological life which created a widespread impression of the unconscious as a chaotic, even hostile region, filled with things too horrible or shameful to be admitted to consciousness. In this respect, Freud's attempt to describe the dynamics of unconscious life was considerably misleading, even though it was also profoundly valuable. Freud was limited in his *conceptualization* of consciousness by his mechanical understanding of reality; further, his depiction of the *contents* of unconscious life was very distorted, because his information was drawn principally from the analysis of emotionally disordered people living in a sexually repressed culture.[3]

The Freudian unconscious, accordingly, is not a very friendly place, and it's not surprising that most people do not develop an especially comfortable relationship with it. But this negative view of the unconscious is precisely the one which most of us have learned—not necessarily as a topic in school, but in a much more powerful way, through frequent reference and repetition in popular culture. So when we come to study any aspect of the imagination—art, myth, Tarot—it is necessary to rethink and outgrow our unexamined Freudian interpretations.

The ideas of Freud's colleague C. G. Jung have proven much more appealing to occultists (and other romantics) than those of Freud. Jung developed his vision of the unconscious in large part by examining the art and dreams of creative people in different cultures, and as a result, Jung's version of the unconscious—while certainly not a complete or perfect model—is much more spacious, and more spiritual, than Freud's. While Jung accepted the existence of the Freudian personal unconscious, with its painful secrets and repressed desires, he saw it as normally a small part of our total psychological life. Jung contended that the localized personal unconscious is connected to a great reservoir of images and patterns which he called the "collective unconscious," and he demonstrated that from this vastly larger realm of images and ideas come the characters, plots, and events with which we create art, religion, and the myths of our own lives.

The simplest delineation between the personal unconscious and the collective unconscious is that the former contains material which was once conscious in the individual, while the latter contains material which was never conscious *for this particular individual*, but which seems to appear recurrently in all human behavior and expression. This "collective" material includes archetypal *images*, such as the mandala or the serpent; archetypal *ideas*, such as conjunction or resurrection; and archetypal *patterns* of experience such as hunting, homecoming, or descent and return. Although we can't observe these unconscious contents directly, we see them everywhere, mysteriously revealed in art, story, ceremony, and all the many manifestations of culture, as well as in fantasy, dream, and other kinds of personal imagining.

Jung gave us a welcome picture of the unconscious as a fertile region filled with creative energy and profound imagery. But again we have to ask: Where did *this* picture come from? Is this the *real* truth about psychological life, or is it, too, based on the metaphors of its times?

To answer that question, I'd like to look back at how the Renaissance magicians conceptualized their own version of consciousness. The dominant metaphor of the Renaissance was exploration, discovery, voyages to new lands; so it may not be surprising that magical philosophers were captivated by the idea of other "planes" or terrains of being to explore. The places they envisioned were inhabited by strange creatures and powerful forces, just like those described in the tales of adventurers who came back from the edges of the "real" world. And of course, the various planes were arranged *up*, *out*, and *beyond*, in the directions of exploration—not *down*, *back*, or *in*, in the nineteenth-century directions of archeology and geology.

Our own time is very like the era of the Renaissance magician, dominated by a theme of exploration; but now our journeys go past the limits of the planet and beyond the reach of the senses, to worlds far away and to worlds vanishingly small. Jung (1875–1961) was just enough younger than Freud (1856–1939) to be affected—consciously and unconsciously—by the new, relativistic worldview emerging from Planck's and Einstein's physics (which, as we shall see in a later chapter, lend themselves to a renewal of magical/mystical ideas), and he brought Freud's essentially nineteenth-century view of the unconscious into the twentieth century, where the dominant metaphors come not from the compressed strata of geologic formations, but from *expansion* into space, energy, and light. So while Freud's mission was to make the unconscious conscious, and thus release the pressure exerted by unconscious materials on the conscious mind, Jung's was to take consciousness on a voyage into the creative mysteries of the unconscious.

Jung's view of consciousness seems to many of us today far richer than Freud's, and much more in keeping with what we know about the nature of reality. Just as science has broken down the old distinctions between energy and matter, the dichotomy between "conscious" and "unconscious" life is rapidly disappearing. Consciousness now appears as a total system, not a collection of oddly different parts (like the Freudian id, ego, and super-ego) at war with each other. We see that conscious and unconscious relate constantly and creatively.

Conscious and unconscious processes *seem* to be two different, somewhat incompatible regions of being largely because the ego insists that things make sense only when they follow the rules of conscious thinking. And so, the rules of conscious thinking have come to define what is rational or reasonable. In the realm of the unconscious, however, different rules apply. These rules may be quite strange when compared to those which govern conscious thinking, but they are just as "logical" in their own way. Information *does* get processed and stored by the unconscious systematically—it's just that the system is not at all obvious to the conscious mind, because the unconscious uses *images* and *energies*, rather than the words and numbers that are used for conscious thinking.

"Psyche is image," Jung said repeatedly. By "psyche" he meant primarily (though not exclusively) the region of consciousness which we usually call the unconscious; by "image" he meant "a concept essentially derived from a poetic figure of speech; namely the *fantasy image*, a presentation which is only indirectly related to the perception of the external object."[4] The processes used in the psyche/unconscious are, according to Jung, "imaginal" processes, concerned with the creation and manipulation of images.

Taking this insight of Jung's many steps further, a group of "post-Jungians," led by noted analyst James Hillman, has defined a new style of psychological investigation called "archetypal psychology." Their work has attracted much attention since Hillman's influential work *Revisioning Psychology* was published in 1975, and it has contributed a great deal to the various movements now seeking to rediscover archetypal structures. Hillman elaborates the role of images in psychic life, considering them the "basic givens of psychic life, self-originating, inventive, spontaneous, complete, and organized in archetypal patterns." This approach is obviously very important to understanding the importance of *image systems* like Tarot, and although most Tarot writers have not yet begun to take advantage of these newer developments in imaginal theory, there is a lot of very relevant insight to be gained from the work of archetypal psychology.

Hillman points out in *Revisioning Psychology* that our most direct observation of unconscious logic is in our own dreams, and he suggests that by examining the dream experience, we can get a sense of how "psyche-logic" operates:

> By employing the dream as a model of psychic actuality, and by conceiving a theory of personality based upon the dream, we are imagining the psyche's basic structure to be an *inscape of personified images*. The full consequences of this structure imply that the psyche presents its own imaginal dimensions, operates freely without words, and is constituted of multiple personalities. We can describe the psyche as a polycentric realm of nonverbal, nonspatial images.

According to Hillman, one of psyche's characteristic processes is "personifying"—another term taken from literature, meaning to endow nonhuman entities with human characteristics. Because it is the nature of psyche to personify, Hillman says, its images are animated, in the sense that they have the *presence* of persons.

It's very interesting to compare Hillman's doctrine of the personifying psyche with what Aleister Crowley describes in *The Book of Thoth* as "a thesis most necessary to the understanding of the Tarot." "Each card," according to Crowley, "is, in a sense, a living being." This is the penultimate sentence of part 1, concluding his whole exposition of the Tarot, and though Crowley (in his typically mischievous way) tells us no more about what he means, it seems

115

very clear to me that his point is in keeping with what Jung and Hillman tell us of the nature of the imagining psyche. Several writers on the Tarot have illustrated Crowley's personifying insight: Richard Gardner, for example, in his book *The Tarot Speaks*, allows the Tarot cards to express themselves in their own "voices," to tell their own stories *as if they were persons*; P. D. Ouspensky's "encounters" with the Tarot images, in *The Symbolism of the Tarot*, work in the same way.

Hillman explains that personifying was given a natural place in traditional cultures, where Fate, Peace, Night and so on are given the status of personages, and daemons of many sorts are presumed to inhabit the individual. Fate, for example, is known to many Native American tribes as Coyote, the Trickster; among the ancient Greeks, Fate was represented in three aspects known as the *Moirae*, who (like the *Horae*, the four seasons) were children of Zeus and Themis, the goddess of order. Similarly, in the Tarot trumps, Prudence (Temperance), Love, Justice, and so on are all represented as characters, *persons*, rather than as abstractions. Only a few of the forces of life portrayed in the Tarot trumps have been "symbolized" (that is, the personifications have been replaced by objects which represent the concept); one is The Wheel of Fortune, which symbolizes Fate. Even these objects, however, are not without personified associations. Though the wheel shown on many Tarot cards looks something like the carnival Ferris wheel, the medieval symbol was in fact taken from the *spinning wheel*, and relates back to the three Greek Fates—the *Moirae*—one of whom was responsible for spinning the thread of life, another for measuring it, and the third for cutting it. Also, in the early Tarot images, the figures "on" the wheel were human, not animals; the change to animal figures, which occurred with the Tarot of Marseilles, was due to a misunderstanding of the animal *ears* worn by the people on the wheel to signify their folly.

Personifying, though it may have been an integral part of many cultures, became unfamiliar to our own culture. In the nineteenth and early twentieth centuries, personifying came to be known as a species of "primitive" behavior (found among backward cultures, children, and mental patients) called "animism" or "anthropomorphism." Only today are we beginning to recover a sense of the importance of personification for the well-being of the whole psychic economy. The techniques of creative visualization and active imagination which have become well-known and widely used in recent years include methods for reaching the deep power of the psyche through the process of personification.

Personification is one of four imaginal activities carried out by psyche, according to Hillman. The other three are pathologizing, psychologizing, and de-humanizing. Each of these psychic processes may also illuminate the nature of the imagination as expressed in the Tarot images, though there isn't time or space to go into all of these ideas here. Briefly stated, *pathologizing* is the need of the psyche to express itself through symptoms of physical and mental disorder; the "dark" Tarot trumps—The Hanged Man, The Devil, The Tower, Death, The Moon—symbolize these de-formative processes, through which new truths may emerge. And Tarot-reading itself, so frequently organized around the tangled problem-realm of life, actually addresses this "pathologizing" activity of psyche.

Tarot-reading is also characterized by the third of Hillman's imaginal processes, *psychologizing*, which is "seeing through," or looking at things in terms other than those immediately presented; this activity of psyche is represented in the spreads or patterns of cards used to constellate psychic material, and also in the attitude of the reader. Finally, *de-humanizing* is the process of psyche by which it relates imaginally to its nonhuman context, through a participation in the soul of "things." Here, of course, is the relationship among reader, querent, cards, and objective events, focused in the shuffling process. All of these processes are *ways of imagining*, and they relate to the Tarot in terms of the different aspects of imagination which the cards engage.

These four aspects of imaginal work described by Hillman may actually be reflected in the structure of Tarot itself. Though it's important to recognize that all things which comes in sets of four are not automatically related to the Tarot suits, nevertheless, there seems to be a natural affinity here: personifying/Cups, pathologizing/Swords, psychologizing/Wands, de-humanizing/Pentacles. (The four suits have also frequently been linked with Jung's four psychological functions—feeling/Cups, thinking/Swords, intuition/Wands, and sensation/Pentacles.)

Underlying all the image-making activity described by Hillman are the deep patterns of psychic functioning called "archetypes." The idea of the archetype is an especially important one for understanding the Tarot, and so it deserves a little more explanation here. This very old concept of an "original model" or "primal form" (literal translations of the Greek word "archetype") for all things was formulated by Plato, revived by the Renaissance philosophers, and given new development in our own time by Jung. In the Jungian sense, an archetype is a *fundamental and generative structure which eludes exact or exhaustive definition*. Putting it another way, an archetype is something (an image, an idea, a pattern) which provokes a strong emotional response, yet can never be fully analyzed.

"The archetype is a force," Jung wrote. "It has autonomy and it can suddenly seize you. It is like a seizure." To illustrate this point, Jung used the following example: King Albrecht of Switzerland was on a journey with his son and several other knights. For reasons of their own, the young men felt it necessary to dispose of the old king; throughout the journey, they discussed whether and how this deed ought to be done, but they could come to no agreement, so no action was taken. In the course of the trip, however, the king and his retinue had to cross a ford at Reuss, not far from Zurich. Suddenly, in the middle of the river, the young men were seized with the decision to act, and all at once, without discussion or hesitation, they fell upon the king and dispatched him.

As Jung interpreted this story, the act of crossing the ford was filled with meaning for the young men. It signified moving from one state into another—plunging into the water, risking peril in order to achieve a goal. The forcefulness of this archetypal event took hold of their imaginations so strongly that their hesitations were overcome and they felt themselves instantly and powerfully committed to the very act they had worried over for many days.

117

This power of archetypes to take hold of the imagination is recognizable by the special *feeling tone* one experiences upon encountering something archetypal. You've certainly felt it in your own life. You hear a news story, perhaps about someone who risks his own life to save the life of another, and you are momentarily overcome with emotion. Why? You didn't know any of the people involved, you weren't there, and the outcome doesn't affect you. Yet there is a sense of pride, a recognition of something irreducibly human, an awareness of the importance of individual action. That choked feeling in your throat is evidence that you've encountered the archetype of the Hero.

Anyone who reads the Tarot cards in public will discover that the images on the cards can have this same type of archetypal effect, even on casual bystanders. Most people, including those who have no interest at all in occult or metaphysical ideas, will find themselves drawn to the cards, intrigued by them. "I'm not sure what it is . . ." they will often murmur, looking at the cards intently. "There's something about the pictures. . . ." This hard-to-describe feeling is of age-old memories stirring; it tokens a sudden connection with something larger than the bounds of the personal ego.

Perhaps the best example of archetypes at work in everyday life is the event we call "falling in love." As everyone knows, this experience comes unbidden, and annihilates entirely the common sense of the people involved. (Not without reason did Shakespeare compare lovers and lunatics!) Falling in love is different from merely loving someone, even loving someone a great deal. "Falling" in love is just that—an uncontrollable tumble into an abyss of emotion, where everything (the sun, the moon, *everything*) revolves around the loved object. And this transformation happens when you meet someone who—for good or ill, in reality or just in fancy—matches up to the archetypal image of "my other soul," which is deeply a part of everyone's imagination. This image is called the "contrasexual archetype," and according to Jung, in a man it takes the form of the *anima*—a feminine figure who embodies his imagining of the soul; in a woman, the *animus* gives form to her imagining of spirit.[5]

For each person, of course, this image of the "other" is different in its nature; a slender, outgoing blonde will fulfill one person's archetypal fantasy, a solid, intellectual brunette will be the ticket for another. Often, we are not even consciously aware of our archetypal prerequisites for a love-object, and are just as much surprised by the person we fall for as everybody else is. ("But I usually date accountants—what am I doing with this race car driver?")

The force of falling in love is undeniable, and the near-madness it brings on either has to be waited out, like a cold, or converted into something deeper and more durable. While it lasts, however, the archetypal seizure completely controls your thoughts and changes your life. This is exactly the state of being which is evoked by the Tarot card called "Love" or "The Lovers." In early decks of cards, Cupid, with his potent bow and arrow, hovers over the lovers, making the archetypal statement of the image quite obvious—the couple is being "attacked" or "captured" by the power of love.

Taking an archetypal view of events reveals layers of meaning which we would otherwise miss intellectually, even though we might experience them

Throughout history, the forces of nature and the abstract qualities of human experience have been given concrete form by means of personification. Here, Fate is shown spinning the thread of destiny, in an illustration from the 1537 edition of Boethius's Consolation of Philosophy. *The distaff or spindle motif used here is associated with the web of fate in a variety of cultures. In the Tarot, the spinning wheel may have been translated into* The Wheel of Fortune.

emotionally and unconsciously. By looking at things in archetypal terms, we also gain the power of organizing into clusters (often called "constellations") many different kinds of events and experiences. A particular archetype can manifest itself on various levels, and so it accommodates all sorts of materials. Hillman explains, in *Revisioning Psychology*:

> The archetype of the hero, for example, appears first in *behavior*, the drive to activity, outward exploration, response to challenge, seizing and grasping and extending. It appears second in the *images* of Hercules, Achilles, Samson (or their cinema counterparts) doing their specific tasks; and third, in a style of *consciousness*, in feelings of independence, strength, and achievement, in ideas of decisive action, coping, planning, virtue, conquest (over animality), and in psychopathologies of battle, overpowering masculinity, and single-mindedness.[6]

119

These multiple levels of the archetype are all present in the Tarot images, and it is for this reason that the Tarot works in a variety of ways. For the Tarot reader, *images* are the point where a process of archetypal analysis begins, and from the images unfold the behaviors and styles of consciousness. The images are keys to understanding the archetypal forces which currently govern how the querent acts, feels, and thinks. In this way, good Tarot reading is often perceived to be like good psychoanalysis; the Tarot process runs parallel to the therapeutic process, in which the images produced in dreams, fantasies, and free association provide the openings into the archetypal *constellations* which are shaping the life of the analysand. When using the Tarot for oneself, in meditation, the same process takes place, although the dynamics are different.

These uses of Tarot are personal in nature, but of course archetypes do much more than express themselves in the lives of individuals. They are the organizing principles of myth and ritual, of art and poetry, of religion and science—and yes, even of magic. Families, groups, whole societies have "egos" and "psyches"; they personify and psychologize and pathologize and de-humanize; they are shaped by archetypal forces, and they change as the archetypes shift. From this common base of imagining come the bonds that link Tarot with art and myth.

Noted Jungian Marie-Louise von Franz has observed that archetypal representations are "genuinely graspable in the actual culture of a people or in the work and experience of an individual." We see the archetypes most clearly as we discover them in the myths which give life and purpose to a community, or in the creative efforts of individuals who use art, music, and poetry to give form to their own psychic engagements. For this reason, it's important to understand the cultural context—the "mythoform"—within which the Tarot images originally developed. The magical background of the Tarot, already discussed at some length, is important not just for understanding the occult associations of the cards, but also—and perhaps even more importantly—for understanding the whole imaginal milieu from which the cards emerged. Even if the trump images are much older than the Renaissance, and even if they originated somewhere far from Italy, nevertheless the form in which we know them now is saturated with the feudalism of the late Middle Ages and the mystical enthusiasm of the Renaissance.

Accordingly, Colin Wilson recommends in his book *The Occult* that the student of Tarot begin with an immersion in the medieval/Renaissance background of the cards:

> Simply stare at [the] cards as a child stares at coloured pictures in his favourite book. . . . The mind should be full of images of Gothic cathedrals, of medieval stained glass—which may be the inspiration for the glowing colours of the Tarot—of small towns surrounded by fields, and artisans at their everyday work.

The "myths" of the culture that laid the foundation for the Tarot are to be found in the Middle Ages—the romances of the Grail cycle, Dante's *Divine Comedy*,[7] the structures of feudal society, the hierarchies of the Church, and the fantasy of the Ptolemaic universe.

But the great likelihood is that although the Tarot images were influenced by this static medieval world view, they were in fact *born* from the energy that was created when that world view began to collapse. The emergence of the Tarot trumps was roughly contemporaneous with the rediscovery of Greek philosophy, the introduction of linear perspective in painting, and the recognition (by astronomers, at least) that the Ptolemaic description of the universe was irredeemably inadequate. As we have already seen in several examples, magical philosophy blossoms when old structures of cultural certainty start to crumble—much the way flowering vines will immediately insinuate themselves into the cracking walls of an abandoned building.

In these cycles, we return to the same imaginings over and over again; we remember a golden age, we rediscover correspondences and symbol systems, we attune ourselves to interior messages and seek to recover the power of human will. But in each of these returns, we achieve a higher level of comprehension. When Court de Gébelin found the Tarot cards, he sensed correctly that they must have a mythic background, and he provided one drawn from the imaginary world he knew best, that of exotic, mysterious ancient Egypt. MacGregor Mathers updated the Tarot by integrating it into the mythic structure *he* knew best—the world of Renaissance "*magia* and *cabala*," as transmitted to the late nineteenth century by the Rosicrucian tradition.

Today, there is a virtual cornucopia of mythological universes for the Tarot. Among them the world of the Greek gods and goddesses, shamanic pagan/tribal life, Norse and Celtic sagas, Arthurian legends, and the mysteries of Japan's "floating world." There are decks and books to fit each of these scenarios, and many more. But what is most important is that we are moving away from a literal interpretation of these myths, toward a recognition that the real bond is between Tarot and the nature of myth itself, between Tarot and the cultural imagination.

That bond exists as well between Tarot and the individual creative imagination. But there is a strange fact about Tarot and the arts. The great poet Yeats knew the Tarot well, but never overtly used Tarot symbolism (except for The Tower) in his work; T. S. Eliot referred to several Tarot trumps (and a few cards he made up) in his important modernist poem "The Wasteland"—but he professed to know nothing about the cards. Among serious writers, only Italo Calvino, in his fictional work *The Castle of Crossed Destinies*, and Charles Williams, in his novel *The Greater Trumps*, used the Tarot directly. Similarly, although many Tarot decks have been painted or drawn, none of them can be called important art by any stretch of the imagination, and none—with the exception of Salvador Dali's Tarot—have been created by artists of serious repute. (It is thought that a few Tarot-type designs are attributable to Albrecht Dürer, but there seems to have been no full set of trumps.)

Why have the Tarot images—so potent in their occult context—excited little interest among artists? Rachel Pollack suggests, in her introduction to *Salvador Dali's Tarot*, that visual artists may have found the images "too literal, too embedded in a web of dense symbolism." This may apply to writers as well, for the Tarot is such a sprawling structure, so complex in its internal linkages and so profuse in its external references, that it may seem there is *nothing more* to be said about it.

121

Contemporary Tarot artists are moving beyond the traditional Tarot images to explore diverse cultural, historical, and spiritual connections. Ed Buryn has used collage to combine images from the work of visionary William Blake into a deck of powerfully expressive trumps. Buryn adds other mythical and mystical dimensions to the deck by incorporating cross-cultural allusions, such as the figure of Themis (the Greek goddess of law) shown here in the Assessment card, Buryn's interpretation of the trump Justice.

Sculptor Niki de Saint Phalle has perhaps found an approach to the Tarot which goes beyond its seeming self-completeness, by creating larger-than-life-size, three-dimensional expressions of the Tarot images. Her "Garden of Tarot," built on a rocky hillside in Tuscany, is an ongoing project in which she not only works, but lives. The Empress sculpture, where her residence and studio are located, is large and sensuously curved, inside and out; The Magician is a tangle of brightly painted, tiled, or mirrored shapes; Temperance, a Juno-esque purple figure with gold wings, pours a swath of scarlet from one jar to another.

Saint Phalle has brought to the Tarot a wild imagination, and she recaptures the strangeness of the images, which must once have been far more striking than we find them today. In the Garden of Tarot, the often blinding colors and the vast numbers of mirrored tiles, scattering the sunlight, dazzle the viewer and revitalize the experience of Tarot. Through the process of building this "mythological garden," as she calls it, Saint Phalle has discovered much not only about the nature of the Tarot, but also about the creative process.

> In the end I've learned an important lesson: Not only am I *making* the Tarot cards, I am also *living* them, playing with forces that must be respected. So I've developed a certain prudence in regard to the cards I choose to represent. We recently completed card XIV of the Tarot, which is Temperance, something the modern world has lost sight of. Temperance also implies integrated duality, and the guardian angel is its personification; I think that accounts for my present state of well-being.[8]

Saint Phalle has made the Tarot a part of her creative life by making it a part of her *entire* life—literally, the Tarot trumps have become the controlling images of her life as she works on the project. In this sense, she has done what any magician would do with the Tarot images: She has used them to transform her consciousness. The physical creations, the sculptures, are in a sense by-products of this transformation.

Dali, too, was drawn to the Tarot not for its visual properties, but for its magical nature. Indeed, Dali had long styled himself as a magician, and he painted himself as The Magician on the first of the trump cards. The deck was created for his wife, Gala, whose fascination with the cards inspired Dali to create perhaps the most beautiful—and certainly the most artful—of all Tarots.

Dali's Tarot, though it was not created until the 1980s, was the culminating expression of the Surrealist interest in Tarot which dated back to the beginning of that movement early in the century. The Surrealists were the only group of modern artists to take and express a coherent interest in the occult, and I will discuss them in greater detail in the last chapter of part 2, "Tarot and the Life of the Spirit." For now, suffice it to say that the new metaphors of the twentieth century—scientific, social, aesthetic—have created a new vision of consciousness, a vision which gives enhanced meaning to the Tarot. In our contemporary understanding of consciousness, imagination plays a very important role, and through this recognition, our appreciation and understanding of image-based systems such as Tarot has been greatly expanded.

123

It may well be that Tarot resists poetic expression because it *is* a poetic expression, in and of itself. With that suggestion, I will leave the last word to someone who speaks with authority on the matter—philosopher Jacques Maritain, whose classic book *Creative Intuition in Art and Poetry* explores the nature of imaginative life.

By Poetry I mean, not the particular art which consists in writing verses, but a process both more general and more primary: that intercommunication between the inner being of things and the inner being of the human Self which is a kind of divination (as was realized in ancient times; the Latin *vates* was both a poet and a diviner). Poetry, in this sense, is the secret life of each and all of the arts.

Notes

1. The ego was not seen by Freud as being entirely conscious, but as making up the bulk of consciousness and as mediating between the instinctual id and the demands of the external world. As the most casual student of Freud will see at once, I am seriously oversimplifying his theory here and in what follows, but I am speaking in terms of how Freudian theory is typically perceived in the public mind, which is generally less complex than what Freud said himself, and in some ways quite different.
2. Jaynes argues that people, up to and including the Homeric Greeks, were not "conscious" in the way we think of it today—that they communicated their own thoughts to themselves in some degree by means of "voices" heard as if they were external (for example, the voice of Yahweh heard in the burning bush, or the voice of Athena heard by Homer's characters). This is a thought-provoking book, in which Jaynes makes some very intriguing points about the real role of consciousness in our lives.
3. A book by David Baken—*Sigmund Freud and the Jewish Mystical Tradition*, written in 1958—suggested that Freud's ideas were actually influenced by Kabbalism as well as by the scientific and cultural factors usually cited. Though Baken's contention is generally rejected by Freud scholars, the student of occultism will find it of interest.
4. *Collected Works*, Vol. 6, par. 742.
5. The animus and anima are important concepts in a Jungian approach to the Tarot. They are generally thought of as corresponding to The High Priestess (Papess) and The Hierophant (Pope). The contrasexual archetypes can be investigated further in "Is the Animus Obsolete?" by Mary Ann Matoon and Jennette Jones, included in *The Goddess Re-Awakening*, edited by Shirley Nicholson; and in *Anima: An Anatomy of a Personified Notion* by James Hillman.
6. It was only while proofreading the galleys for this book that I noticed the resonance between Hillman's description of the Hero archetype and the Tarot trump Strength. In early decks, the figure on the Strength card was frequently Hercules or Samson, usually subduing or threatening a lion with a club. Those decks which had female figures sometimes substituted a pillar—perhaps reminiscent of the pillars of the temple brought down by

Samson—for the lion. There has been much controversy about the meaning and placement of the Strength card; it seems to me this identification with the Hero may aid in the interpretating of the card.

7. Joseph Campbell uses Dante's works as a basis for interpreting the Tarot in his essay "The Exoteric Tarot," included in *Tarot Revelations* by Joseph Campbell and Richard Roberts. Campbell accepts the early dating of the trumps in the late fourteenth century, thus placing them much closer to Dante's time than they probably were, and this limits the validity of his observations; but his intuition that the medieval ideas summarized by Dante were formative for the Tarot is probably quite accurate.

8. Saint Phalle's remarks are quoted in "House of Cards," in *Architectural Digest*, September 1987.

Bibliographic Note:

Jung wrote an incredible amount of material, all of which can be found in the *Collected Works*; access to the astonishing array of information and ideas in these thousands of pages is by means of the index which comprises the last volume. An excellent sampler of Jung's work is *The Portable Jung*, edited by Joseph Campbell. Of special interest is the memoir *Memories, Dreams, Reflections*, which is one of the few works by Jung which is easy to read. The rest are so daunting that you may prefer some of the commentaries written by his associates and students. Among these, I especially like Edward Edinger's *Ego and Archetype* and Barbara Hannah's *Jung, His Life and Work*. Probably the best-known of the works by/about Jung is *Man and His Symbols*, a picture book with text by Jung and his closest colleagues.

James Hillman has also written a great deal, most of it addressed to professionals in the field of psychology, but still intelligible to the general reader. His most important books are *The Myth of Analysis* and *Revisioning Psychology*; a brief overview of his approach is offered in *Archetypal Psychology*. *Loose Ends* contains a collection of his early essays, and *Insearch* is concerned with the relationship of psychology and religion. In *The Dream and the Underworld*, he explores the nature of the dreamworld in depth.

For the study of myth and mythology, the works of Joseph Campbell are excellent and readily available. His best-known works are *The Hero with a Thousand Faces* and the four-part series *The Masks of God*; more recently, he produced a beautiful large-format multivolume series called *Historical Atlas of Mythology*. Also of interest is his short book *The Flight of the Wild Gander: Explorations in the Mythological Dimension*. *The Power of Myth* contains material from his conversations with Bill Moyers, and offers a good overview of his work.

A periodical of interest with respect to myth and imagination is *Parabola*.

7.

TAROT AS A WAY OF KNOWING

Divination is seemingly the most mysterious aspect of Tarot. Even those who are drawn to the Tarot are frequently put off by its fortunetelling associations, as Tarot consultant Sandor Konraad demonstrates in the amusing story of how he found himself agreeing to give his first Tarot reading, against his better judgment.

My involvement with Tarot stemmed from its probable inclusion in the survey course on the occult that I was preparing. If I were to take up the Tarot at all in the course it would be in a scholarly vein: I planned to approach it historically and trace its origins and evolution over the centuries. Probably too, I would get into the symbolism of the beautiful and mysterious cards and discuss how the images related to ancient mythology and medieval history.

But to spread the cards and peer into the future—that was something else. Connected as it was in my mind with sleazy gypsy store-fronts and all one's questions on love and marriage, and career, there seemed to be something disreputable about it.

As the story continues, Konraad undertakes the reading and struggles to find some order in the cards, but finally is tempted to tell the querent that "as intelligent human beings we should realize that attempting to divine the future with pieces of colored cardboard had to be an exercise in futility and the last word in silliness." Yet in the midst of his frustration, he is amazed to find that as he spreads and respreads the cards, the same ones keep turning up, despite his frenzied shuffling.

Konraad eventually became a full-time Tarot reader, and he tells the story above in his book *Classic Tarot Spreads*. His tale is so much like my own, and like that of many other readers I've known, that it is doubly entertaining to me. But Konraad's account is also very indicative of the way the rational mind seeks to find a way of drawing Tarot safely into its own orbit. We are often attracted to the "scholarly vein" because such an approach to the Tarot is manageable. When seen as mere examples of the mythologizing imagination, the cards are tame; but as tools of divination, they are wild and powerful and unpredictable.

"To divine" means "to know the will of the gods," to gain access to the divine mind. Through most of history, throughout the world, it has seemed obvious to people that divination is possible, even necessary. The ancient Chaldean priests gathered portents from fire and smoke, from gemstones, from weather and animals; the Biblical prophets foretold the unfolding of divinely inspired events; the Navaho have long employed stargazing and hand-trembling to discover the origins of sickness and the whereabouts of water. But today, in our own society, there is wide doubt concerning the existence of a divine mind, let alone access to it. Divination is cut off from its sacred roots, and withers into "fortunetelling."

Yet almost every Tarot book, even the most determinedly historical or metaphysical or psychological or symbolic, includes some sort of instructions for divination. The divinatory power of the Tarot is part of its perennial fascination, and the reason for this continuing interest is that Tarot actually *does work* in a divinatory way. Not always, of course, and not perfectly—but still well enough to impress intelligent and critical people.[1] The noted Tarot publisher and collector Stuart Kaplan makes this interesting statement in the preface to his *Tarot Classic*:

> The primary fascination that the cards hold for me is as mysterious pieces of art with substantial, historical background. However, numerous public readings have actually resulted in startling and perceptive results. There is no question in my mind that the proper shuffle and spread of the pack can enable a diviner to read from the cards a perceptive revelation of events almost always clearly associated with the person who shuffled the cards.

Renowned mythologist Joseph Campbell's interest in the Tarot was primarily scholarly, but he too responded to its divinatory power. At the close of his reading from Richard Roberts (recorded in Roberts's book *Tarot and You*), Campbell remarked, "That is a pretty good story. Quite astonishing to me. As I look at it, it fits all right, and the high points are the ones that came up."

W. B. Yeats and his wife consulted the Tarot frequently, not merely for its artistic symbolism, but for guidance in matters of living. And Jung, though he did not actively work with the Tarot, certainly affirmed the power of divination in his memoir *Memories, Dreams, Reflections*:

> During the whole of those summer holidays I was preoccupied with the question: Are the *I Ching*'s answers meaningful or not? If they are, how does the connection between the psychic and physical sequence of events come about? Time and again

TAROT DIVINATION

There are as many ways of reading the Tarot cards as there are Tarot readers. But here is a description of some basic elements and steps which are used by a great many readers, and which form the traditional structure of Tarot divination.

1. *The Significator*. Traditionally, the querent or the reader chose a card to represent the querent—usually a Court card, chosen to correspond with the querent's birth sign or physical type. Many readers no longer use a significator.

2. *Shuffling*. Either the reader or the querent or both may shuffle. The usual procedure is to shuffle the cards until they "feel" right or until they give some sign—such as refusing to meld. Some readers request the querent to cut the cards with the left hand before the spread is laid out. Sometimes the querent is asked to hold a problem or question in mind during the shuffling process.

3. *Laying out the cards*. The reader will usually have chosen a spread before the reading begins. The most popular spread by far is the Celtic Cross, which is shown on the facing page. Some readers lay all the cards face down and then turn them over one by one as the reading progresses. The conventional method, however, is to lay out the entire spread with the cards face up. There are specialized spreads for use under particular circumstances, such as answering a particular question, exploring past lives, or amplifying the natal chart.

4. *Assessing the cards*. Most readers begin by looking at all the cards and making the following determinations:

   - What is the proportion of major arcana to minor arcana cards in the reading? (The higher the proportion of trumps, the more energy there is thought to be in the reading. Trumps usually signify the effects of forces beyond the individual's direct control.)
   - Which suit dominates the reading? (A preponderance of Cups will usually indicate that the reading is concerned with emotional matters and relationships; Pentacles, financial and business matters; Wands, creative and spiritual matters and conflicts. Frequently, two suits will share dominance.)
   - Are there special combinations? (There are pairs of cards which often occur together in readings, and which have a combined meaning. For example, the Four of Cups and The Devil together in a reading, especially in close proximity, may indicate a problem of addiction.)
   - How many Aces are there? (Aces represent areas of life which are opening up. Several Aces in the same reading may indicate that significant life changes are beginning.)

Readers will usually have their own "keys" to the reading, as well—special cards or patterns they look for, time markers, and so on.

5. *Giving the reading*. The reader may tell the querent what is seen in the cards, and then answer the querent's questions. Or the reader may engage in a dialog with the querent, asking and answering questions as the reading evolves. The style used may depend on the reader's preferences, or on the nature of a particular reading. A general reading usually begins with the past and works toward the future, with the greatest concentration on present events and forces. Some readers will do additional spreads in order to answer questions raised in a general reading. Most readers try to focus on possibilities rather than limitations, and on solutions rather than problems.

THE CELTIC CROSS SPREAD

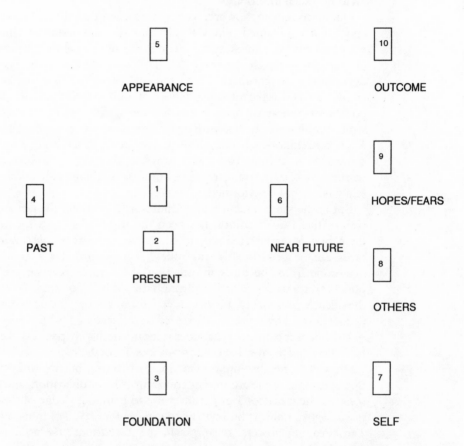

This is the most basic form of the popular Celtic Cross layout. There are many variations, however. Readers today often double the entire spread, using two cards in each position from two through ten.

I encountered amazing coincidences which seemed to suggest the idea of an acausal parallelism (a synchronicity, as I later called it).

Jung went on to develop the idea of synchronicity as a *meaningful coincidence or equivalence* between psychic and physical states (as when the Tarot cards in a spread reflect actual happenings in the life of a querent).[2]

Contrary to popular thinking, "divination" is not the same as "prediction." *Divining* is gaining knowledge by other than ordinary means; the knowledge may concern the past, the present, or the future, physical events or psychological states. Nor does divination require elaborate rituals or secret skills; almost everyone has experienced this kind of knowing spontaneously, in the form of a hunch, a feeling, or a sudden conviction. From one point of view, any systematic approach to divination is merely the practice of cultivating—rehearsing, inviting—such intuitions.

Questions remain, however, concerning *where* the information comes from and *how* it is obtained. The difficulty of either answering or ignoring such questions has led, I think, to the trend in recent years among serious students of Tarot toward emphasizing "higher" uses of the cards, such as self-development, psychotherapy, and spiritual growth. By looking at the Tarot exclusively as a vehicle for psychological and/or spiritual work, it becomes possible to ignore or dismiss the difficult "fortunetelling" aspect of Tarot, while simultaneously acknowledging the great value of the Tarot images. Many contemporary books adopt this position, which is not surprising, because such an attitude is one way to rescue the Tarot from its identification with the "tall, dark stranger" school of fortunetelling—a mission which certainly needs to be performed.

But at the same time, it's important not to overlook the fact that a major part of the Tarot tradition has been the use of the cards for purposes of divination. Moreover, the experiences of many worthy people confirm that the cards can be used in this way today. It *is* possible for a good reader to determine from the cards information about future events; and it is also possible for a reader to gather through the cards important knowledge about the client's personality, his hopes and fears, his present problems, and the factors beyond his control which may be influencing his life.

How does it happen? What does it mean? In this chapter, I'd like to look at how these and many other questions about Tarot divination may be answered. There will be no absolute explanations, of course; but we will try to reason through some of the arguments concerning Tarot divination, and to explore some of the practices Tarot readers use to gain knowledge of the otherwise unknowable. Our method will be to explore four levels of thinking about the Tarot reading process: the *rational*, the *psychological*, the *psychical*, and the *metaphysical*.

There is a popular theory that tries to account in so-called *rational* terms for the fact that some card-readers actually do appear to know things about the people they read for and to make accurate predictions about the future. It says the reader notices very small details about the client, quickly draws generalized conclusions (based on statistical probabilities and stereotypes) from those details, then subtly probes for further information by asking the client leading questions. Finally, according to this explanation, the reader makes "predictive" statements which are so vague they can be interpreted in a wide variety of ways; the client, who *wants* to believe in the power of the reader, cooperates by interpreting events according to these predictions and imagines that the reading has "come true."

Certainly there are quite a few card-readers (and other fortunetellers) who operate in exactly this way. It can be done, I assure you—and so skillfully that even a very acute person might be fooled. But of course, that scenario describes a form of charlatanry, not the art of Tarot-reading. For a true reader of the Tarot, the object is to get the *least* possible information about the client from sources other than the cards, for not only is such outside information of little help in obtaining a good reading, it may actually be of harm. (Invariably, when I have trusted the information taken in by my conscious mind rather than the information revealed by the cards, I have been misled, and most serious readers would tell you the same thing.)

The next level of theorizing about Tarot divination is *psychological*. Here we can begin with the idea that the archetypal power of the Tarot images, together with the whole ambience of the reading process, lowers the wall that ordinarily blocks the querent's access to unconscious knowledge. Querents are almost always surprised, after an initial session with a good reader, by how much they have learned about themselves and their lives in a short period of time. But of course, they knew some of these things before; it's just that they didn't *know* they knew. We all possess a great deal of information to which we have little or no conscious access, and the Tarot is just one of many ways—such as crystal-gazing, *I Ching*, dream analysis, and hypnosis—that have been created over the centuries to get in touch with parts of ourselves which are hidden, out of "normal" reach. As the discussion of Tarot and imagination has already suggested, the images on the Tarot cards can be catalysts in a complex process by which such inner knowledge comes into conscious awareness.

Yet even if the *querent* knows in some way the nature of his or her own personality and problems, how does the *reader* find out? Seen on the psychological level, the answer may be that good readers are simply supersensitive to the behavior of their querents; without realizing it, they draw out the querent with general observations or leading statements, notice nuances of the querent's reactions, and, unconsciously or "intuitively," put these clues together to form sophisticated guesses—which they in turn project into the cards. The card images, by their archetypal nature, become vehicles through which readers convey unconsciously gathered information to their own conscious minds.

This process of unconscious, averbal, image-organized communication may well be helped along by certain psychological states created in the reading situation, states called "trance" and "flow." Bernie Zilbergeld and Arnold Lazarus describe the trance state this way in their book *Mind Power*:

> Have you ever been so involved in a movie, a book, a piece of music, a sports event, or a work project that you lost sight of your surroundings . . . and you didn't notice the passage of time and were surprised to find that hours had passed? Have you ever gotten so caught up in a daydream . . . that you had to spend a few seconds reorienting yourself in time and space after you were interrupted? . . . These naturally occurring trances are common human experiences, by no means confined to situations in which a person is meditating or under hypnosis.

The authors of *Mind Power* are describing a very light trance state, such as can be induced by relaxation techniques and used with auto-suggestion to change habits, improve memory, and so forth. (Deeper trances may block physical sensation and/or produce complete dissociation from the normal personality, but for most of us, they are much harder to achieve.) While in the trance state,

131

one is more than usually susceptible to suggestion—both from within and from without.

The trance state, I think, may characterize the experience of the querent, brought about by the special circumstances of the Tarot-reading. One of the compelling qualities of being the "object" of a reading is the feeling that *one's own life* is the absolute center of attention, and that all cosmic forces are for the moment centered there. This impression of seeing one's life objectified in the powerful images of the cards is truly fascinating, in the particular sense of that word which means "spellbinding." So—bound by the spell, captivated by the cards, the querent slips into the rapt state of attention defined above as trance. As a result, unconscious messages are heard more clearly—*and* the observations of the reader are accepted more easily. Suggestions made by the reader may also take hold and persist into the future, thus shaping the unfolding of events to conform with the future portents of the reading.

For an example of this process, we can look at a very typical querent response, taken from one of the taped readings in Richard Roberts's book *Tarot and You*. Near the end of this session, the querent—who had been noticeably skeptical in the early stages of the consultation—remarks:

> This is the first good news I've heard about it [his problem]. . . . Amazing is all I can say. Looking at all the cards now, I see the whole problem laid out just as you said. But I don't think I could have seen the same things by myself.

In part, at least, the querent has "seen" what he has been led to see in the cards, through the reader's interpretations. The process of "entrainment," or coalescence of the reader's and querent's perceptions, has been going on throughout the reading, during which this querent says several times "I see," or "I think I see it." (Some form of "I see" or "I understand" is a frequent response from several of the querents in Roberts's book, and I have noticed a similar pattern in querents I have worked with.) The agreeableness exhibited by Roberts's querent doesn't seem especially characteristic of the man's personality, judging from his remarks at the beginning of the session; though he has never seen the Tarot, the querent instinctively chooses Swords over Cups for his significator, and he makes several challenging statements to Roberts. But the querent's acquiescence is noticeably more pronounced as the reading progresses. He becomes increasingly absorbed in the reading, and responds more and more positively to the reader.

It may be the development of a light trance state which makes a querent more open, more agreeable. The same process may also bring the querent closer to his or her own intuitions and unconscious knowledge. A sample reading included in Mary Greer's *Tarot Mirrors* shows how the querent ends up making a connection between something deeply buried in her past (something she had never told anyone) and the problems which are destroying her present happiness. Her unconscious awareness of the connection is released *as she projects herself into the Tarot images*. Near the beginning of the reading, the querent says in response to The Devil, "Even though I use my mind, it's this feeling of something that happened to me, but I don't know where it's coming from." She is not consciously aware at this point of what is troubling her. Later the querent says: "I'm working with my logic—I think that's the thing—and I'm just getting like. . . ." Here she points to the Two of Swords. She sees herself in one of the card images, and through that identification, she is able to recognize a pattern of her own behavior.

The reader, Ms. Greer, then follows up by drawing the querent further into the card images:

> [Greer:] Is there any card here that shows what you get from the process you've been involved in—destroying your happiness, or keeping your physical body under control? Keeping all those obstacles in the way?

> [Querent:] I think it arises from the Hierophant. I think it's the part of me that's judged myself. . . . And early on—I had a very strict Catholic upbringing. And I know it's got to do with a lot of that.

By focusing on the "priest" figure in the cards, the querent begins to explore feelings of guilt, and from that point her free association becomes a journey back through buried memories. Finally, the querent produces the "hidden" information from her childhood, the "something that happened to me" which she couldn't recognize at the beginning of the reading.

If the description of this event sounds more like a psychotherapy session than a Tarot reading—well, there you are. The Tarot situation and the therapy situation have something in common: Each offers a space and a time for the querent or the patient to study his or her own myths. This ritualized self-focus is seductive, and lowers the barriers which separate conscious and unconscious knowledge. But the Tarot situation actually has an advantage over the therapy situation in that it is much less threatening; the querent doesn't usually put up defenses against divination the way a patient puts up defenses against therapy. As a result, the mild suggestibility that accompanies the trance state is especially effective. The querent in the Greer reading, for example, mentions that she has been working with a counselor with whom she isn't very satisfied, but she's rejected opportunities to change to a more meaningful form of therapy. Greer encourages her in the reading to consider a change, and within three weeks, the querent has begun work with a new therapist.

If the querent in a Tarot reading can be described as experiencing trance, the reader may be seen as experiencing "flow," an altered mode of consciousness we all find ourselves in from time to time.[3] Daniel Goleman, in *The Meditative Mind*, explains the flow state this way:

> The key elements of flow are (a) the merging of action and awareness in sustained concentration on the task at hand, (b) the focusing of attention in a pure involvement without concern for outcome, (c) self-forgetfulness with heightened awareness of the activity, (d) skills adequate to meet the environmental demand, and (e) clarity regarding situational cues and appropriate response.

In other words, the flow state occurs when we are engaged in some activity which transcends immediate self-awareness, and which requires all our

133

concentration *without exceeding our abilities*. If the demands of the situation are too high in comparison with our skills, the result is stress; if the demands are too low, the result is boredom.

The process of Tarot-reading meets all these criteria remarkably. Tarot is designed to engage the reader not only through the intellect, but through the body and the senses. With Tarot, you have the *visual* stimulation of the images and the *tactile* involvement of shuffling and/or laying out the cards. Moreover, Tarot skills are almost always adequate to the demands of reading situations; most readers start out reading for friends in a playful way, and progress to more serious readings only if they become more confident with the cards. Providing that dire predictions are sensibly avoided, the Tarot-reader can as a rule be deeply involved in the cards without having to be too heavily concerned about the outcome of the reading. Yet the event of the reading is intensely involving, inviting the reader to a deep level of concentration as he or she attempts to trace out the patterns of circumstance and fate revealed in the cards.

The flow state brings increased receptivity and clarity, which may account for the reader's alertness to the querent's responses and to the cards themselves. Also, flow is a highly creative state. This increase in imaginative activity may enable the reader to discover connections in the cards and weave stories from the images they portray. The state of flow—which contains an element of dissociation from the "normal" personality—could explain as well why readers often feel they have gone "beyond" or "outside" themselves during a reading.

Both flow and trance bring heightened states of awareness, and it is easy to see how these modes of consciousness, interacting through the medium of the Tarot cards, could produce remarkable results. It's also worth noting that both states are typically followed by a sense of refreshment and well-being. This, too, seems to fit the Tarot experience, for although the reader may be tired from the reading effort, and the querent may be emotionally moved or mentally concerned about issues which arose during the reading, as a rule, both will feel *better*—often in an undefinable way—afterwards.

A final note about flow. The most frequently used example of an activity that leads to the flow state is *playing games*. This fact sheds a very interesting light on the early history of Tarot as a game. A great many explanations of Tarot history have been thought up to get around the fact that Tarot seems originally to have been used for playful purposes, but perhaps they all miss the point. It may be that the very reason the game of *tarocchi* had such enormous popularity was the combination of the flow state induced by the game-playing process *and* the archetypal content of the cards. Five hundred years ago, all those players of the game of Tarot may well have had especially delightful, uplifting, and even mind-altering experiences without ever realizing why!

Flow, trance, unconscious knowledge, intuitive perception—put them all together, and the psychological approach to Tarot-reading seems to promise an impressive explanation. But there is something missing. This scenario still doesn't account successfully for all that actually happens in reading situations. How, for example, do we explain *psychologically* the fact that a reader will frequently lay out two or three spreads in a row for a querent, and despite

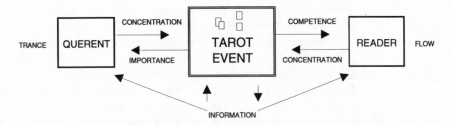

The Tarot-reading event may serve as a point of focus for both reader and querent, allowing the acquisition and exchange of information through the medium of the cards. Where does the information come from? Perhaps it travels through the medium of the collective unconscious, through the process Jung calls "synchronicity."

careful shuffling in between, turn up a significantly larger number of the same cards in each spread than random chance could reasonably account for? A recently developed mathematical model demonstrates that it takes seven complete shuffles of a fifty-two-card deck to achieve an acceptable level of randomness. (After that, the number of additional shuffles makes little difference in increasing the level of randomness.)[4] Allow ten shuffles, then, for a seventy-eight-card deck. Most readers will shuffle or have their clients shuffle a deck many more than ten passes before laying out a spread; they will then take the cards from the top of the deck and arrange them in a predetermined structure. So—with the deck thus randomized between spreads, where do those recurring cards and patterns come from?

And what about that residue of information which *can't* be accounted for in terms of the querent's "unconscious" knowledge? And how does the reader become aware of specific *future* trends and events which really do, in many instances, come to pass? These are the questions about Tarot divination which take Tarot-reading out of the realm of the "merely" psychological, by suggesting that transpersonal and transtemporal levels of being actually must exist.

So let's move from the psychological level to the *psychical*. Begin by assuming that the reader's "intuitive" grasp of information about the querent comes not from complex behavioral observations and averbal communications based on unconscious processes, but from *telepathy*—the ability of one mind to achieve direct contact with another mind. This is a simpler and actually more elegant explanation. Moreover, the trance and flow factors still apply here, since these states are well known to improve psychic abilities. So far so good.

As for the order in which the cards fall, the psychical approach will still account for this phenomenon if you add *telekinesis* to telepathy. In this way, querent or reader (or both) could transmit unconscious knowledge, obtained telepathically, to the cards during the shuffling and spreading process. Next, we can take care of "knowledge the querent doesn't have" by a similar means. Since the information will have to be obtained by the reader from some other source than the querent's own mind, include *clairvoyance* on the list of psychic

135

activities required for a Tarot reading. And to account for the "future" aspect, we'll also need *precognition*.

A successful Tarot reading would seem to require just about every psychic skill identified by parapsychology. But calling these activities by their official scientific-sounding names doesn't do much to explain what really takes place. Unfortunately, parapsychology has not proven to be a very successful means of illuminating so-called psychical phenomena. Lawrence LeShan, an experimental psychologist and well-known writer on parapsychology, writes in his 1987 book *The Science of the Paranormal*:

> The field of psychical research, which started out as a great dream and adventure, is now in a sad and depressed state; indeed, it is extremely doubtful whether it can be rescued from this situation by those now working in it. Most of them are apparently hopelessly mired in a bog of outmoded science and philosophy. Hardworking and dedicated, they remind one of no one so much as Cervantes' Don Quixote of La Mancha, who set out on a great quest fully equipped to deal with a world that had long passed away.

LeShan feels that parapsychology has failed because it hasn't responded to the new worldview which has evolved through contemporary physics, and about this there will be more in the next chapter.[5] In the meantime, it's enough to note that words like "telepathy" and "precognition" don't actually mean much.

They do, however, offer us labels for certain kinds of abilities, and parapsychology has encouraged a general awareness that these abilities are widely distributed in the population. But though it may be true that we all have psychic abilities in varying degrees, there are certainly some people who are more naturally talented in this arena—and it's interesting to note that these people typically do *not* seem to take up the Tarot. It may be that people with these ready psychic gifts are more drawn to freeform pursuits such as crystal-gazing, automatic writing, or psychometry than to Tarot. Why, after all, spend the considerable amount of time and energy required to learn the language of Tarot, if information can be gathered in easier ways? Most people come to the Tarot (as to *I Ching* or astrology) precisely because they expect, or at least hope for, some kind of inspiration and power from the cards themselves (or the hexagrams or the birthcharts). These types of divination are systematic, and they promise a way to exercise and amplify and organize the lesser psychic abilities that most of us seem to possess.

In any event, the psychical explanation of Tarot divination does not seem too illuminating. Even if we assume that all Tarot readers use psychic abilities without necessarily being aware of it, the net result is only to create more questions. Where "is" the information which the reader draws on clairvoyantly? Where "is" the future which is seen precognitively?

To find these answers, we must go on to a fourth level of Tarot theory, the *metaphysical*. It is not easy to penetrate this level, however. As we saw in chapter 5, divination has long been regarded by Western metaphysicians as a poor relation at best. In ancient cultures, divination was a vital activity,[6] and even today, it plays a strong communal role in a few remaining traditional societies (the Navaho, for example, and the Huichol) and in certain religious traditions (such as Brazilian candomblé and Haitian voodoo). But in mainstream Western society, divination has been progressively trivialized. In the Christian era, divinatory practice was condemned by the Catholic Church, both for its flavor of paganism and for its supposed association with devilish spirits. (There was no lack of it going on even in the Middle Ages, however; Dante found many diviners in the Inferno, their heads twisted so that they could see only backward for all eternity.)

Divination was somewhat elevated in the Renaissance, but among serious magical philosophers like Ficino and Pico, from whom so many of our modern ideas of the occult have descended, it was of secondary interest at best. The whole thrust of Renaissance "high" magic was toward active influence in the astral realms rather than passive knowledge; popular divination, which focused on the world of human events, was thought of as part of *mundane* magic, quite inferior to the higher *religious* magic of the philosophers.

In our own time, divination has been closely identified with superstition. One wry definition of superstition is "what other people believe that you don't," and that is often the criterion by which things are labeled as superstitious. But we have to keep in mind that there actually is a category of psychological activity which can fairly be called "superstition." It can be described variously as naive, primitive, or prescientific thinking, as an immature compensatory device to combat feelings of existential helplessness, and as Freudian wish-fulfillment. All of these descriptions accurately reflect real phenomena. Many people *do* adopt supernatural explanations for natural occurrences simply because they are unable to understand them; there *are* people who use belief in the supernatural to boost their own self-esteem or to support a neurotic fantasy world. But the fact that these kinds of "superstition" exist does not in any way invalidate the study of occult phenomena, nor does it mean that divination has no genuine metaphysical basis or power.

Israel Regardie, who is certainly an acknowledged voice in the serious discussion of modern magic, offers an elegant view of divination, placing it firmly in the highest occult tradition:

> [The magical hypothesis] holds that divination is not ultimately concerned with mere fortune-telling—nor even with divining the spiritual causes in the background of material events, though this latter is of no little importance. On the contrary, however, the practice of divination when conducted aright has as its objective the development of the inner psychic faculty of intuition. . . . That this mechanism is concerned at the outset with providing answers to apparently trivial questions is by itself no objection to the technique itself. . . . Nor is the objection valid that the technique is open to frequent abuse by unscrupulous charlatans. But practised sincerely and intelligently and assiduously by the real student, consciousness gradually opens itself to a deeper level of awareness. . . . A sense of the spiritual aspect of things dawns upon the mind—a sense of one's own innate high wisdom, and a recognition of divinity working through man and the universe.[7]

From this point of view, divination can be considered a sophisticated approach to the process of integrating imagination, spirit, and consciousness—a path to higher awareness. "Surely," argues Regardie, "such a viewpoint

137

elevates divination above the level of a mere occult art to an intrinsic part of mystical endeavor?"

Regardie's interpretation does give divination a much higher place among metaphysical interests than it is usually accorded. In large part, this is because Regardie takes a very psychological approach to magic. Once again, in Regardie's treatment of divination, it is the *process* which is the key, not the *content*, just as—on a psychological level—the process of reading Tarot in itself brings about the benefits of the flow state, and just as the experience of the Tarot reading brings about for the querent a clarified and objectified state of mind, regardless of what is actually discovered in the cards.

Regardie's magical explanation, like the psychological and the psychic, is still too "human." All these interpretations assume that the complex network of interrelations reflected in the Tarot-reading process is encompassed by the human psyche, ignoring what James Hillman describes as the "dehumanizing" faculty of psyche—the ability of the imagination to participate in an organization of reality which is *not human-centered*. The only modern idea which does come close to acknowledging the nonhuman aspect of divination is Jung's theory of synchronicity.

Jung was among those relatively few "civilized" persons who are spontaneously aware that human experience is not exhaustive of reality; this faculty—which Jung cultivated in a six-year-long "self-experiment" of controlled surrender to fantasy life—enabled him to perceive the nature of synchronicity. In his memoir, *Memories, Dreams, Reflections*, Jung tells of one of his own psychic experiences. He was awakened by the impression of someone entering his hotel room. There was no one there, but he felt a dull pain, as if he had been hit in the head. The next day, he received word that a patient had committed suicide—a gunshot to the head. Jung comments:

> The experience was a genuine synchronistic phenomenon such as is quite often observed in connection with an archetypal situation—in this case, death. By means of a relativization of time and space in the unconscious it could well be that I had perceived something which in reality was taking place elsewhere. The collective unconscious is common to all; it is the foundation of what the ancients called the "sympathy of all things."

The "sympathy of all things"—the correspondences of the magicians! Jung seems to be saying that the connections which form these magical correspondences have their ground in the collective unconscious. More than that, he is telling us that the collective unconscious is *not* a static repository of archetypes (sort of like an internal symbol library), even though we tend to think of it that way; and neither is it just an inherited basis for our own personal imagery. The collective unconscious is a living web of interconnections among all people and phenomena, unbounded by time or space.[8] Through our personal experiences of the human unconscious (in dreams, symptoms, fantasies, and associations, as well as in art, poetry, music, and image-systems such as alchemy, astrology, and Tarot) we *participate* in what Jung calls elsewhere "the divine unconsciousness of the world."[9]

Synchronicity is perhaps the most difficult to grasp of all Jung's ideas. It's a comfort that near the end of his major treatment of the topic (in *Synchronicity: An Acausal Connecting Principle*, written with physicist Wolfgang Pauli), Jung remarks, "I have been informed that many readers find it difficult to follow my argument." He points out that "synchronicity is no more baffling or mysterious than the discontinuities of physics"—as if that were reassuring! But it is certainly true that an insight into contemporary physics helps a good deal in understanding synchronicity, and the whole matter may be somewhat illuminated in the next chapter, "Tarot in the Light of Science." Ironically, perhaps, the *metaphysical* explanation of Tarot divination may have its ground in the *physical* explanation of the world.

In the meantime, I'll conclude this chapter with some very tentative hypotheses regarding the reading process. First, I believe that Tarot-reading takes place on all four of the levels I've mentioned. Some readings are nothing more than the subtle trickery described in the rationalist interpretation. Many others take place along the psychological lines, and these are frequently very valid—therapeutic, inspirational, and educational, all at once. Doubtless, readers use psychic faculties according to their own gifts, which may be slight in some instances, potent in others, to supplement the reading process.

Mary Greer has identified, in *Tarot Mirrors*, four different fundamental approaches to reading, and she suggests that each reader will typically use two or three of these in varying measure, usually with one predominating. They are:

Analytic: Analysis of correspondences between symbols and meanings to determine relevancy.

Psychic: Intuitive use of inner "sight" and subtle sensory "feelings" to know things.

Therapeutic: Assisting the querent to discover personal meaning, options, and goals.

Magical: Affirming the querent's ability to create what she finds worthwhile and valuable.

I am principally an *analytical* reader, and we are the ones who are probably most dependent on the cards, for reading analytically involves actually *reading* the card images, as if they were a symbolic language. The *therapeutic* reader also uses the cards extensively, but in this case as catalysts in the process of creating a dialogue with the querent. ("What does this card remind you of?") Readers who follow the *psychical* style make the least direct use of the cards, often employing the shuffling-and-spreading process mainly as a method of focusing their own psychic abilities. The *magical* method, meanwhile, uses the cards in what I would call a partial way, since the meanings taken from the cards are selected and arranged from a specific point of view—that is, in terms of revealing and affirming opportunities for change and growth.

Although Greer uses the terms "magical" and "psychic" in a perfectly acceptable way, she is not really speaking of either as an esoteric matter; the magical method is merely encouragement of the will, and the psychic method is just a higher degree of dependence on the intuitive faculty. In reality, the

SYNCHRONICITY

The idea of synchronicity is fairly easy to summarize: The term refers to psychic/material events separated by distance, but connected in a way that is not causal and is not accidental. ("Not causal" means that there is no apparent mechanism by which one event creates or affects the other, "not accidental" means that the co-incidence of the events is not randomly generated.) But the mechanism of synchronicity is much more difficult to explain—if, indeed, it can yet be explained at all.

How can connections be "not causal" and "not accidental"? These diagrams, taken from Charles Poncé's intelligent book *The Game of Wizards: Psyche, Science, and Symbol in the Occult*, may offer a helpful image of the nature of synchronicity. On the left, a sphere represents objective reality. Within the sphere are individual psyches. The unshaded tips of these individual psyches represent the conscious mind, the shaded bands, the personal unconscious. Each individual psyche is connected to the "objective psyche," another term for the collective unconscious. The asterisks mark the presence of archetypes.

On the right, a detail of the larger diagram describes the difference between causal and synchronistic connections. Causal connections proceed from and are perceived by consciousness. Synchronistic connections travel through the medium of the objective psyche and are perceived by means of the continuity between the objective psyche and the individual psyche. Because synchronistic "information" must be transmitted to the individual consciousness by means of the personal unconscious, it is frequently manifested outwardly—in "events"—which are in turn experienced and interpreted by the individual. The exact mechanism by which all this takes place, however, has still not been explained in a satisfying way.

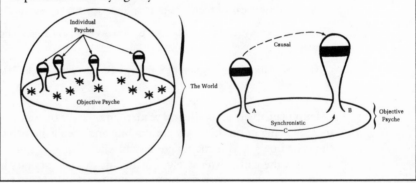

magical, analytic, psychic, and therapeutic approaches she describes are all psychological; they are just distinguished by different emphases. Each actually corresponds to one of the four Jungian functions—the analytical method belongs to the thinking type, the psychic method to the feeling type, the therapeutic method to the intuitive type, and the magical method to the sensation type.

Insofar as these are "styles" of reading, ways that different readers employ and approach the cards, I suspect that the psychological level is all that *can* be described, for to the extent that there is a metaphysical component of Tarot-reading, I believe it is not present as a matter of choice or of personality. Where a metaphysical component enters the Tarot process, it does so in a way that is beyond the control of human factors. There may be attitudes and methods which draw the reading process toward a connection with the nonhuman, and there may be other approaches which work to prevent the nonhuman element from entering the reading. But by and large, the meaningful "co-incidence" of our conscious activities with the greater context of reality is something which, in my opinion, occurs spontaneously and unpredictably. We might think of it as the action of "grace," which can't be commanded, but which comes where and when it is needed. Or, in the much better expression of the *Upanishads*,

> Divine knowledge is not sought in mere words; to speak concerning it were hard as iron. By God's grace man obtains it; skill and order are useless therefore.

Notes

1. No one—so far as I know—has undertaken a controlled and detailed study of how readers use the Tarot cards, how successful they are in gathering information from the cards concerning the querent, or how well their predictions fit the actual events of the future. We have to rely on anecdotal evidence to support the assumption that Tarot is a valuable tool for knowing, but fortunately, there is a good deal of such evidence, from respectable sources.
2. Synchronicity can also apply to the equivalence of two psychic states (thoughts, feelings, dreams, etc.) occurring in different places and/or times without any apparent intervening causality.
3. The seminal work on the flow state was conducted by psychologist M. Csikzentmihalyi, and reported in his book *Between Boredom and Anxiety* (1978). "Flow" and "trance" can be seen as different labels for the same phenomenon. However, I feel they can be usefully separated, as I've done here, to describe different *aspects* of the same phenomenon. Generally speaking, I think of "trance" as passively induced, "flow" as actively induced.
4. An explanation of this mathematical model can be found in the January 1990 issue of *Discovery*.
5. There are some intriguing new directions in parapsychological work, however, and two recent books not only give a good picture of what's happening in this area, but also offer interesting and original ideas. They are *Parapsychology: The Controversial Science*, by Richard Broughton; and *Margins of Reality: The Role of Consciousness in the Physical World*, by Robert Jahn and Brenda Dunne. For a skeptical look at parapsychology, and indeed, at many of the topics discussed in this book, an excellent book is *The Hundredth Monkey, and Other Paradigms of the Paranormal*, edited by Kendrick Frazier. This is a collection of well-argued and carefully documented articles, all written by scientists critical of "fringe" science and occultism.
6. The methods of divination used to be referred to as the "mantic" arts, from

141

the Greek word for "soothsayer" or "prophet." (The combining form "-mancy" is used to create words such as "astromancy"—divining from the stars—and "cartomancy"—the formal word for a divinatory use of cards, including Tarot.) The word "mantic" shares a common Greek root with our words "mania" and "manic," referring to irrational states of consciousness.

7. From Regardie's *Foundations of Practical Magic*.

8. One occult idea which seems very close to this description is the supposed existence of a "plane" on which there is a record of everything—every event, every detail—that has ever existed. This realm of information is called the "akashic record," a designation taken from the Sanskrit word "*akasha*," which means roughly the same thing as the "ether" of the nineteenth-century physicists or the "astral light" of Lévi. Although one sees this term used in occult literature, I haven't been able to find out where and in what context it originated; I have the impression, however, that it comes to us, like so much else, by the Theosophical route. The akashic record is often referred to today as containing not only all that has "already" existed, but all that exists in all times, past, present, and future, and many occultists believe that divination is the process of tapping into the information contained in the akashic record.

9. In his massive analysis of alchemical symbolism, *Mysterium Coniunctionis*, Jung uses this phrase to describe the primordial unity from which things are differentiated into existence—the *unus mundus*, or "one world," which is expressed psychologically in the mandala, and parapsychologically by the phenomenon of synchronicity.

Bibliographic Note:

Unfortunately, there is very little written on the general subject of divination which is illuminating. On parapsychology, any of Lawrence LeShan's books will be of interest, especially the classic *The Medium, The Mystic and The Physicist* (now retitled *Clairvoyant Reality*) and *The Science of the Paranormal*. J. B. and Louisa Rhine's work in this field is, of course, the best known—Jung refers to it frequently—and any of their books is worth looking at if you are particularly interested in this field, along with the books of Charles Tart and Stanley Krippner. Other classics are Raynor Johnson's *The Imprisoned Splendour* and Arthur Koestler's *The Roots of Coincidence*.

The topics of trance and flow are frequently discussed—by these names or some others—in books on meditation and self-hypnosis. Good books in this field include Lawrence LeShan's *How to Meditate*, and Daniel Goleman's *The Meditative Mind* and *The Varieties of Meditative Experience*.

F. David Peat has edited an informative book called *Synchronicity*. A newer treatment of the topic is *Synchronicity: Science, Myth, and the Trickster* by Allan Combs and Mark Holland.

8.

TAROT IN THE
LIGHT OF SCIENCE

*The essential point in science is not a complicated
mathematical formalism or a ritualized experimentation.
Rather the heart of science is a kind of shrewd honesty
that springs from really wanting to know what the hell is
going on!*

SAUL-PAUL SIRAG

THE process of using Tarot to gain knowledge requires at least two ingredients: people and Tarot cards. We need, then, to examine the process from two angles, both the mental and the material. It goes without saying that these two aspects are interconnected, but it is easiest to discuss them clearly by taking one at a time.

We'll begin with the matter of "matter." First point: Tarot cards are no more than pieces of cardboard. Is it possible for there to be *meaningful interaction* among pieces of cardboard, real life events, and personal perceptions? And second point: The material world reveals a past, but not a future—from which fact we assume that future events on the material plane don't exist "yet." Can we gain information about something that doesn't exist?

If you personally try working with the Tarot cards, and you find that you *can* gain information from them, and you find out that the information *does* contain accurate approximations of future events, then the experientially

143

validated answer to these questions will be yes. That "yes" doesn't fit into our normal picture of the world, however. So it becomes necessary to consider further: In what kind of a "reality" can people use cards (or stars or crystal balls) to see the future? And is there a believable description of such a reality—a description which agrees with known scientific facts?

I believe there is. I cannot explain it in detail (I am by no means a physicist or a mathematician!), but I can give a rough idea of what it's about and where it comes from. Let me preface this discussion, however, with the caveat that most scientists engaged in the studies I'm about to discuss insist that it is impossible to understand these ideas accurately without being well grounded in the mathematical concepts involved. Further, many scientists feel it constitutes a gross misapplication of these ideas to take them out of their proper scientific context and use them to support philosophical speculations. But although these critics may very well be justified on both counts, I think there is still good reason for the layperson to become aware of these ideas, and to consider how they may offer new ways of looking at old questions. You don't have to be an aeronautical engineer, after all, to understand the basic ideas of flight, and no one would dream of saying that psychologists, historians, philosophers, or just ordinary people shouldn't consider how the power of flight has influenced our society. Why, then, should we be dissuaded from trying to grasp fundamental ideas of the new physics, or from speculating on how the shifting paradigms of the sciences relate to our total conceptualization of reality? It is certainly important, however, to approach these ideas in a very critical and responsible way, rather than enthusiastically co-opting them to support our own pet theories.[1]

The next two sections may seem to be ranging far from the topic of Tarot. They may also seem to be delving more deeply into particle physics and other scientific subjects than is required in a book about Tarot. But I believe that a serious study of the "science of Tarot" is the only logical next step in the evolution of this intriguing instrument. As we have seen in previous chapters, the traditional vein of occult investigation is nearly exhausted today, and the psychological approach, while undeniably fertile, can take us only so far into the mysteries of Tarot. The most promising new tool for deepening our understanding of the Tarot is contemporary science—but in order to use that tool, it is necessary to learn a good deal about it. So although what follows may be a bit daunting to those who haven't thought much about science lately, it will, I hope, serve to open a new line of thinking about the very old matter of Tarot.

PHYSICS, OLD AND NEW

To begin thinking about the "new" science, we first have to examine our own relationship to the "old" science. Most of us nonscientists have learned what we know—about the composition of the universe, about what is and what isn't possible, about how and why things work the way they do—from our parents and teachers, and from our common-sense experience. It may be, however, that a good deal of what we have learned is, if not inaccurate, then at least inadequate. Most of us, and certainly most of our parents and teachers, learned about reality from the viewpoint of what is now called "classical," or "Newtonian," physics; that world view leaves no room at all for phenomena which fall outside the bounds of pure, obvious, cause-and-effect relationship. So for those of us who have had experiences which can't be explained in terms of the old world view, it seems very worthwhile to explore the new world view and see if there are some explanatory possibilities to be found there.

Classical physics works very well, it should be said, on the level of things that can be seen with the unaided eye, and it accords with our common-sense experience, so most people who don't go beyond the required science courses in school have no occasion to question the classical interpretation. It's still true, after all, that bowling balls and feathers fall at the same speed, and yes, for every action there really is an equal and opposite reaction; principles such as these describe our day-to-day reality perfectly well, and that's enough for most of our purposes. But the contemporary science of physics has moved very far beyond the simplistic picture of matter most of us grew up with. It appears that at the sub-atomic, or "particle," level of reality, matter behaves quite differently than common sense would expect. Indeed, the particle world is so strange that its most basic constituent, the quark, comes in "flavors," such as "up," "down," "charm," and "strange." (Charmed quarks, you should know, are heavier than strange quarks. But keep in mind that anti-quarks carry anti-flavor!)

The new physics may sometimes sound whimsical, but in fact it is extremely serious about discovering the fundamental structure of nature, and is being pursued on a grand scale, with multi-billion-dollar projects and experiments that require hundreds of Ph.D.s just to monitor them.[2] Emerging from all this work is a picture of reality which many believe will provide a ground for integrating physical and metaphysical speculations. At the very least, it can be said that contemporary physics is introducing some ideas which seem to resonate with "occult" or "esoteric" concepts. This resonance may eventually result in a reunion between magical philosophy and natural science.

During the Renaissance, as we have seen, the investigation of the material world was regarded as an inquiry into the nature of God, as revealed through the order He had created on earth. In those days, religion and science believed themselves to be engaged in the same activity, just approaching it from different perspectives. But that harmonious state changed, with both good and bad consequences. Natural scientists began to realize that by isolating matter from any spiritual component, and looking at it merely as an object, they could learn much more about it. From this recognition there developed a "scientific method," which over a period of time became accepted as the *only* way of acquiring valid knowledge.[3]

In the wake of the first scientific revolution, natural scientists, with their new methodology and their new attitude, went off in their own direction, leaving the philosophers and theologians behind to continue wrangling over such intangibles as the existence of God and the nature of truth—questions that didn't lend themselves to the new experimental techniques. Science took over the study of the material world, and religion was left to try and preserve the idea of a spirituality cut off from this material world. Because the scientific method was so successful in penetrating the mysteries of matter, the "unscientific" methods of religion and philosophy came to seem inadequate and even irrelevant.

The efficiency of the physical sciences in mapping the material world had, by the middle of the eighteenth century, produced the comprehensive picture we now call Newtonian, or classical, physics. Sir Isaac Newton's name has been given to this body of ideas because his work consummated the shift of science from a *magical* approach (as described in chapter 5) to an *empirical* approach. But Newton himself retained some magical attitudes (including an interest in alchemy), and his predecessors—such as Johannes Kepler, another architect of classical physics—are well known to have combined aspects of both the old and the new world views in their work. So the first scientific "revolution" was not, as used to be thought, a sudden, enlightened rejection of old superstitions, but really the gradual transformation of the magical approach into a more detached and practical way of examining natural phenomena.

Whatever its origins may have been, empirical science took up a life of its own, and worked so well that by the nineteenth century, classical physics was a completely self-contained and self-consistent body of ideas. It described a system in which *matter* (taken to be absolute in its "realness") was affected by *fields* (gravitational and electromagnetic—invisible, but still "real"). *Laws of motion* described the behavior of matter in fields, and *field laws* described the source and behavior of the fields themselves. Taken all together, the principles described by these laws were believed to *determine* (automatically and irrevocably) all events in the material world.

Where inconsistencies or unknowns occurred, it was assumed they would be rectified by means of further work. Some of these "difficulties," however, proved very resistant to rectification. For example, black bodies—nonreflecting objects such as chunks of iron—could be seen by any steelworker to glow bright red when heated; but by all calculations of classical physics, the glow of hot iron *ought* to have been *blue*, because excited atoms were expected to emit high-frequency (blue to white) light. Why did hot iron glow *red* instead—and, even more important, why couldn't classical physics explain the phenomenon?

This "black-body problem," along with a few others, remained doggedly inexplicable when approached in terms of classical physics. But around the turn of this century, a few maverick physicists began to question the assumptions of classical physics, and to lay the foundations of the *second* scientific revolution. Max Planck decided to prefer a "working" solution to the black-body problem over a classically "correct" solution, and by this means he found that black-body radiation could be explained. The explanation involved abandoning the classical theory that energy is absorbed and emitted in a smooth stream, and assuming instead that energy is absorbed and emitted in a series of discrete little "packets." (When a black body is heated, it will radiate the smallest energy packets first, and low-frequency red light has the smallest energy packets in the spectrum—hence the red glow of hot iron.)

Planck called these energy packets "quanta." This single notion of Planck's about the relationship of particles and their energy proved to be the key to unlocking all sorts of doors into the world of matter—but it also led to the revelation that light, long "proven" to be a *wave*, had characteristics which were specific to *particles*. This was very problematic, since in classical physics, waves and particles were understood as two entirely separate sorts of things; waves were energy, particles were matter. But in Einstein's 1905 paper on the photoelectric effect, light "waves" were shown to behave at times as *particles*, and, soon enough, matter itself was shown to have not only particle but also wave characteristics—all of which effectively turned the whole of classical physics upside down and inside out. And whereas classical physics had contributed little to the understanding of esoteric matters such as Tarot, the new physics would offer fascinating new opportunities for occult ideas to rejoin the mainstream of science.

What developed from the work of Planck and Einstein, along with that of Werner Heisenberg, Niels Bohr, and others, was the critical recognition that particles on the subatomic level do not follow the same laws that seem to predict the behavior of gross objects. Contemporary physics now focuses almost entirely on this subatomic world, and so is frequently referred to as "particle physics." It is also spoken of as "high-energy physics," because the smallest particles can only be created and observed at very high energy levels. But many aspects of the new physics still carry the name borrowed from Planck's "quantum," or denomination of energy—hence quantum mechanics, quantum theory, quantum statistics, and so on.

The best-known characteristic of the quantum region is that the behavior of particles is *statistically describable* but it is not *predictable*. That is, if you split a stream of particles, you can determine statistically that a certain number of particles will go one way, a certain number the other—but you *cannot* predict

THE MACROWORLD	THE QUANTUM WORLD
Naturally visible	Not naturally visible
Classical laws of physics apply	Classical laws of physics do not apply
Quantum rules do not apply (?)	Quantum rules do apply
Forward direction of time	No direction of time
Behavior of physical phenomena predictable	Behavior of physical phenomena not predictable
Matter and energy phenomenally distinct	Matter and energy phenomenally continuous

Particle physics tells us that the "macroworld" of everyday experience and the quantum world of subatomic particles exist in different conditions and follow different rules. Although this description of a discontinuous reality (sometimes called the Copenhagen Interpretation) is not altogether satisfying, the majority of physicists accept it. Quantum physics has proven to be a very reliable tool in understanding a wide variety of phenomena, but it also creates many problems and questions. Some physicists today are moving outside the traditional interpretations in search of new answers.

147

which way a particular particle will go. This fact is related to another well-known aspect of particle research: It isn't possible to know the behavior of a particle with certainty, because the position *and* the momentum of a particle cannot both be observed with complete accuracy. The more exactly the position of a particle is measured, the less exactly its momentum can be measured, and vice versa.

This principle of uncertainty, perhaps more than any other aspect of the new physics, was initially regarded by the scientific community as shocking. Heisenberg, who defined the uncertainty principle, described in *Physics and Philosophy* how he responded, in 1927, to the emerging revelations of quantum mechanics:

> I remember discussions with Bohr which went through many hours till very late at night and ended almost in despair; and when at the end of the discussion I went alone for a walk in the neighboring park I repeated to myself again and again the question: Can nature possibly be as absurd as it seemed to us in these atomic experiments?

Einstein, too, was distressed by the implications of quantum mechanics, and never accepted quantum theory as a satisfactory point of view. Because it worked so well from a mathematical and experimental standpoint, most physicists agreed to accept quantum mechanics as an effective theory, even though they acknowledged that it did not explain in any way what we think of as "reality." But many of them were not happy about it. One of the chief reasons for their discomfort was the fact that the quantum world does not obey the same laws of causality which we assume to govern our own human-inhabited world.

Physicist Paul Davies, in his book *Superforce*, explains that "at the atomic level matter and motion are vague and unpredictable. Particles can behave erratically, rebelling against rigidly prescribed motions, turning up in unexpected places without discernible reason and even appearing or disappearing without warning." Davies goes on to wonder why the idea of an object abruptly appearing from nothing should be considered so incredible. He speculates that such occurrences seem "supernatural" because we don't encounter them in everyday life. If we did—if we lived in a world where the spontaneous appearance of objects was commonplace—we would regard that phenomenon as just another "quirk of nature."

But, says Davies, in a way we *do* live in such a world, without realizing it.

> If we could actually observe the behavior of atoms directly with our sense organs, rather than through the intermediary of special instruments, we should frequently see objects appearing and disappearing without well-defined reasons.

In other words, events which would be characterized as supernatural if we encountered them in the "real" world are perfectly natural in the "quantum" world.

Now the obvious question is, can the "real" world and the "quantum" world *from which it is created* actually be absolutely and qualitatively different? This is one way of putting the question that bothered Einstein—and it's easy to see why it bothered him. Such an idea violates our fundamental sense of logic. Nevertheless, this very position was adopted by a majority of the physics community in 1927 at the fifth Solvay Conference. In debates with Einstein, Bohr argued that quantum theory was completely discontinuous with experienced reality, and that the one could never explain the other; his position was accepted and is now called the "Copenhagen Interpretation." It is still the ruling point of view in mainstream physics today.

There are physicists today who choose not to be limited by the Copenhagen interpretation, and several of them will be mentioned in this chapter. But no matter how adventurous and imaginative some scientists may be, scientific work is, by its very nature, confined to a certain style of inquiry, and it has certain criteria for results. This is by no means a bad thing, but it does limit certain types of speculation. We who are not part of the scientific profession need not observe these limitations, however—and that freedom does not necessarily mean our theorizing will be valueless. Before going more deeply into the prevailing currents of scientific thought, it might be interesting to formulate a little hypothesis of our own.

Here is a plausible chain of reasoning to begin our speculation: (*1*) The reason we don't see our experienced reality in the same way physicists see quantum reality is that we use different instruments. We use our physical senses rather than particle accelerators and the like. (*2*) As we already know, our physical senses observe only the light found in the middle of the total spectrum of light; light frequencies at the very low and very high ends of the spectrum are invisible to our physical senses, and can only be "seen" with the aid of other instrumentation. The same is true of sound, for only the mid-range frequencies are audible to the human ear. (*3*) It does not, therefore, seem entirely outrageous to think that our senses may pick up only the *middle* of the "reality spectrum." The *low* end—the atomic world—cannot be perceived by us without a special apparatus; so it's possible to suppose that there might be a *high* end of the reality spectrum, invisible to us because we don't have any instrumentation to detect it.

To put this argument another way: Since nature favors symmetry, if there is a "subnatural" aspect of reality (the particle world), it seems likely there is also a "supernatural" aspect. When placed in this context of a total reality spectrum, the word "supernatural" is freed of its associations with superstition and general weirdness; it becomes just another component in a complete description of what *is*. And released from the constraints of natural causality, the behavior of events on the supernatural level makes just as much sense as the behavior of particles on the subnatural level.

So what would "high-end" or "supernatural" reality be like? Perhaps it could be something roughly (probably very roughly!) analogous to the astral regions of the magicians. Or the "other world" of the shamans. Or Jung's synchronistic "divine unconsciousness of the world." If so, we would have to say that although conventional science doesn't have any instrumentation to detect upper-spectrum reality, and although it is not perceptible to our normal

149

senses, it is nevertheless not inherently imperceptible. Many people do, in fact, seem to or claim to spontaneously perceive it. There is also a variety of mystical and magical paths which offer to teach us methods for extending our perceptions beyond the physical sensory level, to encompass high-end reality.

These methods, however, are generally unacceptable to science because they don't "work" from the scientific perspective—that is, they are not measurable, repeatable, and objectively verifiable. Two people following exactly the same instructions will not get the same results, and, furthermore, one person following exactly the same procedure twice will not get the same results both times. If you do A, B will happen sometimes—but not always! Classically, phenomena of this unpredictable type are scientifically inadmissable; they can't participate in an accurate description of events.

But from the *quantum* point of view, this shouldn't necessarily be so. Quantum reality, remember, can only be described statistically, never absolutely. Let's call on Paul Davies again. "The quantum microworld," he wrote, "is not . . . linked by a tight network of causal influences, but more by a pandemonium of loosely obeyed commands and suggestions." If there is not a reliable cause-and-effect relationship at the quantum level, it seems problematic to insist that such a relationship must obtain everywhere else.

Suppose we instead assume that causality is a defining characteristic of the natural, or sense-perceptible, world of our normal experience, but doesn't

SUPERNATURAL REALITY	Imperceptible to the natural senses
	Spontaneously perceptible to some
	Perceptible to the expanded consciousness

NATURAL REALITY	Perceptible to the natural senses

SUBNATURAL REALITY	Imperceptible to the natural senses
	Not spontaneously perceptible
	Perceptible only by instrumentation

This hypothetical model of a "reality continuum" includes aspects of reality which cannot be perceived by the natural human senses. Supernatural reality is perceived spontaneously and unpredictably by some people (mystics and artists, for example), and many people can expand their conscious awareness (by means such as meditation or magical practice) to perceive it. Subnatural reality is never spontaneously perceived, but may be consistently perceived through instrumentation (such as microscopes and particle accelerators).

necessarily apply anywhere else. Therefore, psychic events—which are by definition independent of our sensory relationship to the natural world—would not have to obey laws of causality. They could be *a pandemonium of loosely obeyed commands and suggestions.* (Anyone who has attempted to achieve, through magical or mystical means, participation in the high end of reality may well recognize this as a precise description of the experience.) Statistically speaking, in psychic matters, B will follow A a certain percentage of the time, but there is no way of predicting precisely *which* A-event will precipitate a B-event. Not unlike the reality of the quantum world, perhaps?

So far, I've been using some aspects of contemporary physics to develop a sequence of ideas that might show how Tarot-reading fits into the grand scheme of things. I must remind you that few physicists would agree with my reasoning. But I would add that some are actually thinking along similar lines, and most are forced to admit, as Niels Bohr did (in *Atomic Energy and Human Knowledge*), that quantum mechanics necessitates "a final renunciation of the classical ideal of causality and a radical revision of our attitude toward the problem of physical reality." I am merely suggesting a "radical revision" that has room for some of the phenomena typically abandoned and rejected by science—phenomena which are part of my personal experience, and which I feel ought to be considered continuous with the rest of what is described as "reality."

So let's go at least a bit further and discuss a few other aspects of contemporary physics that may enlarge my argument. First, we can look at *how* the physicists gain knowledge of the quantum world. High-energy particles cannot be directly observed; they (like the archetypes) are known by the effects they produce, and/or by the traces they leave. Moreover, a number of particles which are predicted by quantum theory to exist do not appear under "normal" circumstances; they must be forced into existence by creating very high energy levels, or evidence of their existence must be trapped by elaborate means. (The competition in the international physics community to create or catch these elusive particles is fierce, and the United States has begun the very expensive construction of a gigantic superconducting supercollider to take the quest to new and higher levels.)

When you get right down to it, then, the physicists don't "see" the particles they call leptons and muons anymore than the Tarot reader "sees" the inner processes and future probabilities of a querent. What the physicists see are *indications* of the existence and behavior of the objects they are studying, frequently in the form of collision charts like the one on the next page. Only highly trained experts can read these charts and interpret the meaning of the particle events recorded there. It seems to me that a spread of Tarot cards could be described in a similar way—as a "chart" of traces left by events of a certain type, and readable only by those who have learned to recognize characteristic signs and structures.

One objection to this notion might be that the same spread of cards, laid out for the same person, would almost always be read differently by different readers; this fact may seem to "prove" that card-reading depends not on the traces signified by the cards, but on the subjective impressions of the reader.[4]

151

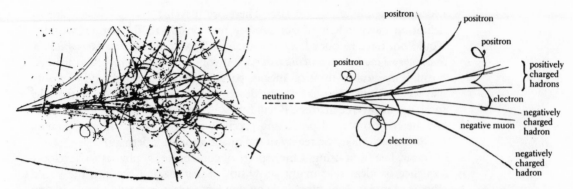

The scrambled mass on the left is a "picture" created by the collision of subatomic particles. By producing these collisions under special experimental circumstances, scientists can record "tracks" of the interactions among the particles and the formation of new particles. The raw data must then be interpreted and described in the form of a collision chart, shown right. This scientific procedure may be a useful analogy for the Tarot-reading process. The cards in a spread may be tracks of events, visible to the trained interpreter.

But there is an alternative way of looking at it. In the case of two different reading events, even if the pieces of cardboard have exactly the same pictures on them, and even if they are arranged in exactly the same pattern, the two events *themselves* are different, and therefore contain different information. For one thing, there are variant human influences, since the querent will be in a different frame of mind and the readers will have different sets of personal characteristics and skills. Environmental influences—from the local to the cosmic—will vary as well. But even if all these factors could be completely controlled, it would still be true that the same card can represent traces of many different events, and one reader might pick up one set of associations, while another reader picks up another set.

Here again, there is a parallel with the world of quantum theory, which acknowledges that in every event, the observer interacts *by the very process of observation* with whatever is being observed. There is no way of proving that an event (such as the collision of two particles) would have taken place in precisely the same way if it had not been observed! Furthermore, the observer brings to the event some "attitude," even if it is only the intention to observe and the decision concerning *what* to observe. As physicist John Wheeler expresses it:

> "Participator" is the incontrovertible new concept given by quantum mechanics. It strikes down the term "observer" of classical theory, the man who stands safely behind the thick glass wall and watches what goes on without taking part. It can't be done, quantum mechanics says.

It's a long way from this statement to the popular metaphysical idea that consciousness creates reality, and the doctrine of participation which pertains to quantum mechanics doesn't necessarily support such an interpretation. But I do think it's fair to say that if participation is a valid principle in the scientific process, then it may actually validate, rather than *in*validate the Tarot-reading process to say that the reader "participates" in the nature of the event.

We have now looked at three of the basic building blocks in the methodology of present-day physics: the quantum, the uncertainty principle, and the doctrine of participation (complementarity). These ideas are accepted by virtually every scientist in the world—there's nothing "out on a limb" here. Let's next take a look at a somewhat more controversial proposition called "nonlocality." While the basic facts of nonlocality are not disputed, there is certainly no agreement on what they mean.

A SHORT INTRODUCTION TO SPACE-TIME

"Nonlocality" is the current best answer to a problem that has been nagging at physicists ever since the famous Einstein-Podolsky-Rosen thought experiment of 1935, usually referred to as the "EPR paradox." An oversimplified description of the EPR paradox goes like this: If you take two "twinned" particles and submit them to a test, they will both behave in the same way, as long as they are both given the same test. But if you change the conditions of the test for *one* particle, that change will also affect the behavior of the *other* particle—*no matter how far apart the particles may be*. Although the two particles don't have any apparent way of "communicating" with each other, somehow the experience of one particle is nevertheless linked with the experience of its twin.

The EPR paradox remains a paradox as long as you assume that reality is "local"—that is, as long as you assume that whatever makes a specific particle behave in a particular way must be local to it, not occurring at a distance (or, put another way, that the real situations of the two particles are objectively and absolutely distinct). But in 1964, physicist John Stewart Bell proposed a mathematical proof—known as Bell's theorem—which suggested a way of resolving the paradox. Bell's theorem has since been experimentally validated, and the result seems to say that the principle of local causes does not hold up. The particles do not have separate objective realities; their realities are connected in some way, and that connection is independent of the distance between the particles.

Bell's theorem is, needless to say, much loved by believers in extrasensory perception, telepathy, clairvoyance, and other so-called paranormal ways of knowing. If particles can communicate with each other at a distance, why can't we? And if reality at the quantum level is a network of invisible interrelationships, doesn't that sound very much like the magical/mystical view of the universe?

John Bell does not share this point of view, but he doesn't entirely reject it either. *Psychological Perspectives*, a journal which explores the relationship between psyche, soul, and nature, interviewed Bell and asked him this question:

> So all the romantic people who want to seize on nonlocality as a scientific basis for ESP and every other mysterious phenomenon that we cannot understand by rational mechanics—you would put a damper on that?

153

Bell answered:

> A damper, yes, but not a condemnation. I'm not going to burn their books or anything. . . . I would say that one should resist the idea that all mysteries should be put into the one box—in particular into this "box" of nonlocality . . . whatever nonlocality there is, it is a *hidden* nonlocality. It is behind the scenes.

Bell's own position seems to be that though nonlocality may be suggestive of alternative ways of looking at reality on the level of the human world, nonlocality alone is not enough to prove that ESP and other paranormal phenomena either (*a*) exist, or (*b*) can be explained by quantum mechanics. He is willing, he says, to leave the area of the mind for another generation.

Generally speaking, Bell and other particle physicists are not interested in the implications, if any, of quantum theory for "macroscopic" (i.e., visible-to-us) phenomena. If something is big enough to see, they reason, it's covered by the laws of classical physics, and so is already well described and explained. Most center their attention on what they can discover with the tools of quantum physics, rather than on what seems already obvious.

But some physicists *are* actively concerned with sorting out the real-life ramifications of nonlocality. Among them is David Bohm, who has become very well-known for his theory of "implicate order." Bohm asserts that beneath the indeterminacy of the quantum world there is a level at which everything is, in fact, interrelated in an orderly way. This *implicate* order is not apparent in everyday life, because it is *enfolded*, Bohm says, in the *explicate* order, or what we commonly experience as the "real" world. "That-which-is"—Bohm's term for the unified whole which encompasses space, time, and matter—is undifferentiated, but it "unfolds" into the world of separate items we commonly experience. For anyone familiar with the magical/mystical view of the universe, or with certain Eastern philosophies, Bohm's idea does not sound like anything terrifically novel. But Bohm has succeeded in engaging the interest of at least part of the physics community because his theory is presented not as a record of personal experience or as an inspired doctrine, but as a way of resolving some of the difficult questions raised by quantum theory.

Bohm offers a very clear model of how the implicate order works. Here's a streamlined version: Imagine a drop of colored ink in a cylinder of glycerine. Spin the cylinder around fast enough in one direction and the drop of ink will disperse into the glycerine and become invisible. Now spin the cylinder in the opposite direction, and the drop will reappear. When the drop is dispersed, its "order" (or coherence) is "enfolded" into the glycerine medium and becomes invisible; when the process is reversed, the order of the drop "unfolds" and becomes visible again.

To explain further how this implicate order is expressed in material reality, Bohm suggests that the universe may be *holographic*,[5] a point of view that has excited interest on quite a few fronts. A hologram, as most people know, is a three-dimensional "picture" created by using the interference between two laser beams to record information on a photographic plate. But unlike an ordinary photograph, a hologram contains *all* the information about the recorded image *everywhere* on the plate. If you cut up an ordinary photo, each piece will have only the information that was stored in that particular part of the photo—an arm, an ear, a tree, or whatever. If you divide a hologram up into pieces, however, each piece will have the entire image "on" it, in the sense that the whole picture could be reproduced from each of the individual pieces. Thus, in a holographic universe, the Statue of Liberty contains all the information about a lotus petal in China, and vice versa, because each has enfolded in it the whole of the implicate order.

Obviously, in Bohm's theory, consciousness is part of the same whole as the Statue of Liberty and the lotus petal, and this again supports the idea that we can know things at a distance—or through objective media such as the Tarot cards. The ability to gather information from nonphysical sources is only one aspect of Tarot-reading, however. There is also the matter of the future, which may be even more problematic. If the future doesn't exist yet, how can we know anything about it, by physical means or by any other means? Is all of time enfolded in the implicate order, too?

In Bohm's view, the implicate order is unrelated to both time and space. All events can be viewed as enfolded until they are unfolded—that is, events are invisibly subsumed in the whole until they become manifest and thus enter the stream of time by becoming perceptible to us. But to understand how this could be true, it's necessary to understand more about time itself. At the quantum level, time—like just about everything else—does not appear as it does in our macroscopic world. Particles can move backward and forward in time, in the sense that they move freely in all directions of *space-time*, the four-dimensional continuum in which quantum-level activity takes place. This is one theoretical explanation of the reason why particles can "appear out of nowhere"; it is actually we, the observers, who at a given moment happen to reach perceptually the time in which the particles already exist. Thus the particles "pop" into view as our field of space-time vision changes.

In his essay "A General Survey of the Scientific Work of Albert Einstein," Louis de Broglie, who first demonstrated the wavelike characteristics of matter, gave this description of our own relationship to space-time:

> [In space-time] everything which for each of us constitutes the past, the present and the future is given *en bloc*. . . . Each observer, as his time passes, discovers, so to speak, new slices of space-time which appear to him as successive aspects of the material world, though in reality the ensemble of events constituting space-time exist prior to his knowledge of them.

This description raises some urgent questions: Does it mean that all events are pre-existing? And, if so, does this mean that reality is deterministic—that there is no free will?

Not necessarily. The generally held position is that while matter/energy may be continuously existing in a total field of space-time, its particular *arrangements* do, in fact, manifest (or, in Bohm's terms, "unfold") according to principles which are organized on the macro-level of reality. This sort of explanation is, of course, somewhat unsatisfying, because it is extremely abstract. But to understand more clearly how our own experience of time relates to quantum-level reality, we have to turn to the laws of classical physics.

The reason that time seems to us to develop in a particular direction (a phenomenon called the "arrow" of time) is contained in the second law of thermodynamics. Simply put, a closed system tends toward disorder. The term for this tendency toward disorder is "entropy." Time's arrow points in the direction of entropy, so we perceive things as getting "older"—that is, more disordered. We also, of course, perceive growth and creation, which are always taking place simultaneously with decline and decay. But *statistically*, the tendency toward disorder is always prevailing.

As we already know from the principle of uncertainty, the behavior of individual particles cannot be predicted, even though the behavior of particles in a group can be predicted statistically. In other words, statistical phenomena are not descriptive of individual particles; so the second law of thermodynamics does not apply at the quantum level. Time's arrow doesn't point in any particular direction in the particle world.

In the macroscopic world, our sensory perceptors and our psychological interpretations are "pre-set," so to speak, to follow the natural direction of time's arrow. Therefore we only perceive time as moving forward, in the direction of statistically prevailing disorder; we see things grow older, get broken, and so on, not the reverse process. But that doesn't actually mean time *itself* develops in a linear way (out of the existent now into a nonexistent future), only that manifestations of the physical world appear to us in that fashion. Time, unlike our perception of it, may be directionless.

This conceptualization of time resonates very sympathetically with the process of divination, for in Tarot-reading, as in other types of true divination, the "future" is always seen as a continuum of possibilities, with certain *tendencies* prevailing. But now we come to a new question: In normal life, we see only a very small slice of space-time on a moment-to-moment basis. Can we go beyond that limitation, to see further into the unfolding of events?

CHAOS AND THE BRAIN

The question just posed has two operative parts, both very important: What is the nature of "events"? and, What are the limits of our own perceptual powers? Let's begin with events. In our macro-world lives, events take place on both mental and physical levels; some events are almost purely mental (a thought, a dream), while others appear to be entirely physical (falling rain, shifting sand dunes, growing grass). But the events we are interested in, as far as divination goes, are principally those events which combine mental activities and physical consequences, often in a complex chain.

So far as I know, there is no current research or even theory in physics that proposes a viable description of such events. This line of questioning crosses into unexplored terrain because very little attention is given to the interaction between the micro-world of the quantum and the macro-world of human events. Such a lack of interest is a natural consequence of the Copenhagen Interpretation, at least as far as the physics community is concerned. But we might have hoped that other disciplines—particularly those concerned with the human mind—would step in to explore this deserted territory. The fact that, for the most part, this has not happened is both disappointing and surprising.

The best sources we can turn to in our search for connections between the micro- and macro-worlds are the information sciences and the new study of "chaos"—that is, of complex events that appear to be random but which are really organized by some hidden order. Chaos science tells us that the formation of patterns in seemingly random (i.e., unpredictable) systems is a result of "sensitive dependence on initial conditions." Weather, for example, is a chaotic system, which is why we cannot make predictions about weather behavior until a pattern has already begun to emerge—and even then, the predictions are only probabilities, because the pattern is unstable; it will continue to ramify according to the dictates of internal feedback within the system, and those ramifications will change their nature in reaction to the introduction of new stimuli. As with all chaotic systems, weather is unpredictable not because there are too many factors to manipulate successfully in forming a model of future behavior, but because the behavior of the system is by its very nature unpredictable; a given set of factors will not interact in the same way twice in a chaotic system. (Which accounts for one of life's great truisms—that no two snowflakes are identical!)

We can, however, recognize *principles* which govern behavior in chaotic systems. The subject is too large (and frequently too mathematical) to pursue further here, but let's consider briefly what chaos science may suggest about Tarot-reading. One suggestion is something of an aside here because it doesn't

Nonlinear fractals, like the one shown here, illustrate the nature of chaotic systems. Fractal behavior follows a mathematical order, but it is not predictable. Fractal systems are "self-similar," meaning that they continuously reiterate themselves—each new part repeats the whole on a smaller scale. This process will continue indefinitely, but the larger the system grows, the more irregular it becomes. Chaos theory is providing new clues to the nature of many seemingly inexplicable phenomena.

157

address the nature of the future, but it's worth mentioning: The fall of the Tarot cards, even if random by usual definitions, may be part of a chaotic system and therefore may have a hidden order. The other suggestion is that our ability to recognize patterns in chaotic systems works exclusively backwards—that is, we can see patterns *after* they have emerged, but not before. It is intriguing to speculate that *all* events are part of a chaotic system. We see meaning in events, and connections among events, after they have taken place, but we are unable, according to our normal rules of perception and interpretation, to predict the patterns which will arise in the chaotic future.[6]

And yet we do seem to perceive, under certain circumstances, "what will happen." This process may be made more understandable by borrowing one of the basic principles of information science. Though information theory is frequently attacked as a poor model for interpretations of psychological processes, it does offer us a useful precept, which is that information itself exists independent of transmitter, receiver, and content. For our purposes, this can be taken to suggest that information *about* an event is not *identical with* the event. By viewing events as informational, we can solve (at least provisionally) part of the problem that seems to separate our present perceptions from future events. When we "intuit"—through the Tarot or by other means—future events, what we are becoming aware of is not the events themselves, pre-existing in a warehouse called the "future," but rather information about possible/probable events. As time moves along (from our point of view), possibilities will collide, canceling or deflecting one another, and some possibilities will collapse while others will continue. Our present intuition of some specific future event may be a "gestalt" grasp of this elaborate network of possibilities, their prevailing tendencies toward interaction, and the probable result of these tendencies.[7]

As for the question of whether we ordinary human beings really *can* grasp such intricacies, the answer is certainly, on the simplest level, that we cannot do so consciously—that is, through conscious "thinking." If such a process takes place, it must take place on some other level. And in search of that other level, we can turn from physics to the human sciences. This is a difficult transition, however. The biological sciences, like the physical sciences, have undergone great changes in this century. But generally speaking, these changes have not been in keeping with the new discoveries and adventurous theories that have marked the course of physics and mathematics. Noted neurologist Oliver Sacks says:

> There has always, seemingly, been a split between science and life, between the apparent poverty of scientific formulation and the manifest richness of phenomenal experience. . . . This chasm—which is smallest in physics, where we have spectacularly powerful theories of countless physical processes—is overwhelming in biology, in the study, above all, of mental processes and inner life, for these are, unlike physical existence, distinguished by extreme complexity, unpredictability, and novelty; by inner principles of autonomy, identity, and "will"; . . . and by a continuous becoming, evolution, and development.[8]

It is certainly true that most of us, if we examine carefully our own *experiences* of being human, will find scientific models of behavior, thinking, feeling, and so on woefully inadequate. The serious study of mind/body interaction, for example, is only beginning—and even the relatively little work being done in this area is opposed by a large part of the medical and scientific establishment.

Perhaps this difference in development between the physical and the biological sciences exists, in part, because philosophical questions are much more obviously involved in thinking about human beings than in thinking about matter. Most physicists were surprised and uncomfortable when it became apparent that the quantum revolution was going to produce questions that not only invite, but sometimes *demand* philosophical speculation. Researchers studying the nature of the brain, on the other hand, are very well aware that their data could be seen as providing answers to the very deepest of human questions: Do we have a soul, a spirit, something other than just physical machinery? If so, how is the nonmaterial part of ourselves related to the material part? In order to exclude such "nonscientific" concerns, scientists engaged in research concerning human beings have elected very often to regard the body/brain as a complex machine, and nothing more. (A tacit version of the Copenhagen Interpretation, perhaps.)

Somewhat ironically, it is actually the physicists who have provided a new basis for thinking about our oldest questions by changing our understanding of the relationship between matter and energy. If matter has wave characteristics, and energy has particle characteristics, obviously there is not such a clear-cut distinction between the two as was once thought. It follows, then, that the relationship between brain and body (matter?) and consciousness (energy?) may need to be reconsidered, along with the relationship between consciousness and the "material" world. Pressed to the wall, research on the human side has now begun to face the necessity of exploring these issues.

There are several areas of biological and medical study which are relevant to our own questions. First, there is the continuing research into the organization of the brain, particularly the relationship between the two halves of the brain. Ever since it was determined, some time ago, that the two hemispheres of the brain seem to have separate and quite different areas of responsibility, it has become widely known that the left hemisphere manages what we think of as abstract and verbal capabilities (such as speech and computation), while the right hemisphere takes care of intuitive and creative matters. But, not surprisingly, the truth is proving to be less simple than it originally appeared. For example, the right hemisphere cannot express itself in terms of language, so if right-brain experience is cut off from left-brain language functions, the right brain will appear to be "dumb." But if the right brain is "questioned" by means of *images* (as when a subject is asked to choose the picture, from among a group of pictures, which would best "answer" an inquiry), the right brain response can reveal, in the words of neurologist Roger Sperry, "the presence of a normal and well developed sense of self and personal relations along with a surprising knowledgeability in general."[9]

It now appears that memory and emotion are distributed throughout the whole brain, and that specific functions are not confined to one side or the other; rather, various areas of the brain participate in specific functions in their own particular ways. (Thus, in drawing, the left hemisphere takes care of details, while the right hemisphere contributes an overall sense of form.) As Howard Gardner explains in his book *The Mind's New Science*,

> Whatever the mission of each isolated hemisphere, there is clearly dynamic inter-action between the two hemispheres. When the left hemisphere is aroused (for instance, by the sounds of language), it promotes certain kinds of analytic and linguistic functions. In contrast, arousal or stimulation of the right hemisphere brings spatial and holistic functions to the fore.

The objects and activities we call "artistic" or "creative" are the ones which stimulate the right hemisphere and encourage its intuitive activity. It is not at all difficult to see that the Tarot images perform this kind of stimulating function precisely. As a simple consequence of contemplating Tarot cards (or any other evocative images), the brain's "spatial and holistic" capabilities are situationally heightened. Of course, this idea of "right-brain encouragement" also supports the suggestion that music and creative movement—other right-brain stimulators—can be used to increase the effectiveness of the Tarot images in arousing intuitive awareness.

Although there do appear to be special complexes in the brain structure which interact with stimuli in a particular way, and express themselves as a particular kind of knowledge or ability, there still remains the question of how the *whole brain* acts as an "organ of consciousness." As a theoretical response to the emerging picture of brain function, neurologist Karl Pribram has proposed a "holographic" model of the brain. "According to Pribram's holographic view," explains Howard Gardner, "all parts of the brain are capable of participating in all forms of representation, though admittedly certain regions play a more important role in some functions, and other regions are more dominant for other functions."

This holographic paradigm for the brain is, of course, reminiscent of David Bohm's idea of a holographic universe. Pribram and Bohm now occupy similar places in their respective disciplines, for while few agree with them, many cannot ignore their ideas. The holographic paradigm has two areas of appeal to brain scientists. First, as we've already seen, since information is distributed across the entire hologram, any piece of the hologram carries the entire image. Similarly, it's been found that, in some cases, when parts of the brain are damaged, other parts seem to be able to take up their functions. And second, multiple holographic images may be "stacked" on one photographic plate; the individual images can be reproduced one at a time, without inter-ference from the other images. This kind of multilayered storage system might illuminate the mystery of memory, as well as of our obviously multilayered "stream of consciousness."

The holographic hypothesis, while intriguing, is still far from being a satisfying explanation of reality, or our consciousness of reality. As investiga-tion continues, "holism" may become a more fully developed method of understanding. Most likely, it will turn out to be a part of the puzzle, or a phase of the solution process. So many areas of exploration are currently going on that it's difficult to imagine how the ideas we glimpse now may all fit together in the future. For example, one interesting avenue opening up suggests that brain function is in some respects chaotic. Neurobiologist Walter J. Freeman, writing in *Scientific American* (February 1991), explains that his experimental research in olfactory perception suggests "chaos is evident in the tendency of vast collections of neurons to shift abruptly and simultaneously from one complex activity pattern to another in response to the smallest of inputs."

Freeman speculates that chaos in the brain arises when two or more parts of the brain excite one another enough to keep any single part from stabilizing, and when, at the same time, they set up a common frequency of oscillation. This chaotic type of activity is profoundly valuable in terms of brain function, because the sensitivity of chaotic systems constantly produces new patterns and associations—which may, in Freeman's view, account for "the ability of the brain to respond flexibly to the outside world and to generate novel activity patterns, including those that are experienced as fresh ideas."

This scenario is interpreted by Freeman along fairly reductionist lines, but more adventurous interpretations certainly seem possible. Is it possible, for example, that something "tunes" the common frequency of oscillation set up between brain parts? Could there be a relationship between chaotic brain functioning and the chaotic nature of future events? Along these lines of speculation, we can imagine that potent images, such as those of the Tarot, could serve as tuning devices for the brain. We can even imagine that the Tarot-reading process might harmonize in some way brain-chaos and future-chaos, providing a common set of "initial conditions" from which both might ramify into new patterns.

These are highly speculative realms, where more questions are raised than answered. Very recently, however, some conventional research has begun to demonstrate clearly certain expanded aspects of our cognitive capability. One of the most interesting areas of research—from the Tarot point of view, anyway—is the study of "covert awareness."[10] This term describes perception, memory, and judgment carried out *unconsciously*—in other words, the structure and process of what you know, but don't know that you know. Though the existence of covert awareness was identified as far back as the turn of this century, only now is it being seriously investigated. In the process of studying the consequences of brain injuries, researchers have encountered phenomena which suggest that there are paths of cognition of which we are not normally aware.

"Blindsight" is one example. According to research at Brown University, stroke patients who are unquestionably blind seem able to perceive some things they cannot physically see; if a bar of light is flashed directly in the blind eye, they are aware of whether the bar is vertical or horizontal. This is described in the report as the activation of a vestigial visual pathway not recognized by the conscious mind. Similarly, a study at the Iowa College of Medicine shows that patients with a certain kind of brain damage who cannot recognize the faces even of their own families nevertheless show physical

161

It is well known that we can see things which are not actually "there"—like the white triangle in the figure here. But it may be surprising to learn that the appearance of the triangle is not merely an illusion created by the mind from the various parts of the image. There are actually highly specialized brain cells which register—that is, "see"—inferred lines such as the ones which make up the triangle. Researchers are only beginning to discover how subtle, complex, and extensive our information-gathering activities really are.

changes (such as an increase in heart rate) when they are shown pictures of people they know. Their *bodies* know something which they are unable, because of their brain injuries, to process consciously.

We have numerous examples in our own normal experience of this type of "body-knowledge," but we're not usually aware of them. We *assume* that because we are consciously aware during the performance of a task, we must be consciously performing the task. The idea that we are doing things consciously, however, is often misleading. Are typists "conscious" of what they are doing while they are typing? Yes and no. Ask touch-typists which letters of the alphabet are located on which typewriter keys, and they will have a hard time telling you. In fact, the fastest typists are the least likely to be able to map the keyboard mentally. After all, if the location of each letter had to be consciously processed for each keystroke, typing would be very slow indeed. The typist's "knowledge" of the keyboard is actually *in the fingers*, as you will discover if you insist that the typist actually specify where the letters are; they won't be able to do it without wiggling their fingers!

Of course, a typist may have purposely memorized the map of the keyboard. In that case, they will know the information consciously. But it's irrelevant to the typing process whether the typist has this conscious knowledge or not. If they *don't* have the information stored somewhere consciously, then when asked to express the information consciously, they will first have to retrieve it from its *non*conscious location in the fingers by questioning each finger about where it would go if it had to type *a* or *r*. And the same thing will be true if you ask a tennis player how to position the racquet to make a certain shot, or a pianist how to play an arpeggio.

Perhaps the most fascinating aspect of the research I've been discussing is a study which strongly suggests that covert awareness is physiological—that its mechanisms are located in the brain itself. This is exemplified by the fact that brain injuries seem to have caused several patients examined in the Iowa studies to lose contact with their covert awareness. When the nonconscious physical responses of these patients were measured while they viewed a series of photographs containing images which were disturbing or shocking, the patients showed some physical response to the disturbing material as long as they were talking about the images. But if they watched the photographs *silently*, they showed *no physical responses at all*. The brain-normal control group, on the other hand, reacted equally strongly under both sets of circumstances.

Researcher Antonio Damasio speculates that the injured patients have lost direct access to what we call "gut feelings," which are apparently part of our covert awareness. When asked to talk about the pictures, the patients could somehow make conscious contact with their unconscious knowledge by routing it through the brain channels used for verbal tasks. But without the verbalization process, the visceral response was somehow cut off. To use the touch-typing example again, it would be as if a typist had to say aloud what was being typed in order to communicate information to the fingers. The results of this experiment seem to confirm that (*a*) we definitely do have unconscious knowledge as well as conscious knowledge, and (*b*) unconscious knowledge can be communicated directly to the body, without being routed through the conscious mind—facts which support the idea that something real, something continuous with our normal experience, does take place in the Tarot-reading process.

A TAROT HYPOTHESIS

While nothing in this chapter has definitively explained how Tarot-reading, or any other type of divination, actually takes place, the facts and speculations outlined here do at least suggest that Tarot can be understood in exactly the same way other phenomena are being understood by our most advanced scientific research. Tarot divination need not be considered something merely imagined by credulous minds, or something that defies the rational understanding of reality. By combining the several different scientific speculations discussed in this chapter with the psychological possibilities considered in previous chapters, it is possible to create a hypothetical scenario regarding divination in general and Tarot in particular.

The ambitious student of Tarot, interested in creating such a Tarot hypothesis, might want to consider these points, summarized from the foregoing chapters on divination and on science:

- The rules which govern reality at the quantum level are different from those we are familiar with in the natural world of material phenomena. In some ways, quantum reality appears to be similar to the mystical perception of reality and to the magical description of the world.
- Time at the quantum level does not have a determined direction of flow from past to future.
- Because we are limited in our perceptions of time, matter, and energy by our dependence on the physical senses, we experience the natural world

163

and the passage of time in specific ways, under normal circumstances. These perceptual limitations may be altered, however, under abnormal circumstances, by changes in brain chemistry and/or brain function.

- The altered states of awareness which produce changes in perception may be induced by a variety of means, including rhythmic stimuli such as listening to music or drumming, meditating on mantras or yantras, and shuffling cards. They may also be achieved in the flow and trance states which spontaneously occur under certain circumstances, such as deep concentration.

- Information about the total expanse of reality (past, present, and future) may be "enfolded" in the material world, much as information about an image is distributed throughout a hologram.

- Information can be regarded as existing independently of any particular source, means of transmission, or point of reception. Thus, information may be "ambient" (or nonlocal) in the natural world, just as it seems to be in the quantum world.

- Certain phenomena can be described as "chaotic"—that is, they are both unpredictable and orderly. Chaotic systems are unpredictable because they develop from varying initial conditions by a process in which sensitive factors continuously influence each other.

- The interaction of forces which produces the actualization of reality over a period of time may also be chaotic. In this case, future events would seem unpredictable, but would nevertheless be the product of an orderly process.

- Certain aspects of brain function, as well as certain aspects of reality, appear to be chaotic. There may be an interactive relationship (in itself chaotic?) between brain function and reality. Such a relationship might be analogous, at the level of the natural world, to the way in which observation affects events at the quantum level.

- The human capability of knowing is not strictly an aspect of conscious awareness. The unconscious is also capable of taking in, processing, and storing information. Unconscious knowledge is directly available to the body, and parts of the body also seem to receive and retain information.

When these ideas are considered all together, they seem to resonate with tantalizing possibilities. Though it is certain that all the pieces of a viable scientific theory of Tarot are not yet in place, it seems very likely that, as scientific research continues to produce surprising new results, many of the mysteries surrounding the Tarot will be illuminated.

Indeed, scientific support for something like Tarot-reading may be simple and tame compared with some of the speculations that take place today on the leading edge of the sciences. As reported in the *New York Times*:

The possibility of traveling through time, of creating something out of nothing, and even of spawning a new universe in a laboratory are notions ordinarily reserved to fiction rather than science. But a rash of articles in some of the most prestigious scientific publications suggests that theoretical physicists have begun to take such outlandish ideas seriously . . . in the domain of quantum physics, the physics of nuclear particles and ultrasmall spaces, scientists have recently spotted potential loopholes in the conventional rules that might seem to verge on magic.[11]

Science and magic reunited. What more could we ask?

Notes

1. Manly P. Hall wrote, "If we wish to be true to the convictions of various peoples and to benefit from these convictions thus enlarging our philosophies, we should consider the meanings of these beliefs as they were held by the peoples among whom they originated." Hall was speaking of metaphysical philosophies, but his remark applies just as exactly to scientific disciplines.

2. "The Ultimate Quest," the cover story for the April 16, 1990 issue of *Time*, gives a very good picture of the scope of contemporary physics, its fundamental theories, "hot" topics, and major players.

3. The scientific method requires that theories be based on observation rather than on metaphysical assumptions and that they be tested by experimentation; these experiments must be controlled in some way to eliminate distortion by variables, must be repeatable, and must yield objectively verifiable results.

4. It should be noted that one reason Tarot readings turn out differently is that some readers are better than others. Some people, in fact, can't learn to read the cards at all—just as, undoubtedly, some people could never learn to interpret high-energy particle collision charts. Moreover, there are certainly points of disagreement among physicists concerning interpretation of data.

5. Bohm uses the hologram only as an analogy, and prefers to employ the term "holomovement" to describe the process from which manifest reality arises. A good place to encounter Bohm's thinking is in his long conversation with Renée Weber, contained in *The Holographic Paradigm*, edited by Ken Wilber. See also *The Holographic Universe* by Michael Talbot.

6. These statements are akin to the position of Ilya Prigogine, Nobel laureate in chemistry and general *provocateur* of the new sciences. Prigogine says (in an interview with Renée Weber in *Dialogues with Scientists and Sages*), "Time is creation. The future is just not *there*." He sees reality as a nonlinear system, developing chaotically, and he is a well-known critic of the approach to physics which ignores the temporal dimension of the macro-world. To employ Weber's description, Prigogine's universe is "creating itself as it goes along. . . . We don't know what the universe is going to do until it does it."

7. This very compressed treatment bears some relationship to the ideas developed by physicist Fred Alan Wolfe in his book *Star Wave: Mind, Consciousness, and Quantum Physics*. Wolfe relates the nature of consciousness to the theory of quantum wave function, and his argument is both

very complex and colorfully presented—I wouldn't even attempt to summarize or paraphrase it. Further, I haven't gone into the whole question of wave functions here because it's just too large a topic to fit in, but Wolfe's book is worth taking a look at in this regard. It's not *quite* as daunting as it appears to be, by the way.

8. This quotation is from Sacks's article "Neurology and the Soul," published in the *New York Review of Books*, November 22, 1990. Dr. Sacks's books—such as *The Man Who Mistook His Wife for a Hat* and *Seeing Voices*—have explored, in a very humane and imaginative way, the strange, complex, and highly meaningful pathologies of brain injury.

9. Dr. Sperry received the Nobel Prize for his split-brain research. This quotation is taken from remarks made in a panel discussion, and later published in *Nobel Prize Conversations* (Saybrook Publications, 1985).

10. Information about the research reports referred to in the subsequent text was taken from an article titled "The Brain May See What the Eye Cannot," by Sandra Blakeslee, published in the *New York Times*, January 15, 1990.

11. This quotation comes from "New Directions in Physics: Back in Time," by Malcolm W. Browne, August 21, 1990. The article summarizes conjectures by noted physicists Kip Thorne (on time travel) and Alan Guth (on the creation of "baby universes"). Their speculations are not idle fantasies, but attempts to work toward a theoretical explanation of gravity, the one force which remains inexplicable in quantum terms.

Bibliographic Note:

My personal favorite book on high-energy physics is *The Particle Explosion* by Frank Close, Michael Marten, and Christine Sutton. It's a big book with lots of color pictures, and it presents the "straight science" of the subject in a very clear and readable way. Heinz Pagels gives a conservative presentation in his book *The Cosmic Code: Quantum Physics as the Language of Nature*; Pagels is a critic of "mystical physics," so his work will, if anything, lean in the other direction. Stephen Hawking's *A Brief History of Time* is deservedly popular for its clear, concise presentation of basic contemporary ideas.

Among the books by supporters of the physics/mysticism conjunction, Nick Herbert's *Quantum Reality: Beyond the New Physics* is perhaps the best. (The nonmystical John Bell prefers Herbert's book among popular presentations, describing it as "very feet on the earth.") The classic in this field is, of course, Fritjof Capra's *The Tao of Physics*, which most everyone credits with having broken important ground, but which is also generally felt to go a bit overboard. The most fun-to-read book in this category is Gary Zukav's *The Dancing Wu Li Masters*, but it too is somewhat overenthusiastic in its presentation. (Both Capra and Zukav have gone on to write ambitious philosophical books, respectively *The Turning Point* and *The Seat of the Soul*, which have interesting aspects.)

Paul Davies has several good books, including *Superforce: The Search for a Grand Unified Theory of Nature*, *God and the New Physics* and *The Cosmic*

Blueprint. Davies's view is generally a balanced one. The ideas of Fred Alan Wolf, on the other hand, are very idiosyncratic, but quite fascinating if you can manage the density of his presentation; see *Star Wave: Mind, Consciousness, and Quantum Physics*, and *Taking the Quantum Leap*. Along the same lines as Wolf's *Star Wave*, with its attempts to explain consciousness in terms of quantum physics (or vice versa) is *Margins of Reality: The Role of Consciousness in the Physical World* by Robert G. Jahn and Brenda J. Dunne; these authors attempt to suggest both a philosophical and an experimental basis for demonstrating that a quantum model of consciousness can account for anomalous events (such as precognitive remote perception).

Regarding chaos, James Gleick's *Chaos: Making a New Science* is very popular, though its focus on people often overshadows the ideas. *Turbulent Mirror: An Illustrated Guide to Chaos Theory and the Science of Wholeness* by John Briggs and F. David Peat is somewhat hampered by its "creative" format, but it brings together a number of interesting ideas in a fairly clear way. F. David Peat has also coauthored, with David Bohm, *Science, Order and Creativity*, containing explorations in the theory of implicate order and the holographic paradigm. Also in the holographic vein is the collection of essays by diverse voices (including some critical ones) gathered by Ken Wilber in *The Holographic Paradigm and Other Paradoxes*.

Ken Wilber has done several other interesting books, including *Quantum Questions: The Mystical Writings of the World's Great Physicists*. (Wilber, by the way, argues that while parallels between physics and mysticism are enlightening, science can never actually reveal the nature of the mystical experience.) In a similar vein, Renée Weber has put together several of her interviews (with the ubiquitous David Bohm, of course, as well as Ilya Prigogine, Rupert Sheldrake, the Dalai Lama, Lama Govinda, Krishnamurti, and even Stephen Hawking) in *Dialogues with Scientists and Sages: The Search for Unity*. David Bohm and Krishnamurti did a book together, as a matter of fact: *The Ending of Time: Thirteen Dialogues between J. Krishnamurti and David Bohm*.

The whole field of research into brain/mind consciousness is so fragmented, and so generally reductionist, that it is difficult to find any recommendable works of mainstream science on these subjects. But two terrific new books by outsiders delve into these areas in most original ways. Roger Penrose, a very distinguished physicist, takes on "computers, minds, and the laws of physics" in *The Emperor's New Mind*. Todd Siler (the first visual artist to receive a doctorate from M.I.T.) explores "art, science, the mind, and the universe" in *Breaking the Mind Barrier*, with fascinating (though sometimes overly creative) results.

Omni and *Discovery* magazines are reasonably good sources of contemporary science reporting on topics such as those included here.

INTERLUDE

Quantum Exercises for Tarot Readers

"A VAST similitude interlocks all spheres, grown, ungrown, small, large, suns, moons, planets, all distances of place however wide, all distances of time, all inanimate forms. All souls, all living bodies though they may be ever so different, or in different worlds. All gaseous, watery, vegetable, mineral processes, the fishes, the fowls. All nations, colors, barbarisms, civilizations, languages. All identities that have existed or may exist in this globe or any globe. All lives, and deaths, all the past, present, future. This vast similitude spans them and has always spanned and shall forever span them and compactly hold and enclose them." This is the way Walt Whitman described the basic unity of all things—as a condition of being which has always been perceived by mystics, but is rarely grasped by most of us. Some people, it seems, are naturally gifted with an ability to see beyond the *apparent* fragmentation of the world. They may use this gift in religious life, or, like Whitman, they may express their visionary perceptions by means of poetry, painting, music, or one of the other arts.

But for the rest of us, a spiritual view of the world does not come readily. Because we are constructed in such a way that our senses take in only so much information, and because we process that information only in certain ways, it is very difficult to be aware of the unity of creation through our ordinary modes of being in the world. This does *not*, however, mean that unity doesn't exist, as we have seen in the previous sections.

There is frequently a distinction drawn between using Tarot for personal spiritual growth and using the cards for divination. Certainly, a big difference exists between either of these activities and "fortunetelling," but it should be recognized that true divination—using the cards to obtain information about the past, present, and future which is not otherwise available—depends on the same world view, and the same skills, that belong to any metaphysical use of

168

the cards. This mystical/magical world view is relatively easy to *learn about*, as is the contemporary understanding of matter and energy and time; but it is more difficult to reach a point of *thinking* and *acting* as if the things learned were true.

Even Jung had difficulty accepting the idea that synchronistic events may be as "normal" as causal events. He tended on the whole to view synchronicity as being occasional, happening in conjunction with unusual levels of archetypal intensity. His colleague, the Swiss analyst C. A. Meier (who was one of the first to investigate seriously the healing power of dreams), reports having had "a great row" with Jung over whether synchronicity was a "special" or a "general" phenomenon, with Jung insisting it was a relatively rare occurrence.[1] Jung did expand his conceptualization of synchronicity, but he never fully adopted the idea that it is an equal counterpart to causality.

Living as we do, in a society conditioned over centuries to causal thinking, it is difficult to let go of that attitude not only intellectually, but *experientially*. Yet if we are ever to achieve an understanding of Tarot divination, we must discard the human-dominated model of reality, in favor of something like the "field theory" model which animates the new physics, or the "systems" approach which is shaping new attitudes in a whole variety of studies, from neurobiology to environmental research. In these paradigms, no element can be considered in isolation from its context; the only way of determining how individual parts of a whole "work" is to understand the nature and process of the whole itself. This approach is not merely a method, it is a point of view, an outlook, an attitude.

It is crucial, if one wishes to go beyond a naive use of Tarot, to move through an attitudinal shift. The following activities may help in achieving a more intuitive grounding in some of the ideas which form the background of Tarot. They are cast not in terms of Eastern philosophy or magical theory, but in terms of our contemporary Western science, in part because I believe that for many of us, these Western images and approaches are more easily absorbed into the imagination, and in part because I think the confluence of the physical sciences with metaphysical concepts is a very exciting part of our world today. The exercises do not make direct use of the cards, and they do not relate specifically to ways of working with the cards; they are not intended to teach about Tarot or to refine Tarot skills. Instead, they are meant to help in creating new frames of mind and points of view—fundamental skills of imagining, if you will—which can broaden and enrich one's work with the Tarot.

Let's begin with this analogy: Sitting where you are right now—unless you are in a very remote spot indeed—you are surrounded by ambient "information" in the form of television signals. But you cannot *see* television unless you have a television set; the mechanism of the television set has resources for recognizing signals invisible to you, and translating them into a form which you are physically able to see. The information contained in the television picture exists all the time, whether you can see it or not; however, you cannot *ordinarily* see it. You must have assistance.

Just as television signals are not visible by means of your own built-in equipment, neither can you perceive the "quantumstuff" of which the

169

universe is made. ("Quantumstuff" is a word I've borrowed from Nick Herbert, who uses it in his book *Quantum Reality* to represent the wave/particle unity/duality which seems to be the nature of matter/energy.) What you *do* perceive is various organizations of this "stuff." You look around and see objects, people, light—all the manifestations of the physical world—as if they were distinct from one another, because that's the way you are equipped to engage material reality. We human beings perceive the world at a level where differentiation of structure has already taken place; by the time our perceptors kick in, quantumstuff has already organized itself into grass or iron or salt or muscle tissue or whatever.

Let's go a step further. When you look at a television program, you seem to see representations of people, places, things. The people move and talk just like real people; cars start, planes fly, flowers bloom, just like in the real world. But of course you are not seeing real things—you are seeing *pictures* of real things. Or are you? No, you're not. It's a double trick. You are seeing a great many dots; when these dots are viewed at a distance while their pattern changes very rapidly, the illusion of moving pictures is produced.

Well, of course you "know" all that. You know that television isn't real, and that people don't live inside the television set. But what you *know* is irrelevant; it's what you *experience* that counts. And what you experience is the sensation of watching the president board his helicopter or the weatherman point at his map. Similarly, we *seem* to see around us cars and clouds and the like, because the patterns of organization of quantumstuff—just like the dots on the television screen—are so fine and function so quickly that we are fooled. And even if we *know* (as we might if we were particle physicists or mystics) that what we are really seeing is quantumstuff at play, we nevertheless *experience* a world made up of discrete and independent objects.

Look around you. Look at everything you can see from where you are. Windows? Ceilings, floors, a lamp probably. Furniture? Your feet? Etc. This is the world as you ordinarily experience it.

Now, concentrate on the idea that all those "things" are in fact merely slightly more dense *clusters* of the same whatever-it-is that you *don't* see all around them. Imagine that they are specialized "thickenings" in the quantumstuff. Try really to *see* everything around you as if it were variations in the weaving of a single piece of fabric.

If you can do this at all, try to extend the exercise further in your imagination—outside the room, outside the building, around the world, into space, to the sun, beyond. Somewhere along the line you may find your usual conceptualizations suddenly skewing crazily; with luck, you may catch a glimpse of what Whitman was trying to describe: the unity of all things.

If the experiment worked, you will have realized that your own thinking about these things was part of the continuity that joined them all. And so was my thinking, as represented by the words on this page. And so were the thoughts of your neighbors and of the people in China and of babies in the womb. An interesting thing happens when you reduce the world back to quantumstuff; you realize that thoughts (and feelings, and dreams, and memories) are as "real" as the furniture around you or the city of Paris or the moon.

If there's no absolute line of demarcation between wave and particle, matter and energy, then there's no boundary between thought and object, form and substance. All the dichotomies we are so accustomed to disappear into the quantum flux.

Don't worry about it if nothing happens when you try the above experiment; try it again some other time. If you keep trying, something will probably happen, and you will have a drug-free psychedelic trip—though probably a very short one. Even for people of a mystical temperament, this unified view of the world doesn't usually last long unless they spend a great deal of time training, working up skill and stamina for the visionary life. For most of us, the world snaps back into its customary, functional configuration very quickly.

Still, at the ultimate reaches of physical and spiritual union, we can actually know that state of cosmic continuousness in which the subject-object distinction is lost. If you would like to experience a "sample" of this possibility, try the following: Become aware of the chair you are sitting in (or the bed you are lying down on, if that's the case). Think about everywhere your body touches the chair. What is the *exact* boundary between you and the chair? Is it where your skin touches the upholstery? No, that can't be, because your clothes (presumably) intervene. Are your clothes part of you? Not exactly; in actual substance, they have more in common with the chair than with you. But—the clothes are an extension of your self-awareness, right? You feel the clothes as if they were a second skin.

So maybe the clothes are a kind of boundary zone between you and the chair—a zone of transition from "you" to "not-you." Wait, though. Why aren't your clothes a zone of transition from "chair" to "not-chair"? Well, you *could* look at it that way.

"But why bother?" someone may say. "I'm the important one here, because I'm conscious, and the chair is not. But I'll bet you're going to ask how I know the chair isn't conscious, and then we'll get off on that silly argument. Where is all this leading?"

I'm trying to establish that there isn't an *exact* boundary between you and the chair—at least, not intellectually. But you can certainly tell the difference between you and the chair experientially, or so it seems in everyday life. Yet . . . isn't that difference actually a product of our habitual way of seeing the world? We divide everything up into subject ("me") and object ("it"). Even another person, though we know intellectually that he is a "subject" to himself, becomes an "object" in this way of thinking, because he is "not-me."

Back to the experiment: Try for a short time to let go of this habitual way of thinking. Concentrate not on the *boundary* between you and the chair, but on the *contiguity*. You and the chair are so close together that you occupy a continuous volume of space; think of the outline in space which is produced by the unit "me-in-chair." Imagine that another person comes into the room and perceives a continuous shape: "person-in-chair." Imagine an outline drawing of the shape person-in-chair, with no lines marking the boundary between person and chair, just lines defining the boundary between person-in-chair and everything else.

Now, finally, try to imagine yourself in the world not as a person, but as a person-in-chair. Can you extend your senses to the edge of the chair, to contact with the floor? You can if you'll abandon your preconceptions about where one thing leaves off and another takes up.

The purpose of all this is to explore the ways in which we construct a subject-object duality, moment to moment, all our lives. It's *not* easy to escape from this habit. But it is possible. Intimacy with another person can be a vehicle for accomplishing this change of perception. But there are other ways as well.

If you were to continue the above exercise, becoming aware of yourself as extending beyond the chair, throughout the floor, the rest of the furniture, the walls, and beyond that, as far as you could go, then you would be having what is recognized as the "mystical experience." In our society, this type of experience is mostly thought of as something you go off to a cave or a cloister to have. But of course, you needn't do any such thing. The mystical mode of perception can be achieved in your daily life, and can become the way you experience your own life in the "real" world.

One of the characteristics which seem to separate life in the real world from the infinitude of the mystical moment is the arrow of time. But as we have already seen, a life cannot be understood merely as a temporal trajectory from the launch point of birth to the crash-landing of death. Time doesn't work that way. We may *perceive* time that way, but that isn't the way time actually *is*.

Under certain circumstances—intense concentration, fear, extreme physical exertion—the passage of time loses its meaning; a very short time may seem an eternity, while a very long time may seem to flash by in moments. This phenomenon tells us that, clearly, experiential time is different from "clock" time, in that the former is variable, while the latter is fixed. Now stop for a moment and think about the nature of clock time. In what sense do such things as "minutes" and "hours" (or "months" and "years," for that matter) exist? They are conventions, conveniences. Since the experience of time is variable for each one of us, we *must* have some standard, commonly accepted units of duration in order to communicate with one another and to arrange our affairs. But each of us knows that an hour for the person making love is of very different duration from an hour for the person shelling peas or climbing Mount Everest.

The units of time measurement that we use are actually mathematical divisions of naturally occurring events—the turning of the earth on its axis, the passage of the earth around the sun, and so on. These time units fit perfectly into mathematical calculations and they are part of the description of the physical world. But—they are *not* part of the description of consciousness. Time units relate to the behaviors of matter well enough, but they are not at all useful in relationship to subjective experience. This is easily demonstrable.

Think back to some experience in your childhood. Now think about ancient Egypt. Now think about your next birthday. *Your imagination can go anywhere in time.* If you concentrate on a memory of your own past, your imagination can make that time quite "real." You can, in a sense, "be there." Or, if you are visiting a medieval cathedral, your imagination can take you back to a very realistic experience of what it might have been like to stand in that same spot nearly a thousand years ago, while the stone was still being carved, the great stained glass windows were just being pieced together, and the architects were worrying over whether the flying buttress system would really work.

"Well, that's very entertaining," you may say, "but it's all just fancy. I can't *really* go back in time." Consider that term—"back in time." We use it in this way habitually because we think of time past as being behind us somewhere, time future as being ahead of us. Yet we're always moving around, turning, shifting; so obviously your past isn't behind you in any *literal* sense, any more than your future is actually in front of you. These are just convenient spatial metaphors we use to differentiate things that have already happened or that haven't happened yet from things that are currently happening. We have to "put" the past and future somewhere in our minds, so we arrange them along the spatial pathway we imagine ourselves to be following through life, placing them so that we move away from the past and into the future.

Instinctively, we describe time as being arrayed in space, and, in fact, contemporary science tells us that our instincts are right: time *is* spatial. But it is *not* linear. Our assumption that it is linear arises because our spatial perceptions are really very limited. We have mapped space for convenience and efficiency the same way we have made working divisions of time, dividing space into directions, planes, and so on. For the most part, we conceptualize reality in the three obvious spatial dimensions (height, width, depth), and then we think of the fourth dimension (time) as if it were arranged in terms of the other three. We speak of a "length" of time, a "span" of time, a "point" in time.

Our basic sensory and mental equipment seems structured to deal with time on this relatively simple level; we remember a "past," we experience a "present," we anticipate a "future." But just as the factory-standard equipment on a car doesn't usually give the highest level of performance (a bigger engine will make the car more powerful, optional accessories will make it more functional, a deluxe interior will make it more comfortable), our own "factory-standard" equipment doesn't usually achieve our real potential for understanding time and space. We have to add on some optional features if we wish to alter our basic, limited perceptions and conceptualizations.

The car analogy is a neat one, but it will hold up only to a certain point. Obviously, we can't order perceptual options from a dealer. We already have them installed, in a sense; the trick is to activate them. And although this activation is not as simple as placing an order, neither is it as difficult as you might think. Here are a few things you can do to explore time sense:

- Run part of a video tape backwards and try to understand what is going on by watching events *enfold* instead of *unfold*.
- Keep a time diary for a few days. Use a stop watch to time each of your activities, and record how long you spend on each one (six minutes starting the laundry, thirty-seven minutes in a meeting, and so on). At the same time, note whether the activity *seemed* to take (*a*) a very long time, (*b*) not very long, or (*c*) just a second. Examine the subjective time patterns revealed.

- Listen to a piece of music, then try to estimate the duration of a minute. (Use a timer to alert you when the real-time minute is up.) Listen to another piece of music, with a different rhythm, and do the same thing again. See if your subjective perception of time is changed temporarily by the rhythmic influences of the music.
- For an hour or two, try to be aware of your trajectory through space-time. Ask yourself constantly, "Where was I one minute ago?" and, "Where will I be one minute from now?" Gradually extend your sense of yourself "now" to include yourself a few seconds in the past and a few seconds in the future.

The activities I've included in this "interlude" will provoke some thought and perhaps change some perceptions. But to precipitate real change, practice what the Buddhists call "mindfulness."[2] Be consciously aware not only of what is happening from moment to moment, but of how you are participating in that process. Consider how your attitudes are shaping "reality," and remember that mindfulness is not judgmental; merely observe and be aware. If you continue to practice mindfulness, you will find yourself and your reality changing—not as a function of will or decision, but as a function of growth and insight. The very nature of such change makes it is impossible to predict just what form it will take, or how, exactly, it will affect any person. But if such change does occur in your life, it will surely deepen your intuitive powers, and thus expand and enrich your work with the Tarot.

Notes

1. This is mentioned in an interview published in the Fall/Winter 1988 issue of *Psychological Perspectives*. The eighty-three-year-old Meier also remarks, "What I would like to do still is write a book on divination and oracles." He describes interesting instances of precognition among his patients.
2. If you wish to pursue the topic of mindfulness, see Ellen Langer's book *Mindfulness*, and also *Chop Wood, Carry Water*, by the editors of *New Age Journal*.

9.

TAROT AND THE LIFE OF THE SPIRIT

Among the many disgraces we inherit, we should do well to recognize that the greatest freedom of spirit is left to us. We ought not to misuse it. To reduce the imagination to slavery, even when it might lead to what one crudely calls happiness, is to evade whatever one finds, in the depths of the self, of supreme justice. Imagination alone tells me what can be, and that is enough to lift for a little the terrible interdict—enough also to allow me to abandon myself to this freedom without fear of self-deception.

ANDRÉ BRETON

TODAY, surrealism is identified by most people with the work of Salvador Dali and a few other artists who painted odd juxtapositions of objects and impossible configurations of ordinary things. But in its pure form in the 1920s, surrealism was a movement based on the phenomenon of automatic writing and dedicated to a revolution against the sterility of rationalism. André Breton described the surrealist idea first in the *Surrealist Manifesto*, published in 1924, and he amended and embellished it in two subsequent manifestos, in 1930 and 1942. Drawing on psychoanalysis and on occult ideas, Breton and others developed an approach to creating art directly from the unconscious. Though surrealism never became the revolutionary

175

movement Breton envisioned, it did engage the imaginations of important artists in many different media—Luis Buñuel, Max Ernst, Yves Tanguy, Hans Arp, René Magritte, Alberto Giacometti.

In 1947, a group of surrealists (including André Breton and Marcel Duchamp, a leader of the absurdist Dada movement) staged an exhibition at the Galerie Maeght in Paris. The themes of the show were esotericism and myth, and its general pattern was structured to recall the successive stages of an initiation. The first stage of the process began as the visitor climbed a flight of twenty-one steps. According to the exhibition catalog, these steps were "shaped like the spines of books inscribed with 21 titles corresponding to the 21 major arcana of the tarot," as follows:

1. The Showman [The Magician]: Maturin, *Melmoth the Wanderer*.
2. The Popess: XXX, *Life and Death of the Facteur Cheval*.
3. The Empress: J. J. Rousseau, *Reveries of a Solitary Walker*.
4. The Emperor: Frazer, *The Golden Bough*.
5. The Pope: Baudelaire, *Flowers of Evil*.
6. The Lover: Hölderlin, *Poems of Madness*.
7. The Chariot: Sade, *Justine*.
8. Justice: Eckhart, *Sermons*.
9. The Hermit: V. Andreae, *Christian Rozencreutz's Chemical Nuptials*.
10. The Wheel of Fortune: Kafka, *The Trial*.
11. Strength: Lefebvre des Noëttes, *The Harness and the Saddle Horse through the Ages*.
12. The Hanged Man: Brisset, *The Science of God*.
13. Death: Apollinaire, *The Rotting Enchanter*.
14. Temperance: Swedenborg, *Memorabilia*.
15. The Devil: Jarry, *Ubu Roi*.
16. The God House [The Tower]: Goethe, *Faust*.
17. The Star: Fourier, *Theory of the Four Movements*.
18. The Moon: Forneret, *And the Moon Shone, and the Dew Fell* . . .
19. The Sun: Hervey Saint-Denys, *Dreams and How to Control Them*
20. Judgment: John, *Apocalypse* [*The Book of Revelations*]
21. The World: Isidore Ducasse, *Complete Works*

The part of The Fool, we assume, was to be played by the viewer, as he or she climbed the steps and then proceeded through several rooms before reaching a hall with twelve octagonal recesses, each one "dedicated to a being, a category of beings, or an object *capable of being endowed with a mythical life.* . . ."

Though I haven't found out just who thought up the Tarot stairs, or how the books were assigned to the trumps, it seems the whole thing must have been conceived by people who knew a good deal about the Tarot, because the nature of each book chosen says something very interesting about the trump it represents. The whole image of the staircase/library, moreover, brings together symbolically two potent traditional views of the major arcana: first, that it is a repository of old and vast knowledge, and second, that it symbolizes a path of ascension through various levels of spiritual attainment.

As I was casting around for some new way to bring together all the elements which make up the mystery of Tarot, it occurred to me that the surrealists' Tarot stairs could provide a unique point of departure. The beauty of the list is not only that each book serves—through its title, its content, and its historical context—to illuminate the trump it represents, but also that, taken all together, the titles comprise references to virtually every aspect of the Tarot: mysticism, alchemy, magic, prophecy, imagination, symbolism, nature, society, and the dreaming unconscious. What's more, the Galerie Maeght surrealists were concerned with themes—of history, poetry, and the modern condition—which have scarcely been considered in most commentaries on the Tarot.

To begin: If you aren't familiar with all the books mentioned (and I hasten to say that *I* was not!), let me take you on a quick tour. I've included, where possible, brief quotes which seem to reflect the connection of the work with the associated trump.

Melmoth the Wanderer: [The Magician] A gothic novel of the Romantic period by Irish writer Charles Maturin (1782–1824), concerning the dangers of the metaphysical quest.

> Then the Wanderer raised his heavy eyes, and fixed them on Melmoth. "The secret of my destiny rests with myself. . . . If I have put forth my hand, and eaten of the fruit of the interdicted tree, am I not driven from the presence of God and the region of paradise, and sent to wander amid worlds of barrenness and curse for ever and ever?"

Life and Death of the Facteur Cheval: [The High Priestess] This is, according to the creators of the exhibition, an imaginary title; they may have chosen a book that never existed to represent an historical figure ("Pope Joan") who never existed.

Reveries of a Solitary Walker: [The Empress] An expression of the "back to nature" philosophy propounded by Swiss-French Enlightenment philosopher Jean-Jacques Rousseau (1712–1778).

> The flux and reflux of the water, its ceaseless stir, swelling and falling at intervals, striking on ear and sight, made up for the internal movements which my musings extinguished; they were enough to give me delight in mere existence, without taking any trouble of thinking.

The Golden Bough: [The Emperor] The pioneering work on magic and primitive religion by Scottish classicist and anthropologist Sir James Frazer (1854–1941).

> The danger, however, is not less real because it is imaginary; imagination acts upon man as really as does gravitation, and may kill him as certainly as a dose of prussic acid.

Flowers of Evil: [The Pope] This poetic exploration of ugliness and sin was the principle work of Charles Baudelaire (1821–1867), the French Romantic poet who inspired the poets of the Symbolist school.

> *I skirmish and I climb to the attack,*
> *I, a worm's chorus on a corpse's back,*
> *O fierce cruel beast, I cherish to the full*
> *The very chill that makes you beautiful.*

Poems of Madness: [The Lovers] A collection of poems by Friedrich Hölderlin (1770–1843), the German poet whose style bridged the classic and Romantic periods—and who really *did* go mad. (I do not know which of Hölderlin's poems may have been included, but this passage is from a prose translation of one well-known poem written during the early years of his mental illness.)

Spring comes. And each thing blossoms according to its kind. But he is far away, no longer with us. He now went astray; for spirits are all too good; now heavenly conversation is his.

Justine: [The Chariot] The most famous novel of the libertine Marquis de Sade (1740–1814), depicting the triumph of force over virtue.

It is not virtue which maintains our criminal associations; it is self-interest and egotism; hence this praise of virtue that you drew from some ephemeral hypothesis is disproved.

Sermons: [Justice] Collected sermons of the German mystic Meister Eckhart (1260–1327), who expressed most of his insights into the process of union with God through his preaching.

When the soul, being kissed by God, is in absolute perfection and in bliss, then at last she knows the embrace of unity, then at the touch of God she is made uncreaturely, then, with God's motion, the soul is as noble as God is himself. God moves the soul after his own fashion.

Christian Rozenkreutz's Chemical Nuptials: [The Hermit] An early seventeenth-century alchemical fantasy, which contributed to the beginning of Rosicrucianism.

> *This day, this day, this, this,*
> *The Royal Wedding is.*
> *Art thou thereto by birth inclined,*
> *And unto joy of God design'd?*
> *Then may'st thou to the mountain tend*
> *Whereon three stately Temples stand*
> *And there see all from end to end.*

The Trial: [The Wheel of Fortune] Perhaps the best-known novel of German writer Franz Kafka (1883–1924), in which the protagonist finds himself inexplicably the subject of an absurd trial.

Under the street lamps K. attempted time and time again, difficult though it was at such very close quarters, to see his companions more clearly than had been possible in the dusk of his room. "Perhaps they are tenors," he thought, as he studied their fat double chins.

The Harness and the Saddle Horse through the Ages: [Strength] Published in 1931, and subtitled "A contribution to the history of slavery," this book argued that the invention of the breast harness in the tenth century contributed to the decline of slavery in Western Europe.

The Science of God: [The Hanged Man] I have been unable to find any information on this book or its author. Neither are included in any bibliographies of either theological works or French literature.

The Rotting Enchanter: [Death] A novel by Guillaume Apollinare, the French avant-garde writer who provided the link between symbolism and surrealism.

When the fruit is ripe, it drops and doesn't wait for the gardener to come and pick it up. Let man, that fruit ripening freely on the tree of light, do the same.

Memorabilia: [Temperance] Emanuel Swedenborg (1688–1772) was a Swedish scientist, philospher, and theologian, but he is best known for his detailed accounts of his many visionary experiences.

Every created thing is finite because all things are from Jehovah God through the sun of the spiritual world, which most nearly encompasses Him; and that sun is composed of the substance that has gone forth from Him, the essence of which is love.

Ubu Roi: [The Devil] This play, by French dramatist and novelist Alfred Jarry (1873–1907) gave rise to the so-called "theater of cruelty." It concerns the rise, fall, and inevitable return of an evil king.

Ubu: You're quite right, it's the Russians. I'm in fine shape now! If only there was some avenue of escape, but there isn't; we're on a hilltop, exposed to every blow.

Faust: [The Tower] Seminal re-telling by German writer Johann Wolfgang von Goethe (1749–1832) of the Faust legend, in which a man bargains with the devil to gain ultimate knowledge.

> *Am I a God? It grows so light!*
> *And through the clear-cut symbolism on this page*
> *My soul comes face to face with all creating nature.*

Theory of the Four Movements: [The Star] A book which presented the theoretical foundation of a utopian movement created by French reformer and economist Charles Fourier (1772–1837).

Voluptuousness is the sole arm which God can employ to master us and lead us to carry out his designs: he rules the universe by attraction and not by force.

And the Moon Shone, and the Dew Fell . . .: [The Moon] This short story was published in 1836, but I have been unable to discover anything else about it, or about its author.

Dreams and How to Control Them: [The Sun] André Breton referred to this work in the opening pages of his essay "The Communicating Vessels," but I cannot find any other information about it. However, since dreaming was a topic of great interest to the surrealists, it seems likely that the book was about just what its title implies.

Apocalypse: [Judgment] The Book of Revelations, last book of the New Testament Bible, attributed to St. John; it records a vision of the events which herald the end of the world, and an account of what happens next.

And now I saw a great throne, all white, and one sitting on it, at whose glance earth and heaven vanished, and were found no more. Before this throne, in my vision, the dead must come, great and little alike; and the books were opened.

Complete Works of Isidore Ducasse: [The World] This is a surrealist joke, for Isidore Ducasse (under the pseudonym Lautréamont) wrote only one work, *Les Chants de Maldoror*—a piece of poetic prose regarded by the surrealists as an early example of "unconscious writing."

In this eclectic group of references, there are several themes being developed through subtle relationships among the books and authors. One theme is the legend of the Fisher King. This story, of a land which is barren because its king is wounded in both body and spirit, is included in Frazer's account of divine kingship, and it is often an element in accounts of the Grail quest—which, as you'll remember from Part One, have been linked with the Tarot (especially through the figures of The Emperor and The Hanged Man). In fact, Jesse L. Weston explored the Fisher King myth in her influential book *From Ritual to Romance*, where she also made a connection between the four suits of the Tarot minor arcana and the four Grail Hallows.

One of the people influenced by *From Ritual to Romance* (and also Frazer's *The Golden Bough*) was Nobel Prize winner T. S. Eliot, who used the Fisher King theme—and the Tarot images—in his famous poem of modern angst, "The Waste Land." Part of the structure of that long poem is set up in a card-reading given the burnt-out protagonist by "Madame Sosostris, famous clairvoyante." Eliot tells us in his notes to "The Waste Land" that his knowledge of the Tarot is slight, and that he has made arbitrary associations, but the images he creates will seem very resonant to anyone who is familiar with the Tarot:

> *Madame Sosostris, famous clairvoyante,*
> *Had a bad cold, nevertheless*
> *Is known to be the wisest woman in Europe,*
> *With a wicked pack of cards. Here, said she,*
> *Is your card, the drowned Phoenician Sailor,*
> *(Those are pearls that were his eyes. Look!)*
> *Here is Belladonna, the Lady of the Rocks,*

The lady of situations.
Here is the man with three staves, and here the Wheel,
And here is the one-eyed merchant, and this card,
Which is blank, is something he carries on his back,
Which I am forbidden to see. I do not find
The Hanged Man. Fear death by water.

Eliot tells us that he associated The Hanged Man with the Hanged God figure discussed in *The Golden Bough*, and that "The Man with Three Staves" (the Three of Wands) he associated, "quite arbitrarily, with the Fisher King himself."

Eliot has borrowed from Shakespeare, of course, in his creation of The Phoenician Sailor; "Those are pearls that were his eyes" is a line from the spirit Ariel's song in Shakespeare's great play about magic, *The Tempest*. And Eliot's Belladonna, the Lady of the Rocks, is reminiscent of the Sirens of Homer's *Odyssey*, whose sweet singing lulls the passing sailors and lures their ships onto the rocks. With these allusions to great works of Western literature, and through his invention of new Tarot images (as he says, "to suit my own convenience"), Eliot seems to be telling us something about the way in which archetypes shape the imagination, and how they are given form through creative expression.

In his notes to "The Waste Land," Eliot also refers several times to Baudelaire's *Flowers of Evil*, which brings us back again to the Tarot stair. Poet Stephen Spender, in an essay written long after the Galerie Maeght exhibition, calls Baudelaire "the Fisher King of the modern Waste Land, lord of somber realms, looking out over the future with eyes that prophesy the downfall of the age of progress, and also looking back to the past when men and women were gods and goddesses." One message of Baudelaire's poetry—which is ironically linked with The Pope on the Tarot stair—is that spiritual values are so absent from the modern world that it is difficult even to become damned! And in keeping with this idea, further along the stair we find that The Devil is represented not by Marlowe's Faust, who, like the other Faust characters of legend and literature, loses his soul to the devil, but by Goethe's Faust, who is saved from his damnation—not by the grace of God, but by the power of secular love.

Goethe's Faust is often thought of as the prototype of "modern" man, whose thirst for technological supremacy and alienation from spiritual values have, in fact, gone a long way toward turning the earth into a wasteland. There are other titles along the Tarot stair which pick up this somber theme: *Ubu Roi* (about the bitter fate of a land where kingship has turned to evil), *Justine* (the brutalization of innocence), *The Trial* (the mindlessness of bureaucracy), *Apocalypse* (the collapse of civilization). In the world depicted on the Tarot stair, divine order is dead, virtue is vanquished, and the only hero is a visitor who wanders around playing The Fool.

But perhaps it is not surprising that the main message of the Tarot stair is a bleak one—that just two years after the end of World War II, a group of artists would discover in the authority figures of the Tarot shades of evil dictatorship

181

and empty religion; or that after the Holocaust, they would see in The Chariot the rape of innocence; or that, remembering Hiroshima, they might imagine Judgment to be the Apocalypse. The astonishment may really be in the fact that there is also at work on the stair a thread of hope. Rousseau and Fourier are there, imagining a return to the beauty and harmony which are functions of the "right" natural order. And a transcendental cast of characters—Meister Eckhart, Swedenborg, Christian Rozenkreutz—represents the possibility of mystical enlightenment and the process of personal transformation.

The surrealists left for us, in their Tarot stair, a message which still speaks out urgently and eloquently. It is a message about the counterpoint—of brutal reality and fragile aspiration, material limitations and spiritual expanses—which illuminates the very essence of Tarot. Through the Tarot, we may encounter both the brilliances and the deep shadows not only of our own natures, but of human nature. We may use the Tarot as a text through which to interpret and to project events on the plane of physical existence; we may also use the Tarot as a ladder, to climb from level to level of understanding, to climb beyond the limited view of our own self-preoccupation and reach a vantage point from which the trials of "real" life may be recognized as part of a larger pattern. From each step on the stair, we may survey the world differently, and it is only by making the whole ascent that all these visions can be combined into a fuller understanding of *what is*.

Part 3
LORE

PROLOGUE

THE world of contemporary Tarot is a diverse and lively one. It includes a host of cheerful amateurs who pull out their decks every once in a while for inspiration and illumination, as well as a growing group of accomplished professional readers, many with training and experience in more conventional forms of psychological practice. In between these two poles are serious students who may spend considerable time and money in the pursuit of Tarot—collecting decks, attending seminars, buying videos and Tarot parphernalia.

Those interested in Tarot have benefitted from the recent wave of "New Age" enthusiasm, for although it has fostered much silliness, it has also created a marketplace that is hospitable to ideas which were once considered "crackpot" or worse. Where once only a few Tarot decks were available, and those had to be ordered by mail or tracked down in obscure locations, today there are dozens of decks, many of which can be found for sale in chain bookstores and in shopping malls.

I have tried, in the first two parts of this book, to provide some tools for navigating in the world of Tarot, and for analyzing the many ideas and experiences to be encountered there. In this part, I shall offer something more along the lines of a catalog, listing the considerable array of supplies available to those who wish to outfit themselves for the exploration. It is my hope that newcomers to Tarot will find in these lists of Tarot lore a useful overview of the territory, and that old hands will discover here some things they had not known about.

It is up to each individual, of course, just how much is needed in the way of Tarot gear. Some would say that the best way to learn Tarot is to buy any deck at random and make up your own way of working with it. Indeed, some Tarot enthusiasts today prefer to leave tradition behind entirely and make their own decks, using photographs, bits of fabric, wallpaper—whatever moves them. But there are many others who feel that a thorough grounding in Tarot tradition is desirable; they would suggest extensive reading, careful choice of a deck, and much practice under the supervision of a teacher.

The upshot of all this is simply that there is no "right" way to go about discovering the Tarot, or deepening your enjoyment of it. There may, however, be something of a "wrong" way, and that is to take literally the opinions of any single person or any Tarot school. That is why I think it's important to be aware of the whole range of Tarot lore, so that ideas can be compared and different experiences can be tried on for size. I hope the following information will make it easier for everyone interested in Tarot to achieve the broadest possible view of the subject, and so to derive the greatest possible pleasure and enlightenment from its pursuit.

A SAMPLING OF TAROT DECKS

Y OU walk into a store that carries Tarot decks. There may be a dozen or two dozen sets of cards to choose from (still only a fractional part of the decks that are commercially available). Many of the decks you see, though they may differ in color and style, have enough elements in common to outweigh their differences; clearly, they are Tarots. But some—those with pre-Columbian designs or photographs of outer space, for example—seem altogether different, not only from one another, but also from the basic concepts of the historical Tarot.

Any thoughtful person, surveying the variety of cards available, is going to ask several important questions. For one thing, how are the various decks related—and can they all be "true" Tarots? For another, why are there so many types of Tarot images—and how can each person choose the most appropriate Tarot deck(s) for his or her own use?

First, let's consider what constitutes a "true" Tarot, by comparing some of the contemporary "Tarot-like" decks, such as Motherpeace, Voyager, and Xultún, with traditional Tarot cards. The Motherpeace deck features round cards and images related to ritual and folk-life, evoking especially the themes of Goddess-worship; Voyager uses photomontage to create other-worldly impressions of the great archetypal structures; and Xultún cards are filled with colorful Mayan-style glyphs. Twenty of the Xultún major arcana cards are named after the days of the Mayan calendar; the Voyager minor arcana, meanwhile, changes Swords to Crystals, Pentacles to Worlds, and court figures to Sage, Child, Woman, and Man.

These are just a few of the many deviations which some of today's "Tarot" decks make from their conventional models. The images on these cards are creative interpretations of Tarot "concepts" rather than renderings of the essential Tarot images; the names and even the shapes of the cards may be different, the content of the images may be completely unrelated to the traditional Tarot subjects, and the deck may have its own distinctive divinatory structure. These alternative decks can be very interesting, mysterious, provocative, and contemporary—but at the same time, they do not have the weight of the long Tarot tradition behind them. They are cut off from much of what has been thought and written about Tarot, for most Tarot commentary has focused on illuminating the "core images": Emperor and Empress, Wheel of Fortune, Coins, Pages, and so forth. Without these core images, can a Tarot card really *be* a Tarot card?

In my opinion, no. Something centrally important about a Tarot card changes when there is a shift in imagery, and there comes a point when the degree of change is so great that something new has been created. For example: The Empress originally depicted a regal woman seated on a throne, and represented the female aspect of civil order; there was nothing at all mythic or metaphysical about her image. Then, in many of the decks that evolved from the occult revival of the late nineteenth century, The Empress was placed in a garden, where she seems to represent the feminine principle of fecundity and natural being. If you look at these two types of Empress cards side by side, it is plain to see that the images evoke different kinds of psychological responses.

But even in these two different treatments, a seated female figure remains the core image of the card, and the card's name—"The Empress"—tells us something specific about this woman's place in the scheme of things. If an alternative Tarot deck were to have a card called "The Mother," depicting a woman suckling a child, or if it had a card called "Overwoman," with a female figure astride a jewel-bedecked horse, there would be not only a significant change in the message of the card, but also a massive departure from the place which this card historically occupies in the Tarot structure. The extra dimensions of meaning that have been added to the iconography of the Empress card by more than a century of interpretation are effectively lost.

So, for both psychological and intellectual reasons, I believe the term "Tarot" is best used when it is confined to those decks which preserve the core images of the cards, either in their early, exoteric versions, or in their later esoteric versions. A factor of continuity is vital, not only for students of Tarot theory and history, but just as certainly for those concerned with divination, because the whole reason *why* there has been so much thought given to the Tarot is that the core images have an exceptionally strong imaginative resonance—and so serve particularly well as "evocators" in the divination process.

Within the parameters of these core images, however, there is much room for diversity, and no reason not to enjoy it. From the reader's standpoint, imaginative and emotional response to the look of the cards is very important, and the wide variety of decks makes it possible for each individual to find a Tarot that excites the imagination. The core images can be portrayed in any way at all—they can be crudely sketched or elaborately drawn, traditional or contemporary, bright or pastel—and they will still remain the same in their usefulness and effect; the figures can be dressed up as Egyptians or as medieval nobility or as American Indians, and the essential imagery can remain intact.

Furthermore, a core image can be surrounded with all sorts of other images, whether meaningful or merely decorative, and the result will *still* be a Tarot card. For example, in the classic Marseilles decks, The Hanged Man holds a small bag, while in the Waite deck he loses the bag but gains a halo, and in Crowley's Thoth deck, a snake is added. Yet all of these renditions of the card are alike in their essence, because they center on a certain metaphysical/emotional concept that is captured in the image of the hanging man.

This unity-in-diversity is possible because the Tarot *as an image system* exists separately from its actualization in a particular set of cards. The core images are part of Tarot as a *mental* structure, while the renditions are part of Tarot as a *physical* system which *evokes* the mental images. Thus, the way in which the images are rendered doesn't change the meaning of the images. Visual style is still quite important, however, since different ways of rendering have different psychological effects. That's one of the reasons why so many different Tarot decks have been created over the years, and why new decks are still being produced and sold today. Among all these decks, each one, whether classic or modern, has a character entirely its own—romantic, dramatic, austere, lush, ethereal, menacing, elegant, rustic, ethnic, futuristic, even erotic.

There truly is a Tarot not only for every reader, but for every mood. Psychological variety, however, is not the only reason why so many different Tarot decks exist. Some Tarots appear because artists can't resist the desire to express themselves through the vehicle of Tarot images. Others are conceived in order to illustrate some particular philosophy or to make the Tarot more "relevant" to modern life. And still other Tarots are published to reproduce early or historically important decks. In one sense, the earliest of these historical decks are the "truest" versions of the Tarot, because they duplicate the cards as they actually looked in long-ago times, near the beginning of their known history. But in another sense, such cards are not very representative at all of the "true" nature of the Tarot, since the cards were looked upon then in a very rudimentary way.

For the beginning reader, the essential question is simply how to choose among the various Tarots, and the advice most frequently given is to pick the one you find especially attractive or emotionally affecting. That advice may not be entirely satisfying, however, given the wide variety of choices available. What's more, it may not be the best advice; some readers find they do best with a deck that is *not* aesthetically interesting to them. Visual intrigue may actually be a distraction which interferes with the dynamics of reading, and a design which "appeals" to you—much as a pet, a song, or a poster might—could be too comfortable to provide challenge, and too weak to counterbalance your own strengths. The same is true for those intending to use the Tarot for magical or meditative purposes, for some tension between the deck and the aspirant can be creative.

I've divided the best-known and most readily available Tarot decks into categories below, and I have some personal suggestions for those seeking a Tarot deck. First, decide what your immediate goal is and pick a deck which will help you reach that goal in the most positive way. If your primary interest is in learning to read predictively, select a deck that is colorful, straightforward in its presentation, well-documented, and filled with conventional symbolism. The Rider-Waite deck meets all these criteria, and it is far and away the most popular choice for beginning readers, but if you don't care for the bright primary colors of the Rider-Waite, the Aquarian deck offers a more muted and stylish rendition of the same iconography. (The three other decks listed below as "classic" decks for readers are probably not the best ones for beginners because they don't use pictorial representations for the minor arcana. Pictures make it *much* easier to develop a sense of the meanings of the pip cards.)

If, on the other hand, you are more interested in using the Tarot for meditation or magical pathworking than for predictive reading, then consider the decks listed under the "esoteric" heading or the "historical" categories. (Among historical decks, some readers feel the more simple and primitive pre-nineteenth-century designs are best for esoteric purposes, while others like the occultist context of the nineteenth- and early twentieth-century decks.) Black-and-white decks are also excellent for these purposes, since the owner of the deck has an opportunity to develop a deep rapport with the cards during the process of coloring them. Crowley's Thoth deck is also found by many to be useful for magical work as well as for reading, though it is not to everyone's taste.

Beyond the beginning stage of Tarot acquaintance, new considerations take on importance. Once you have become familiar with the use of the Tarot, you will want to expand your horizons and explore different decks. In making these next choices, I think it is important to be objective about yourself. Are you too sentimental? Then perhaps it would be interesting to choose a deck that is hard-edged and provocative rather than romantic or fantastic. Too analytical? Try something artistic and archetypal. And if you're too future-oriented, consider a deck from the past.

In other words—the obvious choice of a deck may be a too-easy choice. Consider having one or two decks that you spontaneously enjoy, and one or two that you have to work to establish a relationship with. The following listings will provide a starting point for finding the deck(s) you need/want. I have limited the listings to five in each group, and there are many more decks which are not included here, but I've chosen those which are both interesting and readily available. For further inspiration and information, you can consult the ultimate guide, Stuart Kaplan's three-volume *Encyclopedia of Tarot*, which includes every known Tarot deck, whether commercially published or privately issued. Kaplan provides illustrations from every deck, but offers no analysis. Rachel Pollack's book *The New Tarot*, on the other hand, covers around seventy modern decks published up to 1990, and gives highly personalized commentary on each, along with illustrations.

For a look at virtually all the currently available cards, along with an easy way to order the one(s) you want, just send two dollars to:

U.S. Games Systems, Inc.
179 Ludlow Street
Stamford, CT 06902.

U.S. Games is the central fountain from which Tarot decks flow in this country, and for your two dollars, they will happily send a full-color catalog containing a rich selection of Tarot cards, along with a few books and some related games.

In addition to the mass-produced decks you will find in catalogs and bookstores, there are also some privately published decks available from their authors. The best way to find out about these decks is to join a Tarot networking group and/or subscribe to a Tarot newsletter. Information about these options can be found below in the section called "Tarot Miscellanea."

The ultimately personal deck is, of course, one you make yourself. The books and catalogs already mentioned will provide inspiration, as will some of the ideas shared in newsletters or at Tarot workshops. The books *Tarot for Your Self* by Mary K. Greer, and *The Complete Tarot Workbook* by Nancy Garen also offer useful suggestions for creating your own Tarot. Blank cards may be obtained from U.S. Games if you want to use the typically sized and shaped Tarot card format.

And now, a basic guide to "ready-made" decks for all tastes and reasons.

The Classic Readers' Decks

The Rider-Waite Tarot Deck
The Aquarian Tarot
Thoth Tarot Deck
Tarot of Marseilles
Tarot Classic

These are the decks you are most likely to see being used by professional readers, or to encounter in Tarot classes. The Marseilles deck is the oldest, and has a slightly grotesque appearance to the modern eye; the Classic is very similar in iconography, but has a somewhat more refined style. The Rider-Waite and Aquarian decks are the same sort of pair—virtually alike in content, with the first appearing rather childlike, the second artful and carefully finished. As for the Thoth deck, its swirling backgrounds and haunting images create a unique impression; those who are drawn to the deck find it a very powerful reading instrument.

Esoteric Decks

The Royal Fez Moroccan Tarot Deck
The Golden Dawn Tarot
Gareth Knight Tarot Deck
The Magickal Tarot
Masonic Tarot Deck

These decks have little in common in appearance, but they are all distinguished by their claims to bring special occult symbolism and atmosphere to their renditions of Tarot. How well each succeeds is a matter of personal opinion. The first two are rather delicately drawn, the other three very bold.

Black-and-White

The Brotherhood of Light Egyptian Tarot Cards
Rolla Nordic Tarot
B.O.T.A. Tarot Deck
The Hermetic Tarot
Ravenswood Eastern Tarot

Once again, radically different visual styles with one thing in common: the cards may be colored by hand according to the owner's inclinations. The B.O.T.A. deck is very similar to the Rider-Waite; Rolla Nordic resembles the Marseilles; the Brotherhood of Light deck is Egyptian; Ravenswood uses Persian motifs. The Hermetic Tarot is much more complex and finely drawn than any of the others.

Historical Interest: Fifteenth through Eighteenth Centuries

Visconti-Sforza Tarocchi Deck (mid-fifteenth)
Tarot de Paris (early seventeenth)
I Tarocchi del Mantegna (mid-fifteenth)
Tarot Vieville Deck (mid-seventeenth)
Vandenborre Bacchus Tarot (late eighteenth)

The Visconti-Sforza and Mantegna decks are principally of historical interest, since the Visconti-Sforza is very hard to read with and has little esoteric symbolism, while the Mantegna deck is not a true Tarot. The Paris, Vieville, and Vandenborre decks, however, could be used by anyone who likes the Marseilles-type deck; but unlike the Marseilles and the Classic, these decks do not have English titles added, so you must either read French or recognize the cards!

Historical Interest: Nineteenth and Twentieth Centuries

Etteilla Tarot Deck (early nineteenth)
The Epinal Tarot Deck (early nineteenth)
Oswald Wirth Tarot Deck (late nineteenth)
Papus Tarot Deck (late nineteenth)
Knapp-Hall Tarot (early twentieth)

The Etteilla pack is not a true Tarot, but it is interesting; many of the traditional Tarot images are present but renamed, and additional structures have been added to expand the fortunetelling aspect of the cards. Both the

Epinal and Knapp-Hall resemble the style of popular book illustrations of their times (ca. 1830 and 1930 respectively), which makes them an interesting pair for historical contrast. The Wirth deck, meanwhile, features unexceptional versions of the traditional images, enhanced by a metallic gold background. Perhaps the most interesting of this group is the stylishly drawn, vaguely Egyptian Papus deck, but it is not historically authentic; the cards available today are later versions of the original drawings published in *The Tarot of the Bohemians*.

Artist's Conceptions

Dali's Universal Tarot
Tarot Madonni
Ditha Moser Jugendstiltarock
Pointner Tarot Deck
Ansata Tarot Deck

These decks just have to be seen to be appreciated! Here is the best I can do in hinting at their various qualities: Salvador Dali's deck is wonderfully surreal (what else?), each card filled with surprises which include perfectly rendered little allusions to famous works of art, wrapped in Daliesque ribbons of color. The Ansata deck (major arcana cards only), by artist Paul Struck, is also surrealistic in style, but it adheres more closely to tradtional Tarot images. Silvia Madonni's designs feature pale, flowing people with expressive faces, their clothes and hair billowing everywhere. The Ditha Moser is a 1906 Tarock pack done in the *Jugendstil*, or "young style," which gave a distinctive look to design in turn-of-the-century Vienna. And Rudolf Pointner's cards are covered with wildly colorful patterns and graffiti-like images which create a stunning, carnival-like effect.

Special Interest: Symbolism and Mythology

Jungian Tarot
The Mythic Tarot
Barbara Walker Tarot
The Norse Tarot
Celtic Tarot

Each of these decks is distinguished by its attempt to heighten a certain aspect of Tarot symbolism. The Jungian deck features mandalas integrated into the design of the cards, while the Mythic deck uses figures from Greek and Roman mythology for its illustrations. Barbara Walker's deck is aggressively colored and filled with symbolism relating to Goddess-worship and women's magic. The Norse and Celtic Tarots offer specific adaptations of Tarot imagery by using figures and styles from Scandinavian and Celtic myth and art.

Special Interest: Periods and Styles

> *Medieval Scapini Tarot*
> *Renaissance Tarot*
> *Art Nouveau Tarot*
> *Egipcios Kier Tarot Deck*
> *Native American Tarot Deck*

This group borrows from the visual arts of particular times and places to create special atmospheres for the cards. The titles are probably self-explanatory, but just to pique your art-historical imagination—the Scapini looks like illuminated manuscripts, the Renaissance deck features classical figures, Art Nouveau resembles Tiffany lamps, Egipcios Kier is remindful of Egyptian tomb paintings, and the Native American Tarot features lots of feathers, with motifs that resemble Pueblo pottery. The Scapini deck captures the flavor of the Visconti-Sforza pack, but would be much easier to read with, since the cards are a more manageable size, and unlike the Visconti-Sforza, they have numbers and names on them.

Special Interest: Fantasy and Romance

> *Tarot of the Cat People*
> *Tarot of the Ages*
> *The Merlin Tarot*
> *Hanson-Roberts Tarot Deck*
> *Solleone Tarot*

For fans of fantastic art (1 and 2), players of Dungeons and Dragons (3), followers of fairy tales (4), and/or lovers of Middle Earth (5), these are the cards!

Pop

> *Cosmic Tarot*
> *Tarot of the Witches*
> *Morgan-Greer Tarot*
> *Arcus Arcanum Tarot*
> *The Sacred Rose Tarot Deck*

And for those who still love comic books and cartoons, here is a group of cards which use styles of illustration that will remind you of Batman, *Sleeping Beauty*, and the Illustrated Classics series. These may be fun to read with if they suit your taste, but they probably don't lend themselves to deeper uses.

Whimsy

The Wonderland Tarot
Gatti Originali (The Feline Tarot Deck)
Tarocco delle Collezióne (The Puppet Tarot Deck)
The Topsy-Turvy World (Animal Tarock Deck)
Fumatori Tarot Deck

This group of novelty decks includes, in order: highlights of Alice's adventures underground (suits are Flamingos, Peppermills, Hats, and Oysters!), pen-and-ink drawings of cats doing unlikely things (major arcana only), pictures of very odd marionettes, animals dressed up like people, and Tarot figures smoking meerschaum pipes (major arcana only). What more is there to say?

In A Class By Themselves

The Herbal Tarot
Gipsy Tarot Tsigane
Yeager Tarot of Meditation
Karma Tarot
Tavaglione's Tarot

These decks have nothing in common with each other, and they don't fit into any of the other classifications. For herbalists, the Herbal Tarot is a delight; each card features an appropriate herb, integrated into attractive designs which use the traditional Tarot images. Gipsy Tarot Tsigane doesn't have much (if anything) to do with Gypsies, but it's very pretty, with luminous pointillist designs. The Yeager Tarot of Meditation features figures which seem to glow against perfectly still backgrounds. Karma Tarot uses jolting juxtapositions and illusions of motion to create an eerie, dreamlike deck. And finally, each card in Tavaglione's Tarot—also called the "Stairs of Gold" Tarot—includes just about every symbol and esoteric reference that can be crowded into one design; they are really quite pretty, with the images encircled in ornate gold frames, bearing Sanskrit letters, Latin labels, zodiacal correspondences, Hebrew attributions, Kabbalistic keywords, and more!

Alternative Tarots

The Motherpeace Round Tarot Deck
Voyager Tarot
Xultún Tarot
Morgan's Tarot
Medicine Cards

Some of the cards mentioned in the previous categories—the Mantegna, the Etteila, and the Ditha Moser decks—are not "true" Tarots, and some—the whimsies and the cartoon-style cards—are not "serious" Tarots. But all of them have enough in common with the traditional Tarot to be part of the mainstream. The cards in this group, however, are unconventional in more substantial ways. Though the Motherpeace deck (which I like very much, by the way) uses many Tarot images, it also makes many departures from Tarot tradition, including the round shape of the cards. Voyager, which uses photo-montage to create often-stunning visual effects, shares some of the Tarot's structures, but preserves little connection with the core images. Xultun employs Mayan glyphs that are often reminiscent of the Tarot core image, but substitutes its own structures (such as "twenty steps to enlightenment") for those of the traditional Tarot. And then there is Morgan's Tarot, which can best be described as a set of sixties-style neo-Buddhist aphorisms, illustrated with laid-back pen-and-ink sketches. Last of all, Medicine Cards—forty-four different animal cards and nine personal cards—have absolutely nothing in common with Tarot except that they are frequently liked by the same people who are interested in Tarot, and they are found in the same section of the store!

A TAROT BOOKLIST

BROWSING in the Tarot/Occult/New Age/Metaphysical section of a large bookstore presents the same problem as shopping for a Tarot deck. There are dozens of books—but which ones are worth buying? Which ones do you need for your particular interests?

To provide a starting point for the bewildered book-seeker, I've compiled some descriptions and opinions about a wide range of Tarot books. The listings include the majority of books in print as I'm writing this, along with some out-of-print books which may be found in libraries and stores that carry used books. Though it certainly isn't true (as I sometimes think) that a new Tarot book is published every day, it does seem that more come out than I can keep up with, so there will certainly be several new titles on the shelves by the time you read this. For newcomers to Tarot, however, it may be best to begin with some of the tried-and-true books I've recommended below, especially those mentioned as highly recommended, or as suitable for beginners.

Let me offer right now, to the authors of all the books I've missed, and to authors whose books I may have described or evaluated inadequately or inaccurately, a thousand apologies in advance. I have not tried to list every possible Tarot and Tarot-related title; Stuart Kaplan's *Encyclopedia of Tarot* does that magnificently. But Kaplan's huge bibliographic compilations mix together books that are mainly about Tarot (and actually available to the average book-seeker) with books that don't even mention Tarot, unpublished manuscripts, books in other languages, and codexes that exist only in the Vatican Library or some such. This approach makes the *Encyclopedia* an invaluable reference, but an impractical guide to the real-life process of finding out about Tarot books suited to particular needs.

My own criteria for listing a book are these: (*a*) that it is, or has been, commercially available, and (*b*) that it is significantly concerned with Tarot. In a few cases, where a title would lead one to believe that a book is about Tarot when it really isn't, I've mentioned the title in order to forewarn the reader. An evaluation of a book is offered only if I have seen it, read a review of it from a respectable source, or know someone whose opinion of the book I deem trustworthy. Otherwise, I have just included the title of the book and whatever miscellaneous information I have about it, with the hope that readers will be provoked or inspired to track it down and take a look.

My personal recommendations are based on personal values, of course, and some books I don't like may appeal to others. The basic characteristics I look for in a book are intelligence, accuracy, originality, usefulness, and accessibility. In general, the only books which rate a "no" from me are those which I think actually demean or distort the Tarot in some significant way. In some instances, I've also given a "no" to books which I think are not a good value, because some other book does a significantly better job of covering the same material.

The rest of the books mentioned, though I don't recommend against them, are not all described with the same degree of enthusiasm, by any means. I've tried to identify in my remarks which books I found adequate but uninspiring, and which ones I thought were flawed but interesting. There are a few cases where I've indicated my personal fondness, just to reveal my own tastes a bit more clearly. In many instances, however, my impressions of the books are based on casual acquaintance rather than careful study, so I want to stress that my remarks should be taken *only* as suggestions—certainly not as anything definitive.

In order to give the books themselves a voice, I've included wherever possible a quote which I think captures in brief the author's style and approach; in general, I've selected quotes which express interesting ideas and/or convey something about the author's central point. There is only one quote provided for each author, regardless of the number of books listed by that author.

Though most of the books included here are in print (in the sense that they are listed in the 1992 *Books in Print*), they may not be easy to find, especially in small bookstores. Some can be ordered from the U.S. Games catalog mentioned above, and all should be available by special order or directly from their publishers. To contact one of the publishers listed, look up its current address in one of several directories that should be available in the reference section of your public library: the *Literary Marketplace*, *Books in Print*, or the *Writer's Market*.

Many publishers specializing in metaphysical, occult, or alternative publications will be happy to send you their catalogs, either free or for a modest charge. An excellent way of getting on the mailing lists of several publishers—such as Inner Traditions and Bear & Co.—at one time is to use the "Catalog Connection" order card featured in *New Age Journal*'s annual *New Age Sourcebook*. The *Sourcebook* can be found on newsstands throughout most of the year, and though it is oriented more toward "lifestyle" matters than metaphysical ones, there are always quite a few products and publishers represented which might be of interest to anyone involved with the Tarot. To find out about other publishers—such as Samuel Weiser and The Aquarian Press—who will send you catalogs, consult the *Writer's Market*.

Perhaps the best alternative for getting the book(s) you want is to use one of the services that takes phone orders for all titles currently listed in *Books in Print*. Try the following:

The Reader's Catalog
1-800-882-8770

Book Call
1-800-ALL-BOOK

Be sure to look up information on the book prior to ordering. Have the full title, the correct spelling of the author's name, and for extra insurance, the ISBN number (a unique multipart number assigned to every book published, appearing on the back cover of most books and in the *Books in Print* listing).

Tarot titles will sometimes be found in the listings of discount book services; these books are generally "remaindered," which is to say all remaining copies of the book have been sold by the publisher to a company which then sells them to the public at substantially discounted prices. If you are interested in building your Tarot library and doing a little bargain-hunting at the same time, you may want to receive these catalogs:

Edward Hamilton
Box 15-700
Falls Village, CT 06031

Strand Book Store
828 Broadway
New York, NY 10003

I've noted in the book listings below those titles which are currently out of print. Given the brisk interest in Tarot books, some of these books may have been reissued by the time you read this. But some good books are, for one reason or another, out of print forever; and some books of specialized or primarily historical interest just will not generate a big enough market to justify reprinting. So if you want any of these out-of-print titles, you will have to be resourceful. They don't appear as often in used bookstores as one might like, but keep an eye open; they may also turn up in the discount catalogs listed above. If there is a title you are particularly interested in, contact a company that specializes in finding out-of-print books. You may have such a service locally, but if not, try one of these:

Avonlea Books
Box 74T
White Plains, NY 10602
1-800-423-0622

Phoenix Bookfinders
P.O. Box 527
Plainview, NY 11803
(516) 938-8192

Book services which specialize in metaphysical titles include:

Raven Rare Books
P.O. Box 595482
Dallas, TX 75359

Todd Pratum Books
P.O. Box 1214
Glen Ellen, CA 95442

These sources (along with many others which can be found through advertisements in some of the periodicals I've suggested) will also send catalogues of selected stock for mail order purchase. An extensive stock of rare and out of print books is also maintained by Samuel Weiser. Write:

Glen Houghton
Weiser Antiquarian Department
Box 612
York Beach, ME 03910

Finally, you can at least *read* some out-of-print books—and even some current ones—by borrowing from a library. Most public libraries, even small ones, have at least one or two Tarot books; if you live in an area of small towns, it might be worthwhile to contact several of the libraries near you, since there's no telling what may have found its way onto their shelves. Check college libraries, too.

One other option is the Olcott Library, operated by the Theosophical Society since 1926. A small annual fee entitles you to receive up to three books at a time by mail; all you have to do is pay the postage and get the books back within six weeks. The Olcott has quite a few titles specifically on Tarot among their more than twenty thousand books and periodicals, which cover all aspects of philosophy and spiritual growth. The staff there is extremely helpful, and you can request lists of the library's holdings on specific topics. For further information, write:

Olcott Library & Research Center
P.O. Box 270
Wheaton, IL 60189

THE BOOKS

Almond, Jocelyn, and Keith Seddon. *Tarot for Relationships*. Aquarian, 1990.
Although this book does not offer a deep treatment of relationship issues, or of the Tarot, it is nevertheless distinctive because it presents both traditional meanings of the cards and interpretations constructed specifically along the lines of sexuality and personal relationship. It brings out more of the sexual content of the Tarot than is usually shown, but this is done in a tasteful way. It is illustrated with the Norse deck.

For instance the conceptual relationship between the masculine, extrovert, energetic Magician, and the masculine, powerful, radiating energy of the Sun, is a fairly obvious point, and typical of Tarot symbolism and philosophy; as is the conceptual relationship between the feminine, introspective, mysterious High Priestess or Papess and the feminine, pale, mysterious, eerie Moon.

Anonymous. *Meditations on the Tarot*. Elements, 1985.
This is an a very long and wide-ranging book, written in the format of letters to an aspirant. It deals extensively with Hermetic Christianity. There is a sweet, unassuming spirit to the book, and much interesting lore. The Tarot, however, is more a vehicle than a subject.

The High Priestess warns us of the dangers of gnosticism in teaching the true gnosis.

Arrien, Angeles. *The Tarot Handbook: Practical Applications of Ancient Visual Symbols*. Arcus, 1987.
This is a fine book—intelligent and practical. It places Tarot in a much broader theoretical context than is commonly found in Tarot books. Arrien offers an array of interesting ideas and connections, drawing on various cultures and disciplines to create a multifaceted approach to Tarot.

Just as psychological and spiritual information is revealed to us in our dreams or in contemplative states, the Tarot functions as an outer mirror of external experiences and internal psychological states as well. In using the Tarot and looking at it from a humanistic and psychological perspective, these symbols can teach us a lot about our own psycho-mythology.

Blakeley, John. *The Mystical Tower of the Tarot*. Watkins, 1974.
A very esoteric book which presents a fascinating and detailed case for connection of Tarot with the Ancient Mysteries, with a focus on the Sufi tradition; although Idries Shah has hinted at a connection between Tarot and Sufism, Blakely is the first to examine the idea in depth. Within a wide-ranging and most scholarly framework, Blakeley includes the complete text of Sir Fairfax L. Cartwright's 1889 Sufi-inspired allegory, "The Mystic Rose from the Garden of the King," and analyzes its resemblances to Tarot imagery. A rewarding book for the serious student. Out of print.
According to the Tarot symbolism, the path [of return] is from Pentacles, through Swords or Shuttles, through Cups for reabsorption into the initial sheath of consciousness as signified by the unifying power of the Wand. This is the Ascent of the divine spark from incarceration in the constricting sheath of matter, through withdrawal of mental activity; through the sheath of knowledge; with final absorption in the sheath of bliss where only the life principle remains.

Buess, Lynn. *The Tarot and Transformation*. DeVorss, 1977.
This book is a slightly odd—but interesting—combination of psychological ideas and Theosophy-style metaphysics. It's illustrated with Egyptianized Tarot images (reminiscent of the Church of Light deck, but less refined), and deals with topics, such as reincarnation, the seven rays, and the divine spark, which are not generally addressed on Tarot texts.
The very nature of dualities provides the basis of free will, for if total predeterminism prevailed, duality would not exist. The aspiring mortal on the Path restrains himself from attacking divergent ideas.

Butler, Bill. *Dictionary of the Tarot*. Schocken Books, 1977.
Bill Butler has created a very useful book, though it is not what one might expect from the title. There is a short (and very eclectic) glossary, but the main part of the book is devoted to a card-by-card examination of the Tarot deck, comparing the designs of several decks, including Marseilles, Waite, Aquarian, Crowley, and the interpretations of various commentators, including Papus, Case, Crowley, Mathers, Waite, Gray, and a shifting cast of others. This unusual approach allows us to see differences as well as similarities in the way the cards have been understood by various artists and authors. Butler's book is wonderful for acquiring (or restoring) a sound perspective on the nature of the Tarot, as well as for tracing the historical development of Tarot ideas.
Jung recalls, in Symbols of Transformation, *the Mithraic saying: "I am a star that goes with thee and shines out of the depths." And many of the meanings attributed to stars involve, in some way, the quality of movement: the Star of Bethlehem guiding the Three Wise Men, the order of stars and their function in primitive as well as scientific timekeeping, the forces of the spirit struggling against the forces of darkness, the force of the universe expanding and thus implying the mystic centre.*

Campbell, Joseph, and Richard Roberts. *Tarot Revelations*. Vernal Equinox, 1982.
The bad news about this book is that Joseph Campbell's short essay is disappointing. Misled by a too-early dating of the Tarot's appearance in Europe, he writes about the exoteric Tarot in the context of the images and ideas in Dante's works, but unfortunately, the comparison doesn't hold up well. Nevertheless, it's interesting to see Campbell's creative imagination at work on the Tarot. And Roberts's material, which makes up most of the book, is very valuable, since he develops in great detail the alchemical connections of Tarot which have only been hinted at elsewhere. Advanced.

As we recall, alchemy commences with an ascent, the subsequent descent uniting above and below. Since Tarot begins with a descent, Keys 1–15, we shall begin our discussion from the place of the abyss, Keys 13–15. The archetypal, unmanifest One descended to duality down the Stairway of Planets, where at the abyss, in Saturn's realm, the help of the alchemist had to be sought to liberate (volatilize) the now-concretized One.
(Richard Roberts)

Case, Paul Foster. *The Tarot: A Key to the Wisdom of the Ages.* Builders of the Adytum, 1974.
This book offers a clear—if sometimes laborious—exposition of the "modern" (i.e., early twentieth-century) approach to Tarot. Case focuses mainly on the symbolism of the trumps, which he discusses in relationship to Kabbalism and Hermetic science, as well as in psychological terms. Serious students will find this book rewarding, for two reasons. First, each card's chapter contains some interesting, occasionally unexpected ideas; this is a good book to turn to when having trouble "getting in touch" with a particular card. (Though one must wade through a fair amount of useless information in the process.) Second, the book provides the attentive reader with an insight into the atmosphere of early modern occultism, as "Americanized" by Case. It is keyed, of course, to the B.O.T.A. deck.

The High Priestess wears a blue-white robe, suggesting coldness and moisture, which are the astrological properties of the Moon, and the characteristics of the element of water. The folds of this robe show a shimmering radiance, like that of moonlight on water, and, below the white pillar, this garment seems to flow out of the picture, like a stream. It symbolizes the "stream of consciousness" familiar to students of psychology. In Tarot, the robe of the High Priestess is the source of the river and of the pools which appear in several subsequent major trumps.

Cavendish, Richard. *The Tarot.* Crescent Books, 1986, 1975.
This oversized and heavily illustrated book is much more than just a coffee-table adornment. Cavendish, an authority on magic and its history, provides excellent information about the cards and their interpretations. (The information on divination, however, is scanty and very traditional.) A lengthy section devoted to each of the trumps traces symbolic associations from many cultures and times, drawing together various aspects of occult history and relating them to the Tarot. Illustrations are wide-ranging and thought-provoking (rather than merely decorative), and each is thoroughly documented. Altogether, a beautiful and informative book, of special interest to the intermediate student and the collector. Highly recommended, but out of print.

Crowley was not the first to see the cards in this light. On the contrary, sexual symbolism is seldom far beneath the surface of the most pious and outwardly respectable of the earlier books on the Tarot, including Waite's, which is riddled with innuendo. This does not mean that the earlier authors practised sexual magic, as Crowley did, but it does imply a less austere attitude to sex than is attributed to them by pure-minded admirers.

Clarson, Laura E. *Tarot Unveiled: The Method to its Magic.* U. S. Games Systems, Inc., 1988.
Clarson conveys the basic principles of Tarot readership in a friendly, uncomplicated way, providing many practical hints, along with helpful keywords and combinations. The book is compact and well-organized, making it an excellent handbook for the beginning to early-intermediate reader. More experienced Tarot students may want

to take a look at it as well, since Clarson's creative approach to reading will spark some ideas. Keyed to the Hanson-Roberts deck.

The Tarot reader acts as the intermediary between the universal mind and the client. The Tarot does not and will not reveal all that the client would like to know—only the information he should know *to handle most successfully the situation in question.*

Compton, L. C. *Archetypes on the Tree of Life: The Tarot as Pathwork.* Llewellyn, 1991. Another book on magical pathworking with the Tarot, this one with Jungian embellishments. The book is very thorough and orderly, and it will be useful to those who want to pursue the pathwork approach. Each card is given detailed treatment, including an explanation of the imagery, a list of correspondences, an exercise, a guided visualization, and a group of affirmations.

We must keep in mind that, although many modern Qabalists include in the Tree [of Life] *gods and goddesses from a variety of cultural pantheons, the system arose because the* attributes *of such deities matched the attributes of the Sephiroth. We know that there are many correspondences between the Greek and Hebrew myths—the* Aeneid *is very similar to* Exodus, *for example—probably because they both stem from the same Palestinian source.*

Connolly, Eileen. *Tarot: A New Handbook for the Apprentice.* Newcastle, 1979.

_____. *Tarot: A New Handbook for the Journeyman.* Newcastle, 1979.
These are attractive books, and they are among the very few which actually try to teach the skill of reading. "Thought tracks" created by the author to aid learning, focused exercises, and a format which makes it easy to access several dimensions of meaning for each card all contribute to create the appearance of a useful textbook for the aspiring serious reader. And to some extent, this appearance is valid; there are some good ideas here, and the step-by-step approach is very helpful. But on closer inspection, one realizes that Connolly's presentation of Tarot is unnecessarily complex and somewhat idiosyncratic. There are many very particular religious/esoteric ideas assumed in the books, presented as if they were more central to Tarot than they are.

Remember that the Tarot always reveals what the client needs *to know—not necessarily what he* wants *to know.*

Crowley, Aleister. *The Book of Thoth.* U. S. Games Systems, 1977.
The definitive key to the symbolism of Crowley's famous Thoth deck, this book also includes many snippets of good thinking, along with occasional insights into the mind of the self-styled "Great Beast." It's surprisingly sensible, pungently written, and rich with ideas. A classic—anyone seriously interested in Tarot should take a look.

It has consequently been the endeavour of the present Scribe to preserve those essential features of the Tarot which are independent of the periodic changes of Aeon, while bringing up to date those dogmatic and artistic features of the Tarot which have become unintelligible. The art of progress is to keep intact the Eternal; yet to adopt an advance-guard, perhaps in some cases almost revolutionary, position in respect of such accidents as are subject to the empire of Time.

Curtiss, Harriette, and F. Homer Curtiss. *The Key to the Universe.* Newcastle, 1983.

_____. *The Key to Destiny.* Newcastle, 1983.
The Curtisses were founders of "The Order of Christian Mystics," and these books (originally published in 1919 and 1923) were among many they wrote on metaphysical subjects early in this century. Their personalities come through so vividly

here that a whole bygone world of esoteric movements seems to come alive. The two books provide unusual connections between Tarot and esoteric Christianity; *The Key to the Universe*, for example, explicates ten of the trumps through the ten commandments. The many specific Biblical references—along with wide-ranging references to other traditions, and clear accounts of many metaphysical doctrines (some peculiar, some naive, and some quite appealing!)—make this a valuable work in spite of its old-fashioned presentation.

> *The evolution of the planet has taught us that out of imperfection is perfection builded up and brought forth, hence there is nothing to grieve over or regret if an experience has tended toward our perfection and completion, for the earth today is of the same substance as that which was breathed out as fire-mist in the beginning, but under a different phase of expression.*

D'Agostino, Joseph. *The Tarot, The Royal Path to Wisdom*. Samuel Weiser, 1976.
A thoughtful book, focusing on the symbolism of the Rider-Waite deck.

> *Fundamentally, the Hermit is a portrayal of the collective unconscious, the recorder and preserver of all manifestation, and the container of all potential possibilities available to man at any given time.*

Denning, Melita, and Osborne Phillips. *The Llewellyn Practical Guide to the Magick of the Tarot*. Llewellyn Publications, 1983.
The books in the Llewellyn series, in spite of their somewhat popularized presentations, frequently offer interesting ideas. This volume describes an approach to the Tarot which uses the cards not only to predict, but to change, the future. There are lucid explanations of the nature of the unconscious and its powers; the fundamentals of "magickal" practice; and the nature and use of archetypal imagery. Also covered are ideas for ritual and psychological activities, including meditation, visualization, dramatization, and dance. Throughout, there are concrete details, examples, and suggestions, along with concise study guides and summaries for each chapter. While the tone sometimes seems simplistic, many of the ideas are valid and the approach is provocative.

> *Unlike "passive" meditation, a Tarot Ballet needs for magical purposes only one complete performance: but there is nothing adverse in repeating it as often as you wish, either for practice or for delight. On the other hand, unlike Tarot Drama, Tarot Ballet neither needs nor should have any "locking" meditation afterwards.*

Doane, Doris Chase, and King Keyes. *How to Read Tarot Cards*. Harper & Row, 1979.
This book, originally published as *Tarot-Card Spread Reader*, is based on the ideas of C. C. Zain, but its emphasis is on fairly ordinary fortunetelling. Roughly half the book is devoted to a variety of complex spreads, while the individual cards are developed only by providing a list of key phrases such as "unexpected gain" or "hidden forces at work." Perhaps the most useful aspect of the book is its considerable emphasis (following Zain) on astrology in connection with the Tarot; an extensive summary of basic sun sign correlations is provided. Keyed to the Church of Light deck.

> *Being plastic, the subconscious bends to each new thought or idea presented to it. Therefore, to focus it requires control. So the subconscious mind should be impressed with what to expect. Then the required rapport will result if orders were given firmly and backed up with will power. A systematic approach allows the subconscious to know what is expected of it. This approach is based upon clearly defining the question, selecting an appropriate spread, and shuffling and cutting the cards in the same manner each time.*

Douglas, Alfred, *The Tarot: The Origins, Meaning and Uses of the Cards*. Penguin Books, 1972.

This very serviceable book was among the more sensible works published during the "Tarot revival" of the late sixties and early seventies. Douglas offers an even-handed review of various ideas about the Tarot and its origins, including a nice summary of Gnostic influences on the Tarot and speculation concerning the connection between Tarot and the Grail Hallows. Douglas's treatment of divination and the card meanings is quite traditional, but oddly enough, it's illustrated with thoroughly untraditional drawings of the pip cards (the Three of Batons, for example, has a dolphin on it!). The book includes a brief, clear chapter on meditation with the Tarot cards, as well as an explanation of the game of Tarocco and a very eclectic bibliography.

> *How these four ancient and sacred symbols, the Four Treasures of Ireland, or Grail Hallows, came to be used as suit-marks on playing cards (or if indeed there is any connection between them) is a mystery, but it can be seen that the symbolism of the Tarot lesser arcana is not isolated. . . . The Tarot symbolism of cup, baton, sword and coin cannot be restricted to one tradition only, any more than can the emblems of the major trumps. The quaternary of opposing yet complementary symbols is found in many places at many times, and the Tarot suits represent the coming together of several cultural streams.*

Drury, Nevill. *Inner Visions: Explorations in Magical Consciousness*. Routledge & Kegan Paul, 1979.

_____. *Music for Inner Space: Techniques for Meditation & Visualisation*. Prism Press, 1985.

The first of these most interesting books is concerned with the relationship between magic and the creative imagination; the second analyzes the uses of music to "tune" states of consciousness. Both include material specifically on the use of the Tarot for visualization. *Inner Visions* offers a good explanation of the Golden Dawn practice, as well as suggesting how readers may use the Tarot for expansion of consciousness; the book also covers in some detail the concepts of Surrealism, the theories of Jung and of John Lilly, and various visionary trends in contemporary music and visual art. *Inner Space* offers more detail concerning specific activities, and suggests particular musical works to correspond with each of the Tarot trumps. Stimulating books for the serious student.

> [Meditation on The Wheel of Fortune:] *We have come to a mighty gateway—doorway to the peak of the mystic mountain. On this gateway is a wheel of light which slowly rotates, sending forth pulsing waves of energy. As the wheel turns, different gods come into view upon its rim. We are journeying toward the very heart of the Cosmos.* Appropriate music: *"Theme Three" from Colosseum*, Valentyne Suite: *"Dreams Like Yesterday" from Kitaro*, Silver Cloud. (From *Inner Space*)

Dummett, Michael. *The Game of Tarot*. U. S. Games Systems, 1980.

This very large (six hundred pages!) work devotes about two-thirds of its space to the various games played with Tarot cards, but the first third is given over to an historical introduction to the cards which contains much worthwhile information. Dummett's interest in the cards is entirely historical, rather than esoteric, and his critical approach to esoteric theories and writers provides a useful counterbalance to most other Tarot literature. But at the same time, some of his historical presentation seems biased and occasionally even inaccurate.

_____. *The Visconti-Sforza Tarot Cards*. George Braziller, Inc., 1986.
An introductory essay sets forth Dummett's version of Tarot history, and the rest of the book is devoted to the iconography of the Visconti-Sforza deck.

Tarot was first devised in either Milan, Ferrara, or Bologna. My choice would be Ferrara, because the atmosphere of the d'Este court there—irreverent, pleasure-loving, steeped in romance, devoted to play of every kind—was conducive to such an invention, but there is no actual evidence that tips the balance in favor of any one of the three. . . . The three traditions associated with the three principal Italian centers of the game of tarot differ, not in the composition of the packs, but in the manner of representing the trump subjects and, surprisingly, in their order. The cards whose positions in the sequence vary the most are the three virtues of Temperance, Fortitude, and Justice. Apart from these, the only important variation concerns the highest trump, which is sometimes the Angel and sometimes the World.

Fairfield, Gail. *Choice Centered Tarot*. Newcastle, 1985.
An exceptionally open and easy-to-read book, *Choice Centered Tarot* regards the Tarot as a tool for focusing intuition and working on life issues. Fairfield demonstrates no particular philosophical assumptions or esoteric interests, and follows no Tarot tradition; rather, she proposes a kind of do-it-yourself approach to the cards, utilizing a basic understanding of symbolism and some general, growth-oriented psychological models. "Choice centered Tarot" might well be thought of as "humanistic Tarot" or perhaps "relativistic Tarot," since the whole reading process—preparation and interpretation of the cards, pattern of the layout—is seen as a function of the individuals involved, their moods, goals, etc. Fairfield's chapter on choosing a deck suggests some unusual considerations concerning gender, race, class, and other forms of social symbolism in Tarot imagery.

In some traditional [Tarot] texts, a male image on a card immediately indicates a quality of control, command, aggression, or leadership. A female image represents qualities of passivity, nurturing, submission, or receptivity. In this analysis, women who have assertive qualities are seen as going against nature. A traditional text might say something like, "If the querent is a woman, this card shows that she is a shrew and a troublemaker . . . if a man, this card shoes that he is strong and commanding." Men who are sensitive are seen as weak. Another text might read "If the querent is a man, this card shows that he is ineffective and not respected . . . if a woman, this card shows she is strong in wifely qualities."

_____, and Patti Provo. *Inspiration Tarot: A Workbook for Understanding and Creating Your Own Tarot Deck*. Samuel Weiser, 1991.
This is a nifty workbook, which provides just what the title promises. There's a two-page spread for each card—on one side, a large outline, suitable for drawing or composing card images, and on the other, a form for organizing ideas and information about the card. The notebook page for each card features three brief interpretations of the card's meaning, one by Fairfield, one by Mary K. Greer, and one by Vicki Noble.

Fenton, Sasha. *Fortune-Telling By Tarot Cards: A Beginner's Guide to Understanding the Future Using Tarot Cards*. The Aquarian Press, 1985.

_____. *Tarot in Action: An Introduction to Simple and More Complex Tarot Spreads*. The Aquarian Press, 1985.
These are nice practical handbooks for the beginner interested in a traditional fortunetelling approach to Tarot; they are compact, conveniently arranged, and

brightly written. There are some easy-to-apply original ideas, too. However, the use of an uncommon deck (the "Prediction Tarot"), and especially one which has no images on the pip cards, is a limiting factor for beginners. *Fortune-telling* has several nice features, including keys to health problems, and an unusual system of timing.

Lastly, and probably most importantly, one must make a point of "closing down" after any kind of psychic work. If you are familiar with the chakra centres, then close them one by one in the way in which you have been taught. If this is all Greek to you, then I suggest that you use this method which was passed on to me by my friend Davis Bigham, who is a professional psychic. Pretend that you are climbing into a sleeping bag, imagine that you are pulling it up over your head and then tying it up on the top of your head. If you don't do something to close down after any kind of psychic work then you will find it hard to get to sleep and may pick up other people's feelings of depression, or even their ailments! (From *Tarot in Action*)

Franklin, Stephen E. *Origins of the Tarot Deck: A Study of the Astronomical Substructure of Game and Divining Boards*. McFarland & Company, 1988.

The author of this book has certainly worked out an elaborate theory, which purports to trace the Tarot back to a board game and to link it with the history of other games, such as chess. There are many connections, allusions, and calculations, and at first it seemed to me that none of this was very convincing or enlightening, especially considering the effort involved in following the author's reasoning. But after a determined effort, I unearthed Franklin's point (I think!), and armed with this insight, a second go at the book was much more interesting. Approach this book with patience—and to give you a head start, I'll reveal that Franklin believes the Tarot (along with chess and pachisi) to be one fragment of a divinatory instrument dating back to the time of Pythagoras. (One more hint: Stonehenge and Velikovsky and the realignment of the Greek alphabet also figure in here.)

I was left without a board for my hypothetical Tarot men. The rectangular shape of the cards, however, suggested a solution. If one were to take a large illustrated game board and separate it into individual squares, discarding any that were unmarked, the result would be a stack of square pictures resembling a deck of cards. . . . Such an original board from which the cards might be cut would probably have four equal areas of at least 14 squares each, plus enough room to house the 22 trumps, or 21 if The Fool were excluded. Any blank spaces should be readily explainable in terms of the rules of the game or the former use of the board.

Freer, Jean. *The New Feminist Tarot*. The Aquarian Press, 1987.

Though the feminist note here is occasionally a bit distracting (especially the many different spellings of the word "women"—wymn, womben, etc.), this is a thoughtful and distinctive book. Freer's insights into the significance of the Tarot and the subtleties of the reading process will be of interest to intermediate readers looking for fresh perspectives. Traditional interpretations and spreads are given mild "Dianic" (Wiccan) revision, with a result that is provocative but not confrontational. There are excellent remarks on shuffling and on inversions, along with a very good set of keywords for both the major and minor arcana cards. A surprising—and very useful glossary of words pertaining to esoteric studies (and feminist Wicca) rounds out the book.

As Hawaiian Kahuna magic teaches us, the more a channel is travelled, the stronger it becomes. Our intention for the future definitely effects its unfoldment. Hence the importance of only giving our energies to what we wish to accompany us into the self-created future. It is with this insight that we integrate people and nature, earth and heaven, space and time, receptivity and creativity. This vision is an entirely new quality of life.

Gardner, Robert. *Evolution Through the Tarot*. Samuel Weiser, 1970.

_____. *The Tarot Speaks*.

Richard Gardner's eccentric approach to Tarot was for a while considered influential, which is why I've included his books here. They are a matter of personal taste, and are currently out of print.

[Speaking as The Empress:] *Like all female powers, I was greater in the past and taught you many things. You tunnelled the earth at my instruction and constructed many imitations of my womb, and held rituals in them that opened you to feed upon my life and magic giving powers. All places of worship were imitations of my womb where you sought to dance in patterns like those that make life inside.* (From *The Tarot Speaks*)

Gearhart, Sally, and Susan Rennie. *A Feminist Tarot: A Guide to Intrapersonal Communication*. Persephone Press, 1977.

This book pioneered the feminist interpretation of Tarot, paving the way for later commentators like Freer, Noble, and Walker. It's quite short, and does little more than offer mildly feminized meanings for the individual cards; no conceptual structure, no theoretical overview, no historical background. But the commentaries are economical, often elegant, and reflective of a sound philosophical sensibility. The material is well arranged, offering (in amusingly small print) traditional meanings alongside the authors' own interpretations. Out of print.

A mutual movement takes place through the magician: the dark synthesizing powers of the psyche rush to meet the bright analytical powers of the mental. Light makes materiality aware of itself and the dark gives spirit something to be aware of. Experiences are illuminated; thoughts are embodied. The magician is the channel.

Gettings, Fred. *The Book of Tarot*. Triune Books, 1973.

This coffee-table book does have serious content, but it's rather idiosyncratic; Gettings's attributions of meaning to the cards will be unfamiliar to many people who know the cards. Most of the book is taken up with an iconographic analysis of the major arcana cards. Gettings has developed an unusual approach to the cards, in which he isolates certain shapes—squares, diamonds, stars, etc.—formed by the graphic elements of the picture, then interprets these shapes symbolically. There are frequent comparisons with alchemical imagery, early Christian symbolism, and so on. The approach seems to me somewhat limited, and the presentation opinionated, but the book could be thought-provoking.

[On The Star:] *The positioning of the pitcher in the woman's left hand, covering her pudenda, is a clear association of the creative energies with sexual energies.*

Golowin, Sergius. *The World of the Tarot: The Secret Teachings of the 78 Cards of the Gypsies*. Samuel Weiser, 1988.

The author of this book offers a contemporary reinterpretation of the Gypsy theory of Tarot history. He presents some arguments which are intriguing, and even persuasive, though certainly not definitive. There are also some interesting illustrations. Much of the book, however, is devoted to a fairly standard fortunetelling approach to the cards.

The gypsies in Switzerland today call all playing cards (but especially those used for divination) "joni." The "j" is pronounced like the English "y". The Vedic word yoni originally meant path, resting place, seat. Over the ages, this word took on such meanings as source, womb, birth, class, caste, race, homeland, life, lifetime, body (as the container of the soul), etc. The root means "to set in motion."

Gray, Eden. *Complete Guide to the Tarot*. Bantam, 1971.

————. *Mastering the Tarot*. New American Library, 1988.

Eden Gray's books have introduced generations of curious seekers to the basics of Tarot. They offer a clear, easy-to-follow presentation of mainstream Tarot interpretations. *Mastering the Tarot* is in a lesson format, and concentrates on card meanings and basic spreads; *The Complete Guide* takes the reader a little further, into topics such as meditation and numerology.

It may be helpful to think of the Tarot as representing the spokes of a huge wheel upon which each of us travels during his life on earth, experiencing material and spiritual ups and downs. These are reflected in the cards when they are laid out by a Reader— their positions, juxtapositions, and combinations are all significant. The Fool, representing the Life-force before it comes into manifestation on the earth plane, is in the center of the wheel, moves to its outer edge through 21 phases of experience, and then returns to the center whence it came. [From The Complete Guide to the Tarot]

Greer, Mary K. *Tarot Constellations: Patterns of Personal Destiny*. Newcastle, 1988.

————. *Tarot for Your Self: A Workbook for Personal Transformation*. Newcastle, 1984.

————. *Tarot Mirrors: Reflections in Personal Meaning*. Newcastle, 1988.

All three of these books are lovely—well-designed and insightful. *Tarot for Your Self* is entirely concerned with using Tarot cards for personal growth, and provides a workbook/journal format that is more enticing than most similar efforts. Ideas, exercises, rituals, examples, and information are all plentiful. There are chapters on such unusual topics as healing and use of crystals with the cards. Interpretive keys for each card are intelligent, wide-ranging, and useful; each card is also given an unsentimental but inspirational "affirmation" derived from the card's nature. There are many provocative and easy-to-implement suggestions (such as using metallic pens to enrich the colors of the usually pale Rider-Waite cards). All in all, *Tarot for Your Self* is a book for the ambitious, exploratory student of Tarot, and the same can be said for the other two, which go further afield to build connections with a variety of other metaphysical disciplines and to elaborate entirely new ways of using the Tarot. All highly recommended.

The key to all occult and divinatory work is the personal intention of the seeker. If your intention is focused and positive, all things are possible. Therefore, you must intend to make a commitment to explore and experience the meanings of the [Tarot] images at personal, archetypal, and transpersonal levels. The key to transforming these symbolic mirrors into doorways to "non-ordinary reality" is what some call magic: "the art of changing consciousness at will." You can do it by using the light of your imagination and the energy of your emotions to "set your intention" and then move forward through the portals. [From Tarot Mirrors]

Haich, Elizabeth. *Wisdom of the Tarot*. Aurora Press, 1983.

Haich treats the Tarot major arcana images as an initiatory sequence, and attempts— with intermittent success—to combine metaphysical doctrines with psychological interpretations. Unfortunately, there is something about the tone of this book which prevents me from liking it. Others have found it rewarding, however, and I can see that there are some thought-provoking points sprinkled through the book.

A human being at the level symbolised by tarot card 17 [The Star] is like a shining star in the dark sky. Just as the planets shine in the night because they reflect the light of the sun, so man passes on the light he receives from God. He radiates love and light to all who come into contact with him and he shines like a star with his wisdom and deep faith in God.

Hall, Manly P. *The Tarot: An Essay*. Philosophical Research Society, n.d.

As in most of his works, Hall manages to present a great deal of esoteric lore from an objective, no-nonsense perspective. Those who like the approach of this short work will want to see the chapter on Tarot in Hall's masterwork, *An Encyclopedic Outline of Masonic, Hermetic, Qabalistic and Rosicrucian Symbolical Philosophy* (a lavishly illustrated and *very* oversized production, but now available in a relatively affordable paperback edition). Though some of Hall's work seems outdated today, there is still much worthwhile information to be gleaned, and Hall's clearsighted attitude toward esoteric subjects is an excellent model for all seekers.

Always, however, symbols draw their meanings from those attempting to interpret the designs. In this way, symbolism stimulates imagination, strengthens the observation of the soul faculties, and invites the intellect to practice reflection and contemplation. Each human being must interpret formless symbols as he interprets life: that is, in the light of personal experience.

Hasbrouck, Muriel. *Tarot and Astrology*. Inner Traditions, 1987.

This book, originally published as *The Pursuit of Destiny*, is a complete departure from typical Tarot books, but it is surprisingly interesting nonetheless. Hasbrouck discovered, in Israel Regardie's published version of the Golden Dawn papers, a document which inspired her to identify the Tarot pip cards as the key to a system of ten-day cycles, based on the solar year, which she feels offers a more refined approach to defining personalities and their interactions than that of conventional astrology. I was at first suspicious of the whole idea—but every single birthdate I looked up here proved to be remarkably accurate in its description of the person in question. Hasbrouck supplies positive and negative tendencies, along with suggestions for methods of balancing the two. The style of the book is intelligent and appealing, for the most part, and offers an unusual way of using the Tarot.

The ten-day cycle formula serves to throw new light on the question of why the pack of cards is constructed as it is, who constructed it, and the possible object of its invention. This question, too, requires a chapter to itself, which will be found later in the book. In passing, let us merely recall the rather pertinent statement made by Alice—just as she was growing to her full size, and leaving Wonderland for reality—that the human race is nothing but a pack of cards. *Lewis Carroll, who created Alice, was a mathematician in his leisure moments, and many people have suspected that behind the Carroll fantasies lurk hidden truths.*

Heline, Corinne. *The Bible & the Tarot*. DeVorss, 1981.

Heline has written many books on esoteric Christianity, and in particular, on the Bible, which she regards as "the supreme spiritual textbook of life." Here, she explores the symbolism of Tarot and Kabbalah in relationship to the symbolism of the Bible. Though there are some interesting general insights, this book is of interest principally to those seriously interested in the author's interpretation of Christianity. It utilizes the Egyptian Tarot.

Biblically, he [The Magician] is representative of Adam in Paradise before Eve (the rib) had been taken out of his side. He is masculine as he looks out upon the World spreading out before him, for the feminine is hidden inside.

Hoeller, Stephan A. *The Royal Road: A Manual of Kabalistic Meditations on the Tarot*. The Theosophical Publishing House, 1975.

Equal parts of Jungian psychology, Kabbalistic lore, and common sense are blended in this book on using Tarot for meditative practice. Hoeller is refreshingly unmysterious in his explanation of Kabbalah, and he establishes clear, relatively simple relationships between esoteric ideas and individual psychology. After developing this thoughtful foundation, Hoeller offers an easy-to-follow method of Tarot meditation. For each of the major arcana cards, he gives a visual description of the image, a "Keynote" sentence containing the theme of the card, a "Motto" taken from some interesting source—which might be Goethe, the Bible, Novalis, or Shakespeare—and a one-paragraph meditation. (Some of the meditations seem a bit overblown to me, but others are excellent.) There's a brief, interesting appendix on astral travel with Tarot.

[Meditation on The Hermit:] *In the lonely hour of my soul, thou comest to my chamber, O beauty and love sublime. I lean upon the rod and staff of my insight, and though I walk through the valley of solitude, and scale the summits of loneliness, I know that my lover awaits on the mountain-top, from whence ever cometh my help. In the midst of the turmoil of living, I am but a lonely wanderer seeking my love. A pilgrim of eternity am I homeward bound among the stars.*

Huson, Paul. *The Devil's Picturebook*. G. P. Putnam's Sons, 1971.

Huson tries to cover too many bases in this book, but he does offer some intelligent expositions of Tarot connections—with gnosticism, *ars memoria*, and sorcery, for example—which are frequently mentioned but seldom developed elsewhere in Tarot literature. In his treatment of the individual cards, Huson provides little essays, each one different, which is a nice change from the standard-format approach taken by so many authors. It's a shame this book is no longer in print.

In this way the entire Mystery cycle of the pagan initiate's triumphs came to be paralleled in the Christian myth—Jesus' semidivine parentage, progress through the world of the elements toward the initiation of death, descent into the underworld, defeat of death and final resurrection and ascent into the empyrean. Whether the initiate was Orphic or Eleusinian, Mithraic or Christian, the formula seems to have been identical in pattern. In fact, as we shall see, the tarot trumps present a fusion of these cults typical of syncretist thinking.

Japikse, Carl. *Exploring the Tarot*. Ariel Press, 1989.

This solidly written book focuses on what author Japikse refers to as the "real" Tarot—that is, Tarot as a symbol system representing esoteric truths, useful for discovering "inner dimensions" of reality. He does approach Tarot as a means of answering questions, but he's principally concerned with questions of meaning and direction, rather than questions about everyday life. A question-and-answer format is used frequently and effectively in the book, which also presents several sample readings. The style is clear and pleasant; illustrations are from the Aquarian Deck.

To understand the archetypal forces of the Tarot, you must regard each card as a prism that refracts the light of each archetype in such a way that you can comprehend the message that answers your question.

Junjulas, Craig. *Psychic Tarot*. Morgan & Morgan, 1985.

This book is almost alone in its emphasis on developing psychic powers through the Tarot, and using psychic powers in reading. Although this is not a state-of-the-art explanation of psychic processes, it will be interesting and useful to those concerned with intuitive abilities in Tarot readership.

To see an aura you must allow your eyes to relax and go out of focus, while bringing in energy through the top center of the crown chakra, down to the solar plexus, and up to and out through the third eye chakra. To relax the eyes means to look at something while also visually taking in everything around it.

Kaplan, Stuart. *The Encyclopedia of Tarot.* Volumes 1, 2, and 3. U. S. Games Systems, 1990.

This monumental work contains more information about Tarot and other related types of cards than most of us will know what to do with. Kaplan's primary interest is in the historical and artistic aspects of the Tarot; there is relatively little here about esoteric subjects, but there are pictures of every Tarot deck known up to 1990 and a bibliography that includes virtually every publication in which mention of Tarot was ever made. Volume 3 concentrates on the modern Tarot, and includes interesting information about creative uses of the Tarot images; its most intriguing feature is a long chapter on Pamela Colman Smith, the artist who illustrated the Rider-Waite deck. These three volumes are indispensable to the collector, and useful to anyone with a fairly serious interest in the Tarot tradition.

————. *Tarot Classic.* U. S. Games Systems, Inc., 1972.

In addition to an information-filled section on the history of the cards, and the explication of the eighteenth-century Tarot Classic deck, *Tarot Classic* contains a generous section on spreads, some sample readings, an annotated bibliography, and a glossary. It offers good summaries of traditional card meanings, with no overlay of either a personal or a dogmatic interpretive approach.

Through choice or chance, depending upon one's viewpoint, the twenty-two Major Arcana cards from the seventy-eight-card tarot deck are clearly interwoven into our daily lives. Some tarot cards have loaned their titles to popular magazines and newspapers. Time or The Hermit calls attention to Time magazine. Fortune or The Wheel of Fortune is symbolic of Fortune magazine. The Star, Sun, and World are well-known newspapers of their day.

Knight, Gareth. *The Magickal World of Tarot.* The Aquarian Press, 1991.

Knight's newest book offers a detailed and well-organized approach to working with the Tarot. It includes advanced topics, but also provides a good fundamental treatment. Knight's premise here is that the Tarot must be approached as if it were a "real person."

————. *The Treasure House of Images.* Destiny Books, 1986.

The portions of this book which deal with general Tarot topics, such as the history and iconography of the cards, are good but by no means extraordinary. The material on pathworking with Tarot is excellent, however. Knight is a noted authority on Kabbalism and magic, and here he illuminates the use of the Tarot for ritual and expansion of consciousness, at the same time giving valuable insights into the inner structures of the Tarot deck.

Ritual is undoubtedly a powerful technique, as is all group work that involves the controlled use of the creative imagination. We have already described the technique of Pathworking or Initiated Symbol Projection as some transpersonal psychologists call it. Ritual is an extension of this by adding simple physical actions or words in a ceremonial form. Although this is a logical and simple extension it carries considerable power and effectiveness with it. This is because it is an "earthing" of the group's realizations and intentions in an immediate, formal and balanced way.

Konraad, Sandor. *Classic Tarot Spreads*. Schiffer, 1985.
——————. *Numerology: Key to Tarot*. Schiffer, 1983.

Konraad's work is uneven, but interesting. I don't happen to think that numerology is the key to the Tarot, or even that it is very important in understanding the Tarot, but for those who are interested in exploring the topic, Konraad's book provides a good starting point. I also feel that a few basic spreads are all that's needed for good Tarot work, but there are many who find it rewarding to explore a wide variety of spreads (some of them very elaborate), and here again, Konraad's book offers much useful material.

This spread ["Planetary Mansion"] *is reminiscent of the "Chaldean order" of antiquity, which was concerned with the seven original planets and the affairs of life they governed. If done thoroughly, the Planetary Mansions spread could easily constitute an entire reading. It is the logical follow-up to the preceding spread, for* [the Dr. Zodiac spread] *diagnoses and pinpoints the health problem but this spread gets to the root of the matter and* prescribes *what needs to be done.* [From *Classic Tarot Spreads*]

Lammey, W. C. *Karmic Tarot: A New System for Finding Your Lifetime's Purpose*. Borgo Press, 1988.

This book sounds more substantive than it is. It includes a basic introduction to the Tarot, but is generally organized around explaining and exploring a single spread, the "Karmic Spread." This spread is supposed to aid in answering questions through the Tarot in the total context of the querent's life purpose. The ideas presented here are not very thoroughly developed, although the author's karmic method of Tarot reading is quite elaborate.

There are no "bad" cards in the Tarot, only lessons to be learned. That which is flowing and already bringing you joy is the result of lessons already learned or in the process of being learned.

Laurence, Theodor. *The Sexual Key to the Tarot*. New American Library, 1973.

A unique book! Most treatments of sexuality and Tarot are really about romance and relationships, rather than sexual activity, but Laurence doesn't bother with such frippery. Organs, acts, and erotic attitudes of every sort are frankly mentioned here (most of them over and over again), in a style that seems like a cross between a sex clinic journal and a soft-core paperback. His commentaries on the cards are mostly just free sexual fantasies on the symbolism of Pamela Colman Smith's drawings for the Rider-Waite deck, and have little or nothing to with the Tarot tradition. But here and there he does touch on some of the genuine sexual content of the Tarot. (The following quote is the most "tasteful" passage I could find in the entire book.)

The moon represents reflected light; that is, dimmed sexual knowledge. It drops dew of flames as if to burn those beneath it. The two pillars form a gate of entry, implying that phallicism is the way to life. The dog and wolf symbolize lust and dark passion respectively. The crayfish represents the hideous sexual tendencies of those whose propensities are lower than those of the savage beast. The water, at once orgasmic fluids, also suggest the depths of depravity some men plumb in their voracious quest for orgasm.

Leary, Timothy. *The Game of Life*. Peace Press, 1979.

Stuart Kaplan describes this book as "an eclectic, tongue-in-cheek exposition of the tarot as a method to discard societal conditioning." If you can't find a copy of it (I can't), you can see a précis of Leary's Tarot ideas in his widely available sort-of-autobiography, *Flashbacks*.

The Empress card is a valentine from Gaia-Egg wisdom reminding you that your nervous system contains a slow, crawling amphibian Brain Circuit which is still functioning and demanding of affectionate attention.

214

LeMieux, David. *The Ancient Tarot and Its Symbolism*. Cornwall Books, 1985.

This oversized book makes some pretense of being a coffee-table picture book (there are plenty of illustrations), but it is not, as one might expect from the format and title, an overview of Tarot. Rather, it is an extended treatment of David LeMieux's opinions about the Tarot, which are based on rather shaky historical and factual foundations. There are better books available.

_____. *Forbidden Images: The Secrets of the Tarot*. Barnes & Noble Books, 1985.

Though it follows the "Egypt/Alexandria/Gypsy" myth of the cards as if it were literally true, styling itself as a presentation of the Gypsy Tarot method (for which no proof of existence is ever given!), this short book does have some interesting aspects. The interpretations of the individual cards are way off my own ideas, and frequently diverge from traditional interpretations, but they have an internal logic and consistency. The trumps are given both "Cardreader's" and "Philosophical" meanings, which lends the book a feeling of depth, even though the treatments are quite brief. LeMieux subscribes to the idea that there is a secret order to the cards, and explains his theory of same; he also makes numerous connections to various mystical/occult traditions. Though this book is really for beginners, I can't recommend it for newcomers to Tarot because of the somewhat presumptuous way LeMieux presents his own ideas about Tarot as if they were "the truth."

[On The Star:] *With this card, we must deal with another aspect of the universal great mother goddess of antiquity. This symbol adds depth to what we have already discovered in The High Priestess, The Empress, and Strength. Here, Mem, The Star, The Water Mother—maria—are symbolic of man's subconscious realization that he evolved from the pure, cold, clear water—the sea. The Star represents the celebration of the life-giving and purifying properties of water. This is the true secret meaning of the high Gnostic and alchemical mystery: "immaculate conception."*

Lotterhand, Jason C. *Thursday Night Tarot*. Newcastle, 1989.

The book takes its name from the ongoing Thursday-night class/discussion group which Lotterhand—a student and friend of Paul Foster Case—has been leading for some years. It's in a discussion format, and it's frank, interesting, and frequently funny.

Ideally, we are able to go to the heights, which is going to the center of ourselves, and then return to the outer world, gracefully making the transition from the innermost to the outermost.

Martello, Leo Louis. *Reading the Tarot*. Avery Publishing Group, 1990.

A very superficial treatment of Tarot, which I cannot recommend in any way.

Montalban, Madeline. *The Prediction Book of Tarot*.

This is a compilation of material from Tarot columns written by the author for the British astrology magazine *Prediction* over a period of nearly thirty years. It is mostly traditional, fortunetelling kind of material, but there is some treatment of symbolism. Better beginning books are certainly available, but this one is of interest because, from time to time, you get glimpses of a veteran reader's "savvy." Out of print.

In the Minor Arcana of the Tarot, the Sixes have been called the serpents, perhaps because if one studies the shapes of the figures or writes them together, they form serpentine loops. Serpent power is manifold, sometimes representing wisdom, other times healing and, in certain myths, it has sexual connotations. In Tarot readings, however, it relates to those events in people's lives that eventually enmesh them, whether or not they have consciously contributed to the result.

Masino, Marcia. *Easy Tarot Guide*. ACS Publications, Inc., 1983.

A real textbook format—divided into sixteen lessons, complete with assignments, fill-in-the-blank study areas, and quizzes. Some readers will find this educational approach comforting, while others will find it slow and cumbersome, but no one, I think, will find it "easy." The book is a workbook in the truest sense of the word—there is a lot of work for the reader to do in order to get through the book! Masino's approach to the cards is very traditional, and the focus is entirely divinatory. In short, this is a book that will appeal most strongly to those who would like to have taken Tarot 101 in school, but one which is also of interest as a very detailed explanation of the fortunetelling Tarot tradition, presented sincerely and effortfully.

> *This is such an important point that I'd like to explain it another way. With the shuffling, cutting and putting back together complete, you have the deck sitting in front of you as the seeker has left it. Turn the very first card over, right to left, and notice whether it is reversed or upright facing the Seeker. This is your key; if it is upright, then you have to get the deck to face you keeping the first card upright, because that is the way the cards have fallen for the Seeker. The only way to do this is to turn the deck around. By remembering to turn the deck to face you before each reading, you can eliminate this step of turning over the first card.*

Mathers, S. L. *Tarot*. Gordon, 1973.

This book is of more historical than practical interest, but for those who want to understand the making of the modern Tarot, it offers some interesting insights.

> [Mantram for the Major Arcana] *The Human* Will *(I)* enlightened by Science *(II) and manifested by* Action *(III) should find a* Realisation *(IV) in deed of* Mercy *and Beneficence (V). The* Wise Disposition *(VI) of this will give one* Victory *(VII) through* Equilibrium *(VIII) and* Prudence *(IX) over the fluctuations of* Fortune *(X).* Fortitude *(XI), sanctified by* Sacrifice of Self *(XII), will triumph over* Death *itself (XIII), and thus a wise* Combination *(XIV) will enable one to defy* Fate *(XV). In each* Misfortune *(XVI) one will see the* Star of Hope *(XVII) shine through the twilight of* Deception *(XVIII); and ultimate* Happiness *(XIX) will be the* Result *(XX).* Folly *(0), on the other hand, will bring about an evil* Reward *(XXI).* [Mathers is using the standard order of trumps, but with Justice as VIII and Strength as XI.]

Maxwell, Joseph. *The Tarot*. Neville Spearman Ltd, 1975.

Maxwell, a French lawyer, was a low-profile but very intelligent occult hobbyist of the late nineteenth/early twentieth-century period. This book is primarily a translation of his notes on the Tarot, but the material is nevertheless clear and well-organized. Maxwell's legal mind is obvious not only in the way he applies rigorous reasoning to the Tarot, but also in his focus on the moral dimension of esoteric studies. He gives special attention to numerology and color symbolism in his analysis of the Tarot. Out of print.

> *The Tarot is exclusively concerned with symbolic inculcation of an esoteric doctrine and all that doctrine means to us. It therefore codifies measures of conduct based on human liberty and human responsibility, to be worked out through successive lives and reincarnations of indeterminate number. The purport of the teaching is that each individual should recognize the living force of these principles and complement that recognition with the use of energy in all its forms.*

Moakley, Gertrude. *The Tarot Cards Painted by Bonifacio Bembo*. New York Public Library, 1966.

Librarian Moakley picked the Tarot as her research topic for a project to evaluate how well cataloging methods serve researchers. She discovered that very little was known about the historical Tarot, and curiosity led her to a further investigation of the Tarot's origins. Her conclusions—which include linking the major arcana images with Petrarch's *Trionfi*—are very questionable in the light of more recent scholarship, but her book deserves recognition for being among the first to treat Tarot seriously from the standpoint of art history. It will be of interest principally to the collector and to the Tarot scholar.

> *The tarocchi trumps are not so much a softening of the Petrarch story as they are a ribald take-off. Perhaps because, in the merry mood of Carnival, everything possible was done to make fun of the solemn story. . . . The Pope is given a mate. . . . Chastity is banished in favor of her enemy, Fortune. Time is reduced to being an attendant of Death, and Fame is forgotten. . . . Undoubtedly, it was this audacity and irreverence that made the tarocchi trumps so popular, in fact the game of triumphs par excellence.*

Moore, Daphna. *The Rabbi's Tarot: An Illumination from the Kundalini to the Pineal to the Pituitary*. Hughes Henshaw Publications, 1987.

This book is a curiosity, and it's difficult to tell how useful it would be to any particular individual. At first I thought it was unreadable, but after a fairly short period of time it began to seem very clear, and the next thing I knew, I was growing quite fond of it! According to Ms. Moore, the text is actually a transcription of notes taken from years of lectures given by a rabbi named Aaron in the late nineteenth and early twentieth centuries. "The whole object of The Rabbi's Tarot," she writes, "is to tell you the mechanics of purifying desire and of securing the balanced reciprocal creation of the self-conscious and the subconscious." About these topics the books goes on at length, using Kabbalah, the Bible, alchemy, Islam, and just about everything else to make its point. It's hard to read, but frequently striking, and the treatment of "sex energy" is surprisingly balanced and clear—perhaps the most sensible I've read. Keyed to the Rider-Waite deck. Out of print.

> *To pay attention involves three steps: (1) The first step is to see the object plainly, definitely, and functionally. (2) The second step is to see in what class of objects it comes; what it is like. (3) The Third step is to see how it is different from others of its class.* THESE THREE THINGS ARE INVOLVED IN THE ACT OF ADEQUATE ATTENTION IN SEEING ANYTHING DISTINCTLY. *Do you wonder that everybody is deficient in the ability to pay attention? It is more necessary to cultivate attention than anything else in the world, more necessary than the ordinary business of living.* IT IS ESPECIALLY NECESSARY FOR THE OCCULTIST.

Muchery, Georges. *The Astrological Tarot*. Castle Books, n.d.

In spite of the title, this book is not in any way about Tarot. Rather, it is an explication of "astromancy," a method (presumably developed by Muchery) of using forty-four cards bearing astrological designations in a fashion similar to Tarot-reading.

Nichols, Sallie. *Jung and Tarot: An Archetypal Journey*. Samuel Weiser, 1980.

This is a popular book, and it offers a detailed exposition of Jungian archetypes as related to Tarot images. The thematic proposition is that the major arcana images represent (or can be used to represent) the process of individuation. Each major arcana card is discussed at length, but often the commentary is more about society than about Tarot, and I find the writing somewhat awkward. It also seems to me that Nichols reaches too far for some of her associations, but the book is intermittently thought-provoking.

> *As the Tarot Fool in his circular dance will show us, the self is not a thing we create nor is it some kind of golden carrot held by life in front of our nose.*

Noble, Vicki. *Motherpeace: A Way to the Goddess through Myth, Art, and Tarot*. Harper & Row, 1983.

Motherpeace is an exceptional book. Although there are many attempts to "revision" the Tarot along one line or another, Motherpeace is among the few that is fully developed and really satisfying. This book is most useful as an accompaniment to the deck, but it can be read with interest by anyone who wants to expand his or her understanding of the nature of Tarot. The essential idea here is to explore the use of Tarot images as a way of returning to "goddess consciousness"—a shamanistic, holistic understanding of the world. Noble draws on a very wide variety of cultures for the myths and images incorporated into her Tarot, and provides thoughtful (and reasonably well-documented) explanations of the background of her ideas. A creative reading approach is given, though briefly. Highly recommended.

The Strength card represents the power of healing by the laying on of the feminine force, the Indian tapas, *the heat that heals.*

————, and Jonathan Tenny. *The Motherpeace Tarot Playbook*. Wingbow, 1986.

The *Playbook* follows up on the Motherpeace ideas with connections to astrology, and it offers an assortment of specific activities that will enrich the usefulness of the deck.

O'Neill, Robert V. *Tarot Symbolism*. Fairways Press, 1986.

Though this book can rarely be found, it contains perhaps the most carefully reasoned, wide-ranging, and well-supported treatment of Tarot imagery yet written. O'Neill, a research scientist, puts both his research skills and his scientific objectivity to good use, presenting a wealth of information on the historical relationships between Tarot and other esoteric traditions. What Kaplan and Dummett have done for the history of the exoteric Tarot, O'Neill does for the history of the esoteric Tarot. Out of print, unfortunately.

To understand the Art of Memory as practiced in the Renaissance, we must once again begin our story in the ancient world. We must notice the art being picked up and developed by Hellenistic Neoplatonists. We must watch this practical art crossing paths with hermetic and astrological magic, Christian mediation and Kabbalah. We must watch with amazement as artificial memory, like Alchemy, is transformed from memorizing to a methodology of mysticism. In the end, we will find that artificial memory is an important key to understanding the Tarot and the motivations of the designers.

Ouspensky, P. D. *The Symbolism of the Tarot*. Dover, 1976.

Ouspensky, perhaps the best-known disciple of Gurdjieff, here uses the Tarot trumps (in a very unusual order) to tell a story of the journey toward enlightenment. The narrator of the story encounters each of the Tarot scenes and each brings about a transformation.

[On The Chariot:] This is Will armed with Knowledge. We see here, however, the wish to achieve, rather than achievement itself. The man in the chariot thought himself a conqueror before he had really conquered, and he believes that victory must come to the conqueror. There are true possibilities in this beautiful conception, but also many false ones. Illusory fires and numerous dangers are hidden here.

Papus. *Tarot of the Bohemians*. Wilshire, n.d.

This book is of obvious historical interest, but it also worth investigating for its wealth of material. It is very dense, and requires time and patience. The serious student, however, will appreciate it.

Whilst admitting that our work upon the Tarot may have its errors, no one can deny the absolute simplicity of the constituent principles. We will therefore apply the same method to the divining Tarot, and endeavour to establish a system which will enable us to dispense with memory almost entirely, or at least to reduce its work considerably.

Pollack, Rachel. *The Open Labyrinth*. Borgo Press, 1988.
This book expands on some of the ideas in the author's *Seventy-Eight Degrees*, particularly the "mandala" approach to amplifying spreads. Pollack fans will want it, but others may not find it too rewarding all by itself.

_____. *The New Tarot: Modern Variations of Ancient Images*. Overlook Press, 1990.
Pollack, a popular Tarot writer, has produced the first book which explores the many new Tarot designs that have been produced in recent years. She provides detailed discussions of about seventy modern decks, along with examples of the cards and remarks on the several different categories of Tarots which she sees emerging. This is a most useful book for anyone who is seeking the "right" Tarot deck for personal use; it will also interest the collector. Pollack's observations on the relationship of Tarot, creativity, and the visual arts are useful, if not especially original.

_____. *Salvador Dali's Tarot*. Salem House, 1985.
Pollack does little more here than describe Dali's wonderful imagery, but the book is beautiful, with excellent full-color reproductions of all the cards. I've included it because it is a good substitute, if you can find it, for the expensive Dali deck.

_____. *Seventy-Eight Degrees of Wisdom*. Volumes 1 and 2. Borgo Press, 1986.
Pollack's two-volume approach is perhaps the most outstanding feature of this well-known work, because it allows for a more detailed analysis of the minor arcana cards than is found in most books. Due to Pollack's emphasis on symbolism in both volumes, howver, much of the material is more applicable to the Rider-Waite deck *per se* than to the generic Tarot. These books present Pollack's "mandala" approach to expanding the significance of a spread by adding to and re-patterning the cards.
The basic thing any oracle teaches us is that no action or attitude is right or wrong, except in its proper context. As we go further into the Tarot we will see that this concept of the proper time permeates the cards and is, in fact, the true key to their correct use.

Prosapio, Richard. *Intuitive Tarot*. Morgan & Morgan, 1990.
This is a very short book—only about eighty pages—and most of it is in a workbook/notebook format, so it is not too substantial. However, it includes some intriguing material relating the Tarot and the Medicine Wheel, and the "intuitive" style of reading is well presented.
In the Medicine Wheel way of looking at things, what you do in the first process [of looking at a spread] is "mouse vision." You are looking closely at details, homing in on the specifics of each individual card. . . . In the second process, when you look at the entire spread, you are employing "eagle vision," you are seeing the overall picture.

Rakoczi, Basil. *The Painted Caravan*. Boucher, 1954.
I have never been able to see a copy of this book, but I include it here for two reasons. First, Tracey Hoover, in *The Winged Chariot*, describes it as "charming," "engaging," and "beautifully illustrated," noting that the court cards are given "key types" in the form of identifications with "legendary or historical figures." Second, some of the original card designs included in the book are reproduced in volume 1 of Kaplan's *Encyclopedia*, and sure enough, they *do* look charming—though not extraordinary, I hasten to say. The book is apparently organized around outdated

theories of Gypsy transmission, and may be of as much interest for its Gypsy lore as for its Tarot insights. Anyway, *The Painted Caravan* is long out of print, and it might be fun to keep an eye open for a copy.

The fact that the Empress precedes the Emperor in the pack is perhaps a relic of matriarchal rule and there are old wives' tales which hint at the power of the first mothers to be self-fertilizing or virgin parents who held the male principle in the sceptre or phallus.

Raine, Kathleen. *Yeats, the Tarot and the Golden Dawn*. The Dolmen Press (Dublin) 1972, distributed in the U.S. by Humanities Press.

A beautifully printed book, with some interesting and unusual illustrations. It's actually a literary monograph, exploring the extent to which Yeats made use in his poetry of images from the Tarot; there is not a great deal about the Tarot itself. But there *is* some interesting lore (gossip, really!) about the Golden Dawn, and Raine provides worthwhile insights into the relationship between visual symbolism and poetry. Black-and-white photographs show such rarely seen items as Yeats's ceremonial Golden Dawn paraphernalia and pages from the notebooks of MacGregor Mathers, George Polexfen, and other well-known occultists of the period. Out of print.

What has astonished me in even this most superficial study of Yeats's use of the symbolism of magic acquired through the Hermetic Order of the Golden Dawn is the great background of undisclosed knowledge from which he wrote. He gave away no secrets of the Order; and yet he used continually a method won by long and hard work in a language, today studied by few, but which is intrinsically valid and will, therefore, outlast the ignorance of the time. . . . The powerful symbols of the Tarot are among the many emblems of those primordial images by whose means the unchanging, universal aspects of reality may be apprehended; they underlie some of Yeats's greatest poetic images and were a part of that body of symbolic knowledge upon which he constantly meditated in the composing of his poetry and the living of his thought.

Renee, Janina. *Tarot Spells*. Llewellyn Publications, 1990.

Tarot Spells is exactly what the title implies. It includes suggestions for employing Tarot cards for the usual types of spells and charms, including finding or losing a lover, succeeding in business, attracting good luck—and even insuring fertile crops. Those who are interested in spell-casting might certainly find the idea of using Tarot for this purpose intriguing. For others, there is nothing at all substantive about the book, though it does offer a look at Tarot from a different point of view.

Roberts, Richard. *The Original Tarot and You*. Vernal Equinox, 1987.

Richard Roberts can be given a great deal of credit for connecting Jungian theory with practical Tarot readership. In this pioneering book, he presents transcripts of actual readings, including one with noted mythologist Joseph Campbell. (This item alone makes the book interesting.) For those already familiar with Jungian approaches to Tarot, the chief appeal of this book is in the insight about readership to be gained from "observing" the methods of a skilled reader. The variety of querents and spreads included provides an opportunity to glimpse some of the broad structures of the reading process. Keyed to the Aquarian deck.

The next two cards [laid down in the "Jungian spread"], *World Father and World Mother, (may) refer to the mundane parents in the life of the individual. In cases in which the psychic life of the readee is not yet at peace or in harmony with the parents, these cards may stand as representatives of father and mother imagos, images yet residing in the unconscious. Or they may stand as* exalted *images, Rex and Regina, or*

still further, as the fructifying World Parents of the mythological realm. Most often,
however, the cards describe our apple-pie Mom and Dad as we know them.

Roszak, Theodore. *Fool's Cycle—Full Cycle: Reflections on the Great Trumps of the Tarot.*
Robert Briggs Associates, 1988.
Roszak is a well-known historian and social critic, author of the important 1969
book *The Making of a Counter Culture*. His very short—only thirty-six pages—work
on the Tarot trumps is one of the few instances in which a first-rate thinker has
turned attention to the Tarot, and I recommended it very highly. Roszak attempts to
cut through what he calls the "occult clutter" surrounding the Tarot trumps, and
reveal them as symbolic representations of the stages in our life cycle. He presents
amazingly lucid and concise reflections on each of the trumps, and his writing, while
economical, is rich with provocative allusions. Among the little treasures in this
book is a reading-list of works which might illuminate the trumps, a portion of
which is given in the following quote.

> *Once I played with the idea of arranging a reading program that would trace the*
> *Tarot life cycle through its phases, choosing for each trump a work that probes its many*
> *shades and angularities.* The Fool, *for example, might be pondered in connection*
> *with Dostoyevsky's* The Idiot, *and Death in connection with Tolstoy's tale of Ivan*
> *Ilych, or possible Freud's hymn to Thanatos in* Civilization and its Discontents.
> *Plato's* Symposium *would be my chosen discourse for The Lovers, Blake's* Marriage of
> Heaven and Hell *for the Devil.*

Sadhu, Mouni. *The Tarot*. Wilshire, n.d.
Dense, difficult, and unforgettable, this unique book offers 101 lessons that weave
together a wide variety of metaphysical concepts and precepts. The lessons are
organized around the twenty-two Tarot trumps, each of which becomes like a door
that opens to reveal a whole constellation of Hermetic lore. If you have the patience
to pursue the lessons, they could provide the foundations of an excellent metaphysical education, though they must be supplemented and balanced by other sources, for
some of what Sadhu says is doctrinal, inaccurate, or irrelevant. The lessons cover
everything from basic Kabbalism and numerology to magical operations and astral
travel; but the most striking thing about this book is the author's tone of sincerity
and genuine will-to-the-good. (The lessons on Death, by the way, are remarkable.)

> *Now, I would like to stress, that the Tarot in itself does not expound any definite*
> *SPIRITUAL DOCTRINE, but rather has the purpose of expanding the abilities of*
> *the student, that is to teach him an infallible method for developing and using his*
> *mental faculties. . . . Many people have an unquenchable thirst and curiosity to know*
> *mentally much more than recognized philosophical or psychological studies can offer*
> *them. Some want to systematize the degree of occult knowledge which they already*
> *possess, while others are keen to unveil certain secrets, which lie hidden behind the*
> *"security walls" surrounding the main occult problems. For all such, the Tarot offers a*
> *unique possibility to achieve their various aims, and at the same time educate their*
> *minds and open quite new vistas before them.*

Sandbach, John. *Astrology, Alchemy, and the Tarot*. Seek-It Publications, 1981.
This book is not at all the weighty tome implied by its title. In fact, it's only eighty
pages long, and it doesn't say much about the theory, history, or interrelationship of
the three esoteric studies mentioned. What it *does* do is instruct the reader gently on
the way of the Alchemist, as considered through the metaphor of gardening. This
strategy struck a very resonant chord with me, and I found the book charming
without being the least bit "cute," and wise without being pretentious.

The crowning secret of this card [The Hierophant] *is that no true teacher teaches one thing—or even one thing at a time. Everything is always taught at once—and every lesson is complete—a world in itself.*

Sargent, Carl. *Personality, Divination and the Tarot.* Destiny Books, 1988.
An intellectually lively book! Sargent is the only writer on the Tarot I know about who has seriously tried to relate Tarot not just to Jungian ideas, but to psychological theory in a broader sense. He examines the Tarot as an explication of personality, and connects its images with the ideas of Freud and Maslow, as well as Jung and other psychological theorists. The book is not at all dry or scholarly, however, as Sargent is a cheerful believer in the predictive efficacy of the Tarot, and gives insightful consideration to the use of the Tarot as a divinatory tool. Sargent has created a valuable bridge between the Tarot tradition and contemporary ideas.

Sharman-Burke, Juliet. *The Complete Book of Tarot.* St. Martin's Press, 1987.
The author is a psychotherapist, and includes, among other interesting material, suggestions for using "guided fantasy" techniques to achieve a deeper understanding of the Tarot images. Sample readings are included.
The Fool now faces the lightning-struck Tower, the point at which he must split hell open and release himself from the darkness of his underworld journey.

Shavick, Nancy. *The Tarot.* Prima Materia, 1985.
A nice book for beginners. It has an easy, personal style (it's printed out in the author's own hand), and while it is by no means deep, it has some original insights. Shavick makes the whole topic of Tarot seem simple and unthreatening.
If you are sincere as you read the cards, the experience will be uplifting and mind expanding. The secret to clarity in a reading is belief.

Simon, Sylvie. *The Tarot: Art, Mysticism, and Divination.* Inner Traditions, 1986.
Translated from the French, this book is a coffee-table-sized presentation, with lavish illustrations (most in full color) presenting cards of various decks, as well as a number of interesting but largely irrelevant paintings and engravings of gaming scenes. Somewhat in contrast to the slick format, the book attempts to incorporate significant content, with references to a wide variety of ideas (ranging from Taoism to Jungian psychology), as well as information about card-reading techniques and interpretations. But because it is quite short (115 oversized pages), the book necessarily fails in this encyclopedic approach; the style is telegrammatic, ideas are scarcely developed, references are not documented, and the organization of the book is unclear.
The tarot helps in the attainment of the consciousness that helps to control one's destiny. Nevertheless, we will be able to know only what we are allowed to know. Shadowy regions in prophecy guarantee us a margin of freedom. A certain mystery is necessary; otherwise, we would have neither hope nor desire. A life of which too much is known in advance loses the charm of being lived. Happily for us, our potential for choice is almost infinite; we can play the game according to our own tastes.

Stuart, Micheline. *The Tarot Path to Self Development.* Shambhala, 1977.
A beautifully produced little book, unique in its simplicity. Stuart reflects, in a clear, personal style, on each of the cards, revealing their description of the journey toward psychological unity. Though the approach is Jungian in essence, the book is not at all analytical. And in a fascinating inversion, Stuart begins the journey with The World, representing the spirit imprisoned in nature, and traces progress through the cards to

The Magician, representing transcendence over personality. This reversal of the usual order seems surprisingly "right." Illustrated with the Marseille deck.

There are many interpretations of the Tarot because there are many levels of understanding. To grasp the "teaching" given in its fundamental message, we have to be directly involved with it. It is showing the way that can carry us through the dangers of straying and error to the development of our human nature, from our animal innocence to the opening of the sublime life. However much we know of astrology, however much we know of symbology, we shall remain at the level of "The Fool" unless we realize that no amount of knowledge, alone, will develop a practical sense in us.

Thierens, A. E. *Astrology and the Tarot*. Newcastle, 1975.

A very interesting book for two reasons. First, it presents a thoughtful and detailed analysis of the individual cards as seen from an astrological point of view; and second, it provides an example of the approach taken by the British occultists of the early twentieth century, whose influence on the development of modern Tarot was formative. Thierens's musings on the "theory" of each card will be provocative and occasionally illuminating for readers who are familiar with astrology, but may be somewhat exasperating for those who are not. Originally published as *The General Book of the Tarot*, this book contains an interesting introduction by A. E. Waite.

The less dogmatic one is with regard to the process of divination and its interpretation, the greater the chance of being truly "illuminated" by insight or vision. These cards have to be taken as "signs of the Heavens" and in order to understand what Heaven has to communicate, man has to eliminate, wholly and without consideration, his own as well as other people's prejudices and preferences, bigotry and illusions.

Waite, Arthur Edward. *The Pictorial Key to the Tarot*. Samuel Weiser, 1973.

One of the two most famous of all Tarot books (the other is Crowley's *Book of Thoth*), and still selling briskly after more than three-quarters of a century! It is, of course, the definitive guide to Waite's own deck, but beyond that, most of its content is largely of historical interest. Waite offers interesting insights into the occult milieu of the late nineteenth and early twentieth centuries, by means of an annotated (and highly opinionated) bibliography, and a text that concentrates heavily on debunking ideas about the Tarot other than Waite's own. The style with which Waite carries out his assassinations makes for fun reading, however, and many of the ideas he puts forth personally are the foundations for our modern conception of the Tarot. There are, by the way, five different editions of this book, from five different publishers, listed in *Books in Print*.

[On Temperance:] Hereof is some part of the Secret of Eternal Life, as it is possible to man in his incarnation. All the conventional emblems are renounced herein. So also are the conventional meanings, which refer to changes in the seasons, perpetual movement of life and even the combination of ideas. It is, moreover, untrue to say that the figure symbolized the genius of the sun, though it is the analogy of solar light, realized in the third part of our human triplicity. It is called Temperance fantastically, because, when the rule of it obtains in our consciousness, it tempers, combines and harmonises the psychic and material natures. Under that rule we know in our rational part something of whence we came and whither we are going.

Walker, Barbara G. *The Secrets of the Tarot: Origins, History, and Symbolism*. Harper & Row, Publishers, 1984.

This book is substantial in appearance—250 pages long and packed with references and footnotes. Unfortunately, on close examination, Walker's treatment seems flawed. Her view of the Tarot is developed along very determined feminist lines, and it seems to me that she distorts and omits information in order to support her theories. The material is developed in the form of sweeping assertions which appear to be supported—but often actually are not—by the piling up of cross-cultural references and linguistic similarities. Further, her premises are frequently shakey. For example, she begins with the assumption that the playing-card deck is a remnant of the Tarot deck, left after the suppression (by patriarchal religious forces) of the trumps—a scenario which has been known for some time to be historically questionable. Here, as elsewhere, Walker never points out conflicting evidence or alternative interpretations. I am personally very interested in the links between Tarot and women's mysteries, but I feel that this treatment does not serve the subject well. It should be added, however, that the book has many admirers, and also that it contains a number of ideas and references which, if critically assessed, may be of use to the careful reader.

> *The primacy of the female principle in Tantrism may explain why the feminine-numbered Major Arcana Tarot cards were trumps or Greater Secrets, while the Lesser Secrets added up to a masculine number. Among the trump cards, important figures were more female than male—including a female pope. Fifty-six, the number of the Lesser Arcana, was associated with male gods. . . . When the Enlightened One was born, he took fifty-six steps, fourteen in each of the four cardinal directions (seven forward and seven back), forming a cross. The same cross can be made of the four Tarot suits of fourteen cards each, which total fifty-six. In the East and West alike, the cross was generally assimilated to Phallic gods and the masculine principle.*

Wang, Robert. *Introduction to the Golden Dawn Tarot.* Samuel Weiser, 1978.
This book is intended to accompany the Golden Dawn deck, which was drawn by Wang under the personal direction of Israel Regardie. But the book itself is perhaps more interesting for its detailed presentation of the Golden Dawn approach to Tarot. Wang's solid introduction to the Golden Dawn is followed by the actual texts of the Golden Dawn materials on the Tarot. Of great interest to the student of the historical Tarot, as well as to those interested in the magical and imaginative uses of Tarot.

> *The documents of the Golden Dawn may seem archaic in their approach by comparison with materials on the occult appearing today. They represent a careful intermesh of symbols described in almost clinical terms. An effort to humanize these symbols, i.e., to integrate them into the individual system, and translate them into palpable concepts was required of each member who received the documents.*

————. *Tarot Psychology: Handbook for the Jungian Tarot.* Urania Verlags Ag, 1990.
This rather slight book is distinctive in that it suggests both personal and collective meanings for most of the cards. It also includes an outline of a 34-week course of self-analysis utilizing the Tarot deck. The book is specifically keyed to the Jungian Tarot deck, but it would be of general interest to anyone pursuing a Jungian approach to Tarot.

Wanless, James. *The New Age Tarot.*
This is a very attractive book—both visually and conceptually—in which each card serves as the theme or point of departure for an imaginative spread pattern. Many aspects of Tarot are developed, and there is much opportunity for the reader to become actively involved in Tarot processes. Wanless (who is also the creator of the Voyager deck) has a distinctive approach; it won't be for every taste, but those looking for a change from the traditional may find it refreshing. Keyed to the Thoth Deck.

The dark side of tarot is in your mind. "Dark" interpretations of the cards reflect the residue of mold and an age past and gone. Use the tarot to expose the dark past. Use the "Tower-eye" of tarot to illumine and burn out, the Death card to cut free, and the Devil card to laugh at your ignorance.

Willis, Tony. *Magick and the Tarot.* The Aquarian Press, 1988.

Willis gives his own rather selective explanations of "magickal" practice, then provides clear and simple suggestions for utilizing the tarot cards in a variety of spells and rituals. Magical *theory* is presented in a very oversimplified way, while at the same time, magical *practice* is made to sound more grand and mysterious than it is, but Willis's tone is pleasant and he offers occasional genuine insights, along with some shrewd comments on the practical aspects of practicing magic. The spells and rituals are, for the most part, little more than mildly therapeutic activities such as writing out one's problem in a mysterious alphabet, lighting a candle of a certain color, pinning a particular Tarot card to the wall, and so forth. Careful and critical readers will find some interesting material in this book, but it is not really a very satisfactory introduction to the magical uses of Tarot.

When I first bemoaned the fact that I was unable to supply myself with even a few of the items which I so fondly believed would turn me overnight into an Adept, First Class, I was bluntly informed by my Supervisor: "Then buy, or make, something you can afford. If the instructions ask for gold, make the object out of wood, or some other material, and paint it gold. But don't let the lack of exactly the right magickal artifact deter you from embarking on the practice of magick, or you will never make a start."

Wirth, Oswald. *The Tarot of the Magicians.* Samuel Weiser, 1990.

This is a re-issue of Wirth's 1927 classic. It's a must-have for anyone interested in the history of the esoteric Tarot, and it also has some good ideas and observations.

There is nothing easier than discussing ad infinitum a collection of symbols, such as the Tarot, but chatter is just what the authors of all silent books do not intend.

Woudhuysen, Jan. *Tarot Therapy: A Guide to the Subconscious.* J. P. Tarcher, 1979.

This book is perhaps best described as "irreverent," and though I find the no-nonsense tone refreshing, the content of the book is only intermittently interesting. This is certainly *not*, as the subtitle claims, a "guide to the subconscious." Woudhuysen spends much time belaboring the mechanics of everyday communication, and illustrating her points with familiar jokes and trite anecdotes. The Tarot images specially drawn for the book are just plain silly—they look like the pictures on toy cartons. But on the other hand, the author includes some possibly interesting spreads and some useful tips about the reading process; the chapter on "Payment and Sacrifice" is excellent.

How much to charge in order to make the contribution a "sacrifice" and not just an expense is a matter for the intuitive insight of the Reader. Obviously, the same fee, which is a prohibitive amount for an under-paid student nurse, is small change to the idle wife of a rich company director. . . . One way out is to realize that a sacrifice can be made using other media than money. . . . An idle person should be given an appointment before eight in the morning, or be told that until you have finished the task of folding five thousand business letters you can't begin to read, and could he give a hand meanwhile.

Younger, J. Kelley, editor. *New Thoughts on Tarot.* Newcastle Publishers, 1989.

This is a collection of transcripts, taken from the speeches of Tarot writers and teachers who gathered for the First Newcastle International Tarot Symposium. Among the speakers: Angeles Arrien, Gail Fairfield, Mary K. Greer, Rachel Pollack,

James Wanless. They address a wide variety of topics, and some of the material is very good. One good way of using this book would be to sample the ideas and styles of various popular Tarot writers, as a guide to further reading.

Zain, C. C. *The Sacred Tarot*. Church of Light, n.d.

This volume is part of the teaching series disseminated by the Church of Light. Each chapter is a lesson, exploring various aspects of the Tarot trumps and their connections with astrology, magic, Kabbalah, alchemy, masonic material, etc. The text is hard to read, and—to me, anyway—lacks the direct inspirational quality of Mouni Sadhu's similarly difficult series of lessons. If you are interested in the Church of Light deck and ideas, you might want to start out with the much less demanding exposition in *How to Read Tarot Cards* by Doane and Keyes, listed above.

Arcanum XVI [The Tower] *illustrates one of the most certain principles of magic, that any destructive force, when the period of its orbit has been completed, will return to inflict punishment upon the sender.*

Ziegler, Gerd. *Tarot: Mirror of the Soul*. Samuel Weiser, 1988.

This book is of interest mainly to those who want to explore the symbolism of the Crowley deck, for it concentrates on interpreting the illustrations of those cards. But since the Thoth deck is of such continuing interest as an approach to Tarot, this book may be of interest to the general reader as well. In addition to rather detailed explications of the individual cards, it also offers a brief, useful list of symbols commonly occurring in the Thoth drawings.

The long umbilical cord, connection to cosmic oneness, wraps the Fool in four spirals. The possibility of rebirth is given on all four planes of human existence: spiritual, intellectual, emotional, and physical. The prerequisite is your readiness to change in all areas; your responsibility is to self-development.

Periodicals

Tarot periodicals are typically informal, and are published at unpredictable intervals. Still, they are a marvelous source of information about new decks and books, as well as a way of getting into contact with others interested in Tarot. Frequently, readers share ideas, experiences, and innovations which will enrich your own work with the cards.

Tarot Network News. 2860 California St., San Francisco, CA 94115. Gary Ross, editor.

The Winged Chariot. P.O. Box 1718, Milwaukee, WI 53201. Tracey Hoover, editor.

The Symbolist. P.O. Box 1227, Carmel, CA 93921. Jim Wanless, publisher.

Tools and Rites of Transformation (*T.A.R.O.T.*). P.O. Box 31123, San Francisco, CA 94131. Mary K. Greer, publisher.

Manteia. Sankt Hansgalle 20, DK 4000 Roskilde, Denmark. K. Frank Jensen, publisher.

CLOSURE: A DOZEN TAROT IDEAS

1. *Create an idea deck.* Get a blank deck of cards, and write the following ideas (or any others that you find or think up) on the cards. Then shuffle and deal them into spreads to reveal new connections. Or draw one card from the deck whenever you need "inspiration."

2. *Photocopy your Tarot cards.* Black-and-white cards will copy best, of course, but some colored decks will yield fairly good reproductions. You can enlarge the copies for more detailed view of the images. These copies can be used for practice coloring, and for several other projects, as suggested in the next several ideas.

3. *Make a Tarot notebook.* It's very helpful to record ideas about the Tarot, experiences with the cards, etc.; also, you can compile your own card meanings and associations, drawing on different sources. Special pages can be created for the notebook: for example, make enlarged copies of the cards, using the lightest setting on the copy machine, and you will be able to write right over the images. (This technique can be used to make lovely Tarot stationery, too; just use colored paper.) Another idea is to reduce the card images as small as possible (place the card in the corner of the page-frame) and you will have plenty of room to write on the page, with the card image right there for reference.

4. *Record your readings.* You can use a tape recorder to make sound recordings of your readings; if you have a video recorder, and want to go to the trouble, you could even videotape them for later study. These are good ways to analyze the reading process, including your own skills, the dynamics of the reading event, differences among querents, and so on. Also, you can use these records as a point of reference for evaluating the effectiveness of predictions. But I strongly recommend that, even if you do use audio or video taping, you supplement the tapes with charts of the cards. It's very simple to keep this type of chart if you first create a form. Draw the outlines of the cards on a page as they would be laid out

for a spread; create one form for each of the different spreads you like to use. Make plenty of photocopies of these chart forms and you are always ready to record a reading. Comments can be made on the back of the sheet, and the collected sheets will fit right into your notebook. If you want to get very organized about this, include a space on the chart form for a cross-reference to audio or video tape if made.

5. *For beginners: create a "learning deck."* It's helpful in the early stages of working with Tarot to have suggested meanings and keywords right on the cards, rather than having to page through books or refer to your notes. You can write on a standard deck by using an indelible pen (the kind sold especially for writing on plastic or freezer wrap) which will write legibly over the patterns on the backs of your cards. If you don't mind going to a little more trouble, however, there is a better approach. Use the copy machine to make very small card-images by making a reduced copy—put several cards on a page—and then reducing that copy again. Get a blank deck of Tarot-sized cards and paste a reduced copy of a Tarot image in the corner of each card. (Use rubber cement to reduce wrinkling.) You will then have plenty of space to write on each card the meanings you want to remember/explore. The cards can be shuffled and laid out in the normal way.

6. *For more advanced students: create a composite deck.* If you own several decks, use the technique just described to build a deck with several versions of each image pasted up together on one card. This won't be an aesthetically wonderful deck (many images don't photocopy well, and reducing the images will lose detail), but it will provide an excellent opportunity to study the resonance of the Tarot images by viewing several different renderings at the same time. Here again, you can shuffle and lay out the cards in the regular way, but the spread produced will have extra dimensions of imagery.

7. *Use the cards to explore and develop your "other" senses.* Get into a relaxed frame of mind and hold one card at a time, face down, in your left hand. Don't try to "guess" which card it is—just let your mind receive impressions and, after a few minutes, compare these impressions with the card you've been holding. My own impressions are usually of colors and shapes, but it's also possible to have ideas or emotions which correspond to the meaning of the card. As you try this over a period of time, notice what works best for you and develop an approach to suit your own needs.

8. *Use the Tarot images to "incubate" dreams.* Dream incubation was used by the ancient Greeks as a method of healing, and there are several interesting uses for the technique today; see Patricia Garfield's book *Creative Dreaming* for more ideas. To use the Tarot for this purpose, select a card and look at it for a few minutes before turning out the lights at bedtime. Then try to construct a mental image of the card as you are falling asleep. When you wake up, record your dreams. (Be sure to have a notepad or tape recorder by the bed.) The connections between the card and your dreams may not be immediate, so be patient;

and the connections may not be obvious either, so be creative in your interpretations.

9. *Use the Tarot images as objects of imaginative meditation.* One approach to cultivation of the imagination involves developing the ability to visualize; the Tarot images are perfect for this practice, though they are too complex to work with at a beginning level. For a simpler starting point, the *tatvas* (a black oval, a blue disk, a silver crescent, a yellow square, and a red triangle) are often recommended. (You may find it helpful to create tatva cards for exterior visualization before working on the interior visualization; see Mary Greer's *Tarot Mirrors* for more concerning the tatvas.) If you are successful in creating and sustaining mental images of the tatvas, try working with one of the Tarot images. First build in your mind the basic outlines of the image, then fill in the details. The object is to make the image as vivid as possible and to hold the whole thing clearly in your "mind's eye" for as long as possible.

10. *Choose a Tarot figure to accompany you through the day.* This activity helps give personality and dimension to the Tarot characters, and will enrich your understanding of the cards. Just think about the character as you make choices and decisions. What would the Empress or the King of Wands wear today? What would they choose for lunch? Which movie would they be likely to go to?

11. *Practice telling stories.* Reading the Tarot cards is a lot like story-telling; it involves the same flow of imagination, the same aim of engaging the audience. If you haven't had much story-telling experience lately, find one or more children and persuade them to let you practice on them. Start with traditional tales, then add embellishments, and when you are comfortable with being a narrator, have your audience suggest two or three elements at random (a princess, a pizza, and a trip to the moon, for example) and improvise a story which weaves them together. Be sure you give equal attention to developing plot, characters *and* theme as you tell your stories.

12. *Read for strangers.* If you are interested in Tarot readership, you will make the greatest progress by reading for people you don't know; since you have no conscious knowledge of their lives or problems, you will be forced to depend on the cards and your interpretive skills. One way to find some strangers to read for is to start or join an informal Tarot circle. If there is a metaphysical or occult bookstore near you, they may know of such a group, or they may have a bulletin board where you can put up a note. There may also be Tarot classes offered in your area, and these frequently offer the opportunity to practice reading with other people in the class.

The Baker's Thirteenth. Use books to learn more about Tarot, but don't depend on them. Develop your own relationship with the cards. You won't learn to read successfully by looking up card meanings in books, or by trying to memorize lists of keywords. Instead, study the images on the cards and construct your own imaginative interpretation of what the cards "mean."

Compare many different authors and approaches to the Tarot, taking what is best from each, rather than following the dictates of a single method. And try, if you can, to work with an experienced reader, for no amount of reading can replace personal interaction; but don't try to emulate someone else—create your own style. Finally, take care with the cards. Always be honest and gentle when you read for someone else, and remember that a reading is not a lecture or a performance, but a shared event. Real value will come out of a reading only if real care is put into it.

INDEX

PICTURE CREDITS